21.95

The Poetic Debussy

Debussy, circa 1913, by
Armand Rassenfosse

The *Poetic* *Debussy*

A Collection of His
Song Texts and
Selected Letters

collected and annotated by
Margaret G. Cobb

translations by Richard Miller

Northeastern University Press
Boston   1982

Designer: Catherine L. Dorin

Northeastern University Press
Copyright © 1982 Margaret G. Cobb

Library of Congress Cataloging in Publication Data

Debussy, Claude, 1862–1918.
  The poetic Debussy.

  Original French texts with English translations.
  Bibliography: p.
  Discography: p.
  Includes indexes.
    1. Songs—Texts. 2. Debussy, Claude, 1862–1918.
3. Composers—France—Correspondence. I. Cobb,
Margaret G. II. Title.
ML54.6.D42C62   784.3'05   81-19010
ISBN 0-930350-28-6   AACR2

87 86 85 84 83 82 8 7 6 5 4 3 2 1

Printed in the United States of America

to the memory
of
Stefan Jarocinski

*"La musique et la poésie sont les deux
seuls arts qui se meuvent dans l'espace."*

Claude Debussy

Contents

Illustrations

frontispiece. DEBUSSY, c. 1913,
BY ARMAND RASSENFOSSE
(From the author's collection)

Following page 148

1. TITLE PAGE OF THE FIRST EDITION OF *NUIT D'ÉTOILES* (1882) (Photo Bibliothèque Nationale, Paris)

2. TEXTS OF *MANDOLINE, PANTOMIME,* AND *PIERROT* (c. 1882) (Reproduced by permission of the Houghton Library, Harvard University)

3. FIRST MANUSCRIPT PAGE OF AN EARLY VERSION OF *MANDOLINE* (c. 1882) (Reproduced by permission of the Houghton Library, Harvard University)

4. PROGRAM FOR THE FIRST PERFORMANCE OF *FÊTE GALANTE* AND *LES ROSES* (12 May 1882) (Reproduced by permission of Éditions Richard-Masse, Paris)

5. FIRST MANUSCRIPT PAGE OF *APPARITION* (1884) (Reproduced from the Collections of the Library of Congress, Washington, D.C., © 1969, Société des Éditions Jobert. Used by permission of the publisher, Theodore Presser Company, sole representative U.S.A.)

Foreword

There are few subjects on which the music lover speaks with such authority as he does on the relationship between music and poetry. Because a musician's understanding of a poetic text defies objective analysis, everyone feels free to voice an opinion as to a particular song's felicity. An abundant body of commentary on Debussy's works already exists, which treats his relations with poets, with the nature of his selections of song texts, with his most successful collaborations, and with the various influences that can be discerned in his works. Although it may be pertinent, this exegesis is rarely attuned to our perception of Debussy's unique and innovative musical vision, particularly evident in his orchestral works and those for piano. The survey of Debussy's poetic universe Margaret G. Cobb has so successfully made will, I am certain, open up reconsideration of this entire subject, representing as it does a precise and objective research that includes not only all of the texts the composer employed but, in addition, a highly original anthology of Debussy's own writings through which she has traced the truly poetic thread in his vocabulary and his thought. The world of dreams in which Debussy felt so at home is made vividly present in the many quotations that were an integral part of his everyday thinking and self-expression. An avid reader, the composer never wrote directly about anything he had read, and thus the only way in which we can reconstitute his personal library, now dispersed, is through the method employed in this volume.

We do know that the composer spent considerable time finding the path proper to him, and the majority of the experiments he undertook in his search for his own personal musical diction were carried out primarily in his vocal works. Half of these—some of which have never been published—were composed while Debussy was between the ages of seventeen and twenty-five. As these working sketches piled up, Debussy gradually began to realize that he would never be able to "confine his music in too straight a mold." Having begun with the Parnassians, he was to become a part of the development of the Symbolist movement, not out of any desire to be fashionable but rather because he lived in close proximity with poetry, and because his mature style, when it did emerge, was to be rooted in both music and literature. The great turning point in his work was the *Cinq Poèmes de Charles Baudelaire* (particularly *Le Jet d'eau*), which were to be followed by a whole succession of masterpieces: the *Chansons de Bilitis* (written after the first version of *Pelléas*); the second series of *Fêtes galantes*; the *Chansons de France*; *Le Promenoir des deux amants*—culminating with works on texts by Villon and Mallarmé. As this book shows, however, the dates of his songs are widely spaced—might he have become increasingly uninterested in the form? However that may be, his principal efforts were henceforward directed toward a renewal of his method of composition for orchestra and for the piano, and to several uncompleted operatic projects. It is also true that the developments taking place in poetry itself were beginning to lose something of their former intensity, and that Debussy no longer had an interpreter of whom he was fond close at hand.

The task of guiding us securely along this branch of the composer's development demands a flawless grasp of French culture. Margaret G. Cobb, more than most, has devoted herself to Debussy and has earned her qualifications as an expert. Not so long ago, she unhesitatingly moved to France for a time, to Paris and Saint-Germain-en-Laye, the composer's birthplace, where she organized the newly founded Centre de Documentation Claude Debussy, enriching its collections and infusing it with life. After publishing a historical discography of Debussy's music, she began work on this book, intended to be as useful to the interpreter as to the serious student. It is now available to all of us. I hope that every singer will keep this excellent volume within reach. Rarely has enthusiasm yielded so effective a result.

François Lesure

Preface

Around the turn of the century, French composers played a significant role in the renewal of the art song, an art form that had flourished earlier, chiefly in Germany. The most important of these composers were Chausson, Debussy, Duparc, Fauré, and Ravel. Of these, none surpassed Debussy's contribution to the genre. Few French *mélodies* are as perfect from both a literary and a musical standpoint. Undoubtedly, his secret lay in his equal sensitivity to the poem and to the music. Besides achieving a perfect union of the poetic and the musical ideas in his songs, he was able to discover in a poem that inner meaning of which the poet had allowed only a glimpse. With his sensibility, impeccable taste, and understanding of the rhythm of speech (Messiaen called him one of the greatest rhythmists of all time), he was uniquely equipped to blend words and music in a way that would never betray the poem's integrity. This is not surprising for the musician who wrote: "la musique et la poésie sont les deux seuls arts qui se meuvent dans l'espace"[1] (music and poetry are the only two arts that move in space) and "Les musiciens qui ne comprennent rien aux vers ne devraient pas en mettre en musique. Ils ne peuvent

---

[1] *La Revue blanche*, 1 June 1901.

que les gâcher."[2] (Musicians who do not understand poetry should not set it to music. They can only spoil it.)

The purpose of this book is twofold: first, to make available in one volume the texts of all of Debussy's songs, together with translations and notes; and second, to reveal through a selection of his letters and articles what his friend G. Jean-Aubry called "son esprit nourri de poésie" (his mind nourished by poetry).

Part I contains the texts of all of Debussy's songs: published, unpublished, unfinished, and fragmentary. Each text is immediately followed by a prose translation and notes. The notes include such information as date of composition, source, dedication, any changes Debussy made in text or title, location of the manuscript, and publisher and date of first publication. Much of this material has never been published.

In all, Debussy composed eighty-seven songs, including two that are unfinished, and he left preliminary sketches for four others. Nine songs were published after his death, and twenty-three still remain unpublished (one of these has appeared in a doctoral dissertation). The songs span Debussy's entire career as a composer. His first published work was *Nuit d'étoiles,* a song composed in 1880 and published in 1882. His next-to-last published composition was *Noël des enfants qui n'ont plus de maisons,* a song for which he wrote the words and music in December of 1915.

For his texts, he drew upon the works of twenty-three poets, and he himself wrote the texts of five songs. Almost half of the songs are settings of verses by six great poets: eighteen by Verlaine, five by Baudelaire, five by Charles d'Orléans, four by Mallarmé, three by Tristan Lhermite, and three by François Villon. (The three songs with texts by Charles d'Orléans, for chorus a cappella, are included here.)

Between 1879 and early 1887, Debussy composed forty-five songs to poems by thirteen poets. With the exception of Alfred de Musset, Théophile Gautier, and Leconte de Lisle, they were his contemporaries, and he probably knew most of them personally. Musset's verses yielded the texts for four songs, only one of which has been published, and that since Debussy's death. The two Gautier songs have never been published; of the three by Leconte de Lisle, only one has been published. Debussy's favorite poets during this period were Théodore de Banville, who provided him with eleven texts, although he published only one of these songs,

---

[2] *Musica,* March 1911.

three others were published after his death; and Paul Bourget from whose single volume of verse he chose nine poems, five of these songs were published. The six Verlaine settings of this period were all either slightly altered or completely rewritten before their publication. The early Mallarmé song *Apparition* was also composed during this period. Of each of five lesser poets—Charles Cros, André Girod, Edouard Guinand, Armand Renaud, and Léon Valade—and one unknown poet, he set one poem only. Except for Girod's *Fleur des blés*, the other songs are unpublished. Lastly, there exist an unfinished song and a short fragment on two poems by Maurice Bouchor.

From 1887 to 1915, Debussy composed thirty-nine songs, only one of which, the *Berceuse*, is unpublished. Two small fragments for the *Nuits blanches* also belong to this period. While remaining faithful to Verlaine and Mallarmé, he chose a new group of poets. Foremost among these were Baudelaire, Pierre Louÿs, and the three medieval poets Charles d'Orléans, Tristan Lhermite, and François Villon. The others were four minor contemporary poets: Vincent Hyspa, Grégoire Le Roy, René Peter, and Paul Gravollet.

Among the great songs of this period are the *Cinq Poèmes de Charles Baudelaire*, termed "oeuvres de génie" by Gabriel Fauré, the *Chansons de Bilitis* by Pierre Louÿs, *Le Promenoir des deux amants* by Tristan Lhermite, and the *Trois Ballades de François Villon.*

It was not until 1892 that Debussy composed the first of the songs for which he himself provided the texts: the four *Proses lyriques*. In 1899, he wrote to Georges Hartmann, his publisher, that he was sending him "*Nuits Blanches*: 5 poèmes pour une voix avec accompagnement de piano." (*Sleepless Nights*: 5 poems for one voice with piano accompaniment.) A single page is all that remains of this project. In December of 1915, haunted by the war, he wrote his last song, *Noël des enfants qui n'ont plus de maisons,* the last of his song texts.

Three poets merit our special attention: Verlaine, because he provided the greatest number of texts; Mallarmé, because of the long gap between Debussy's use of his texts; and Charles d'Orléans, because of the special rapport Debussy seems to have felt with the medieval poet.

Debussy's interest in Verlaine spanned a period of twenty-two years, during which he set eighteen Verlaine poems, including two versions of *Chevaux de bois*. As early as 1882, when Verlaine was as yet little known, Debussy had set six of his poems, having early appreciated the musical quality of his verses. Of these songs,

Mandoline was the only one he published; the others were published posthumously. By 1887, he had composed the six *Ariettes*, which he published the following year. In 1891, came two Verlaine triptychs, a form that would become a favorite of his. The *Fêtes galantes*, first series, consisted of three of the 1882 songs, two with entirely new settings, the third only slightly altered; these songs were published that same year. The *Trois Mélodies* were composed next, but these were not published until 1901. In 1903, he made slight changes in the *Ariettes* and published them under the title *Ariettes oubliées*. In 1904 came the last Verlaine settings, the *Fêtes galantes*, second series. One of the manuscripts of these songs bears the dedication: "pour remercier le moi de juin 1904." (This was shortly after Debussy met Emma Bardac, who was later to become his wife.)

Mallarmé was a somewhat unusual choice in 1884 because he, like Verlaine, was little known at the time. *Apparition*, only the second of Mallarmé's poems to be published, appeared in the periodical *Lutèce* in late 1883. Debussy set this poem early the following year, but he never published it. It first appeared in 1926 in a supplement to *La Revue musicale* and then in 1969 as one of the *Quatre Chansons de jeunesse*.

In 1913, nineteen years after the completion of the *Prélude à "l'Après-midi d'un Faune"* and fifteen years after the poet's death, Debussy returned to Mallarmé for his last triptych, the *Trois Poèmes de Stéphane Mallarmé*. A small notebook containing sketches for one of these songs, *Soupir*, also contains several pages of sketches for a new version of *Apparition*—twenty-nine years after Debussy's first setting of that poem.

Debussy first turned to the poems of Charles d'Orléans in 1898, setting two of them for an amateur choral group of which he was the director. These songs, for chorus a cappella, were not published until 1908 when, after significant alterations and the addition of a third song, they became the *Trois Chansons de Charles d'Orléans*. In 1904 he had chosen two rondeaux by this poet and three stanzas of a poem by Tristan Lhermite for the *Trois Chansons de France*. Although Debussy set only five poems by Charles d'Orléans, his letters indicate that he was familiar with many others.

It is in the letters that we sense the feeling of intimacy Debussy felt with this poet. He refers to him, in turn, as "mon oncle Charles d'Orléans," "le gentil Charles d'Orléans," and "doux prince aimé des muses et si gentil français" (sweet prince beloved of the muses and most noble Frenchman). No other poet is referred to in such terms; and with the exception of Jules Laforgue, none of whose poems he set, no other poet seems to be quoted or mentioned as frequently.

What may be one of Debussy's last notes, found in a small notebook, contains the first two lines of Rondeau CCLXXXVII by Charles d'Orléans: "Il n'est nul si beau passe temps / Que de jouer à sa pensée." (There is no more pleasant pastime / Than to toy with one's thoughts.)

Early on, Debussy found inspiration for his songs not only from the poets but also from a singer who was to have a great influence on him in more ways than one. She was his first great love and was to inspire him to write most of his early songs.

When he left in early 1885 for a two-year stay at the Villa Medici, his reward for having won the Premier Grand Prix de Rome with his cantata *L'Enfant prodigue* in 1884, he had composed forty songs—almost half of all he was to write. Of these, twenty-five were dedicated to Madame Vasnier, and several others were certainly composed with her in mind; the texts alone indicate this. She was a handsome, haughty bourgeoise with a soprano voice of high tessitura whom he had met at the singing classes of Madame Moreau-Sainti, where she was a pupil and he was the accompanist. Used to adulation, this femme fatale was flattered at being idealized by a promising young musician. Before long, Debussy was completely infatuated with her. Their liaison is now well known, and the dedications on *Caprice* and *Tragédie* alone reveal his feelings for her. Less well known are the fifteen unpublished songs he dedicated to her, the texts of which are all to be found in Part I.

Before leaving for Rome, Debussy gave Madame Vasnier, as a parting gift, a small volume entitled "Chansons" (the so-called "Vasnier Songbook"). It contained thirteen songs: *Pantomime, En sourdine, Mandoline, Clair de lune, Fantoches, Coquetterie posthume, Chanson espagnole, Romance* (Silence ineffable . . .), *Musique, Paysage sentimental, Romance* (Voici que le printemps . . .), *La Romance d'Ariel,* and *Regret.* The dedication on the title page reads: "à Madame Vasnier. Ces chansons qui n'ont jamais vécu que par elle, et qui perdront leur grace charmeresse, si jamais plus elles ne passent par sa bouche de fée mélodieuse. l'auteur éternellement reconnaissant. ACD" (To Madame Vasnier. These songs that have lived only through her and would lose their charming grace were they nevermore to issue from her melodious fairy mouth. the author eternally grateful. ACD)

While at the Villa Medici, Debussy made three frantic trips to Paris to see Madame Vasnier. However, their relationship came to an end soon after his final return to Paris in 1887. In 1888, she received his last gift: a copy of the newly published six *Ariettes* with the inscription: "à Madame Vasnier—hommage reconnaissant." Later, when *Mandoline,* composed in 1882, was first published in the *Revue illustrée* in 1890, it bore the dedication: "à Madame Vasnier" (the current edition still does). After that, we hear no more of her.

Part II of this book contains a selection of letters chosen to illustrate Debussy's particular interest in and knowledge of poetry. Although his biographers and others have mentioned his use of quotations from poems in his writings and identified a few here and there, no one has indicated the frequency with which such quotations are found or noted how naturally they are included in a given text.

The letters given here were written between 1889 and 1917. They span Debussy's most important years as a composer and demonstrate that his habit of using quotations went on year after year—all include a quotation from or a reference to a poem either by an author of a song text or by some other poet. The first group includes such poets as Banville, Baudelaire, Charles d'Orléans, Mallarmé, and Verlaine. The poems quoted are not always those of the song texts. The second group includes Corbière, Laforgue, Hugo, Malherbe, and Vigny. With the exception of Laforgue, these poets are not usually thought of in connection with Debussy.

Some of the letters are addressed to close friends such as André Caplet, Jacques Durand, and Robert Godet, all of whom would have been familiar with the song texts. Others are addressed to acquaintances such as Alexandre Charpentier, Serge de Diaghilev, and Walter Rummel, none of whom would necessarily have recognized a quotation from one of the songs.

Finally, three articles have been included because of the particularly interesting quotations found in each one. Evidence of the great pains Debussy took writing his articles is found in letters to Émile Vuillermoz, editor of the review *S.I.M.* (Société internationale de musique). In one letter, dated 6 November 1912, he remarks that an article had given him more trouble to write than a symphony. In another, dated 26 October 1913, he warns Vuillermoz that if a single sentence is changed everything will fall. In these carefully written articles we find further proof that poetry was ever in Debussy's thoughts and was an essential part of his very nature.

Occasional references to other quotations are included in the notes to the songs and to the letters. Many others undoubtedly lie hidden in published and unpublished letters, waiting to be identified and added to the ones given here, which are but a beginning. In the meantime, it is hoped that the selection presented here will indicate how great a part poetry played in Debussy's daily life and thoughts.

Debussy's contemporaries frequently mentioned his relationship to poetry, but Pierre Lalo (music critic and son of Edouard Lalo) best expressed it when he said: "Car ce que nous avons aimé chez M. Debussy c'est son sentiment poètique, c'est l'essence même de sa sensibilité et de son esprit." (For what we have enjoyed in Mr. Debussy is his feeling for poetry, the very essence of his sensitivity and of his mind.) Of interest in this connection is Debussy's comment in a letter to Robert Godet of 18 December 1916, in which he describes a concert at which he had accompanied his *Noël des enfants qui n'ont plus de maisons*:

"Cela se passa dans un monde de riches bourgeois au coeur habituellement dur! Ils pleuraient, cher ami, au point que je me demandais s'il ne fallait par leur faire des excuses!

Dois-je remercier *le poète ou le musicien*?" [emphasis added]

(It took place before a crowd of rich and habitually hardhearted bourgeois! They wept, dear friend, to such an extent that I wondered whether I ought not to ask their forgiveness!

Should I thank *the poet or the musician*?)

Part III contains notes on twenty-six other Debussy compositions based on or inspired by literary texts, including poems, plays, and tales. Five of the compositions written while Debussy was a pupil at the Conservatoire are to texts assigned for various competitions. The last of these was the cantata *L'Enfant prodigue*, for which he was awarded the Premier Grand Prix de Rome in 1884.

Fourteen of these twenty-six compositions were never completed, and of some only fragments remain. They range in date from 1882 to 1917. Among the authors of the early texts are two familiar poets, Banville and Leconte de Lisle, whose poems Debussy had used for his songs. Another name less readily linked with Debussy's is that of Henri (Heinrich) Heine. The unfinished song *Tragédie* (c. 1881) was based on one of his poems; *Intermezzo* (1882), also unfinished, was inspired by a poem in prose; and *Zuléima* (1885–1886), which Debussy reluctantly finished and used as his first *envoi* from Rome, was also based on a work by Heine. Two unusual operatic works, which haunted Debussy over a long period and for which he attempted to write his own libretti, are *Le Diable dans le Beffroi* (*The Devil in the Belfry*) (1902–1911) and *La Chute de la Maison Usher* (*The Fall of the House of Usher*) (1908–1917), based on two tales by Edgar Allan Poe. In a letter of 1909 to Gabriel Mourey, Debussy wrote of his remorse for "ce curieux besoin de ne pas finir" (this strange compulsion for not finishing).

The six completed works are all well known. The three most important are *La Damoiselle élue* (1887–1888), *Prélude à "l'Après-midi d'un Faune"* (1892–1894), and *Pelléas et Mélisande* (1893–1902). The text of *La Damoiselle élue* is included here, as it is the only one of these compositions whose text is actually a poem. It is also of interest because it was Debussy's first major composition, and also because of the changes he made not only in the title but in every stanza of the poem. Therefore Debussy's version, which he termed "d'après D.-G. Rossetti" (based on D.-G. Rossetti), Sarrazin's French translation, and Rossetti's original poem have all been included (see Appendix B).

Explanatory Notes
The song texts are given in chronological order of composition, in most cases following the order used by François Lesure in his *Catalogue de l'oeuvre de Claude Debussy.*

The titles and numbering of the songs follow those in the first published editions. Numbers and titles in parentheses indicate those not used in these editions; they are included here for convenience in identification.

The *Quatre Chansons de jeunesse* are not entered as such. These songs—*Pantomime, Clair de lune,* first version, *Pierrot,* and *Apparition*—date from 1882 to 1884, were never published by Debussy, and did not appear under this title until 1969.

The sources given for the poems approximate as nearly as possible those Debussy would have used.

Debussy's songs were all composed for solo voice with piano accompaniment, with the following four exceptions: *Chanson espagnole* is for two voices, *Églogue* is a duo for soprano and tenor, the *Berceuse* is for solo voice without accompaniment, and the *Trois Chansons de Charles d'Orléans* are for four voices a cappella.

The publishers and dates of publication are those of the first edition.

In Part II, "Letters and Articles," Debussy's use of quotation marks has been carefully followed. The italics have been added so as to identify the quotations more easily, especially those which Debussy did not set apart.

Acknowledgments
My first thanks go to François Lesure, head of the Music Department of the Bibliothèque Nationale, Paris. Without his help this book would not have been possible. He put at my disposal many important documents, supplied clues for finding others, and gave me invaluable aid during the course of my research. His *Catalogue de l'oeuvre de Claude Debussy* has served as the basis of my work. At his suggestion I was appointed *animatrice* of the Centre de Documentation Claude Debussy, where for four years I was able to study the many photocopies of manuscripts that form part of the collections of the Centre.

I wish also to express my gratitude to: Mme Dolly de Tinan, who kindly gave me permission to translate and publish the letters to André Caplet and several hitherto unknown letters and to reproduce manuscripts of unpublished songs; Mme Henri Goüin, for her warm reception at the Bibliothèque Musicale François-Lang, Abbaye de Royaumont, where I was able to identify the manuscript of the published version of *Chevaux de bois*; Mrs. Gregor Piatigorsky, for having graciously supplied me with the text of the *Chanson espagnole,* which is given here for the first time; Roy Howat, Jean-Michel Nectoux, Richard Miller, and James A. Hepokoski for their many very helpful suggestions, which they will find duly incorporated in this book; and to Alexis Leger, with whom I first discussed this project and who never failed to show his keen interest and lend me his moral support.

I wish to thank the Houghton Library of Harvard University, the Library of Congress, and the Bibliothèque Nationale, Paris, for permission to publish photographs of their manuscripts, most of which have never before been reproduced; and the Humanities Research Center, The University of Texas at Austin, for being able to verify the date and the form of address on the letter to René Peter from the autograph.

Finally, my family deserve a special tribute for their patience and continued support during the years this book was in preparation.

The following letters have been translated and printed by kind permission of the publishers:

Letters of 22 July 1910, 17 September 1910, 22 July 1915, and 9 October 1915 from *Claude Debussy: Lettres à son éditeur*, © Éditions Durand & Cie.

Letters of 1893(?), 6 May 1898, and 19 August 1899 from *Claude Debussy*, by René Peter, © Éditions Gallimard.

Letters of 10 July 1889, 25 December 1889, 14 July 1914, 6 October 1916, and 28 July 1917 from *Lettres à deux amis: soixante-dix-huit lettres inédites à Robert Godet et G. Jean-Aubry*, © Librairie José Corti.

Letters of 29 November 1910, 4 December 1913, and 9 December 1913 from *Lettres de Claude Debussy à sa femme Emma*, © Librairie Ernest Flammarion.

The following song texts have been translated and printed by kind permission of the publishers:

La Flûte, La Chevelure, and *Le Tombeau des Naïades* from *Chansons de Bilitis*, by Pierre Louÿs, © Editions Albin Michel.

Les Angelus from *La Chanson du Pauvre*, by Grégoire Le Roy, and *La Chanson de la mère*, from *La Tragédie de la Mort*, by René Peter, © Mercure de France.

Beau soir, Romance (Les feuilles s'ouvraient . . .), *Musique, Paysage sentimental, Romance* (L'Âme évaporée . . .), *Romance* (Silence ineffable . . .), *Romance* (Voici que le printemps . . .), *Regret* (Devant le ciel d'été . . .), *La Romance d'Ariel* from *Les Aveux*, by Paul Bourget, © Société des Gens de Lettres de France.

The program of the concert of 12 May 1882 is reprinted from *La Revue musicale*, 1 May 1926, by kind permission of Éditions Richard-Masse.

Margaret G. Cobb

New York, 1981

Part I
Song Texts

Chronological List of Songs

BALLADE À LA LUNE

— *Alfred de Musset*

C'était, dans la nuit brune,
Sur un clocher jauni,
  La lune
Comme un point sur un i.

Lune, quel esprit sombre
Promène au bout d'un fil,
  Dans l'ombre,
Ta face et ton profil?

Es-tu l'oeil du ciel borgne?
Quel chérubin cafard
  Nous lorgne
Sous ton masque blafard?

N'es-tu rien qu'une boule?
Qu'un grand faucheux bien gras
  Qui roule
Sans pattes et sans bras?

Es-tu, je t'en soupçonne,
Le vieux cadran de fer
  Qui sonne
L'heure aux damnés d'enfer?

Sur ton front qui voyage,
Ce soir ont-ils compté
  Quel âge
A leur éternité?

Est-ce un ver qui te ronge,
Quand ton disque noirci
  S'allonge
En croissant rétréci?

Qui t'avait éborgnée
L'autre nuit? T'étais-tu
  Cognée
À quelque arbre pointu?

BALLAD TO THE MOON

There, in the dusky night above the sere steeple, was the moon, like a dot on an i.

Moon, what dark spirit leads you, face and profile, leashed through the shadows?

Are you the eye of the one-eyed sky? What loony cherubim peers down at us behind your pallid mask?

Are you merely a ball? Are you a huge harvest spider toiling along, legless and armless?

Are you—as I suspect—the old iron clock that tolls the hour for the damned in hell?

Do they this evening read on your traveling face the extent of their eternity?

Are you being eaten away by a worm when your blackened disc stretches out into a thin crescent?

Who put out your eye the other night? Did you run into some sharp treetop?

NOTES FOR *BALLADE À LA LUNE*

Date: c. 1879
Source: Alfred de Musset, *Poésies 1828–1833*, Contes d'Espagne et d'Italie, Chansons à mettre en musique. Alphonse Lemerre, Paris 1876, pp. 26–31.
Manuscript: not found
Comments: The complete poem contains thirty-four stanzas. The first nine and the last three only are given here.
Paul Vidal, a friend and fellow student at the Conservatoire, wrote of having heard the song (see *La Revue musicale*, 1 May 1926, p. 12). This is the only known reference to this song.
The song is unpublished.

Car tu vins, pâle et morne,
Coller sur mes carreaux
   Ta corne
À travers les barreaux.

Comme un ours à la chaîne,
Toujours sous tes yeux bleus
   Se traîne
L'Océan montueux.

Et qu'il vente ou qu'il neige,
Moi-même, chaque soir,
   Que fais-je
Venant ici m'asseoir?

Je viens voir à la brune,
Sur le clocher jauni,
   La lune
Comme un point sur un i.

MADRID, PRINCESSE DES ESPAGNES[1]

— *Alfred de Musset*

Madrid, princesse des Espagnes,
Il court par tes mille campagnes
Bien des yeux bleus, bien des yeux noirs.
La blanche ville aux sérénades,
Il passe par tes promenades
Bien des petits pieds tous les soirs.

Madrid, quand tes taureaux bondissent,
Bien des mains blanches applaudissent,
Bien des écharpes sont en jeu.
Par tes belles nuits étoilées,
Bien des senoras long voilées
Descendent tes escaliers bleus.

Because you showed up pale and dejected to stick your horn against the panes of my window, through the bars.

Like a bear on a chain, the mountainous ocean moves slowly beneath your blue eyes.

And I too, wind or snow, what do I do each evening when I come to sit here?

I come to see in the dusky night above the sere steeple the moon, like a dot on an i.

MADRID, PRINCESS OF ALL SPAIN

Madrid, princess of all Spain, many are the blue eyes and the dark eyes that teem through your vast campañas. White city of serenades, many are the tiny feet that pass each evening along your promenades.

Madrid, when your bulls charge, many are the white hands that applaud, many are the scarves that wave. In your lovely starry nights, many are the señoras in long veils who descend your blue staircase.

NOTES FOR *MADRID, PRINCESSE DES ESPAGNES*

Date: c. 1879
Source: Alfred de Musset, *Poésies 1828–1833,* Contes d'Espagnes et d'Italie, Chansons à mettre en musique. Alphonse Lemerre, Paris 1876, pp. 18–19.
Manuscript: not found
Dedication: P. Vidal et Passerieu
[1] The title of the poem is *Madrid.*
Comments: Paul Vidal, a friend and fellow student at the Conservatoire, wrote of having heard the song (see *La Revue musicale,* 1 May 1926, p. 12).
The song is unpublished.

Madrid, Madrid, moi, je me raille
De tes dames à fine taille
Qui chaussent l'escarpin étroit;
Car j'en sais une par le monde,
Que jamais ni brune ni blonde
N'ont valu le bout de son doigt!

J'en sais une, et certes la duègne
Qui la surveille et la peigne
N'ouvre sa fenêtre qu'à moi;
Certes, qui veut qu'on le redresse
N'a qu'à l'approcher à la messe,
Fût-ce l'archevêque ou le roi.

Car c'est ma princesse andalouse!
Mon amoureuse! ma jalouse!
Ma belle veuve au long réseau!
C'est un vrai démon! c'est un ange!
Elle est jaune comme une orange,
Elle est vive comme un oiseau!

Oh! quand sur ma bouche idolâtre
Elle se pâme, la folâtre,
Il faut voir, dans nos grands combats,
Ce corps si souple et si fragile,
Ainsi qu'une couleuvre agile,
Fuir et glisser entre mes bras.

Or, si d'aventure on s'enquête
Qui m'a valu telle conquête,
C'est l'allure de mon cheval,
Un compliment sur sa mantille,
Puis des bonbons à la vanille,
Par un beau soir de carnaval.

———————

Madrid, Madrid, I for one scoff at your thin-waisted ladies in their narrow slippers; for I know one unequaled in all the world—there is no blonde or brunette who is worth the tip of her finger!

I know one, and the duenna who watches over her and combs her hair opens her window for me alone; of course, if you're looking to be rebuffed, you need only try to approach her at mass, be you archbishop or king.

For she is my Andalusian princess! My lover, my jealous one! My beautiful widow in her long lace veil! She is a demon, an angel! She is golden as an orange and lively as a bird!

Ah! when she swoons against my adoring mouth like a mad thing, you should see how, in our struggles, her supple and fragile body becomes an agile snake, fleeing and sliding within my arms.

Now, if anyone should happen to ask what won me such a conquest, I owe it to the appeal of my horse, to a compliment about her mantilla, and to vanilla bonbons on a fine carnival evening.

———————

NUIT D'ÉTOILES[1]

— Théodore de Banville

Nuit d'étoiles,
Sous tes voiles,
Sous ta brise et tes parfums,
Triste lyre
Qui soupire,
Je rêve aux amours défunts.
[Je rêve aux amours défunts.][2]

La sereine mélancolie
Vient éclore au fond de mon coeur,
Et j'entends l'âme de ma mie
Tressaillir dans le bois rêveur.

Nuit d'étoiles,
Sous tes voiles,
Sous ta brise et tes parfums,
Triste lyre
Qui soupire,
Je rêve aux amours défunts.
[Je rêve aux amours défunts.][2]

Je revois à notre fontaine
Tes regards bleus comme les cieux;
Cette rose, c'est ton haleine,
Et ces étoiles sont tes yeux.

Nuit d'étoiles,
Sous tes voiles,
Sous ta brise et tes parfums,
Triste lyre
Qui soupire,
Je rêve aux amours défunts.
[Je rêve aux amours défunts.][2]

———————

STARRY NIGHT

Starry night, beneath your veils, your breeze and your perfume, like a
sad sighing lyre, I dream of bygone loves.

Serene melancholy blooms in the depths of my heart, and I hear the
soul of my love quiver in the dreaming woods.

Starry night, beneath your veils, your breeze and your perfume, like a
sad sighing lyre, I dream of bygone loves.

At our fountain I again see your glances, blue as the sky; this rose is
your breath and these stars are your eyes.

Starry night, beneath your veils, your breeze and your perfume, like a
sad sighing lyre, I dream of bygone loves.

NOTES FOR *NUIT D'ÉTOILES*

Date: 1880
Source: Théodore de Banville, *Les Cariatides*, Les Stalactites. G. Charpentier,
Paris 1879, pp. 269–270.
Manuscript: in a private collection in the United States
Dedication: "à Madame Moreau-Sainti"
[1] The title of the poem is *La Dernière pensée de Weber*.
[2] Added by Debussy
Publisher: Société Artistique d'Édition d'Estampes et de Musique, Paris 1882
Comments: The second stanza and the refrain following it are omitted.
This was Debussy's first published composition. It is the only one of the
eleven songs he set to Banville's poems that he published. Three were published
posthumously; the remaining seven remain unpublished.

CAPRICE

— *Théodore de Banville*

Quand je baise, pâle de fièvre,
Ta lèvre où court une chanson,
Tu détournes les yeux, ta lèvre
Reste froide comme un glaçon,
Et, me repoussant de tes bras,
Tu dis que je ne t'aime pas.

Mais si je dis: Ce long martyre
M'a brisé, je romps mon lien!
Tu réponds avec un sourire:
Viens à mes pieds! tu le sais bien,
Ma chère âme, que c'est ton sort
De m'adorer jusqu'à la mort.

FLEUR DES BLÉS

— *André Girod*

Le long des blés que la brise
Fait onduler puis défrise
En un désordre coquet,
J'ai trouvé de bonne prise
De t'y cueillir un bouquet.

Mets-le vite à ton corsage;
Il est fait à ton image
En même temps que pour toi...
Ton petit doigt, je le gage,
T'a déjà soufflé pourquoi:

CAPRICE

When, pale with fever, I kiss your lips from which a song springs forth, you avert your eyes, your lips remain cold as ice, and thrusting me away from your arms you say I do not love you.

But if I say: this long martyrdom has destroyed me, I'm breaking my bonds! You reply with a smile: Come to my feet! You know full well, dear soul, that you are destined to adore me until death.

FLOWERS OF THE WHEAT FIELDS

Among the wheat that the breeze causes to curl and then uncurl in coquettish disorder, I took the notion to gather a bouquet for you.

Put it quickly in your bodice, it was made in your image as it was made for you... I wager you already suspect why.

NOTES FOR *CAPRICE*

Date: 1880
Source: Théodore de Banville, *Les Exilés*, Améthystes, Nouvelles odelettes amoureuses composées sur des rhythmes de Ronsard. G. Charpentier, Paris 1878, p. 220.
Manuscript: in the Bibliothèque Nationale, Paris
Dedication: "À Madame Vasnier—Ces mélodies conçues en quelque sorte par votre souvenir ne peuvent que vous appartenir comme vous appartient l'auteur Ach. Debussy"
(To Madame Vasnier—These songs conceived somehow in your memory can belong only to you as does the author)
On the title page: "Poésie de xxx très inconnu / Musique de xxxx moins inconnu"
(Poetry by xxx very unknown / Music by xxxx less unknown)
Comment: This song appeared in a doctoral dissertation: Peter Ruschenburg, "Stilkritische Untersuchungen zu den Liedern Claude Debussy," Hamburg 1966, pp. 167–168.

NOTES FOR *FLEUR DES BLÉS*

Date: c. 1880
Source: André Girod (place and date of publication unknown)
Manuscript: not found
Dedication: "à Madame E. Deguingand"
Publisher: Vve Girod, Éditeur, Paris 1891

Ces épis dorés, c'est l'onde
De ta chevelure blonde
Toute d'or et de soleil;
Ce coquelicot qui fronde
C'est ta bouche au sang vermeil.

Et ces bluets, beau mystère!
Points d'azur que rien n'altère,
Ces bluets ce sont tes yeux
Si bleus qu'on dirait, sur terre
Deux éclats tombés des cieux.

—————————

RÊVERIE[1]

— Théodore de Banville

Le zéphyr à la douce haleine
Entrouvre les roses des bois,[2]
Et sur les monts et dans la plaine
Il féconde tout à la fois.

Le lys et la rouge verveine
S'échappent fleuris de ses doigts,
Tout s'entrouvre à sa coupe pleine[3]
Et chacun tressaille à sa voix.

Mais il est une frêle plante
Qui se retire et fuit, tremblante,
Le baiser qui va la meurtrir.

Or, je sais des âmes plaintives
Qui sont comme les sensitives
Et que le bonheur fait mourir.

—————————

These golden ears are the waves of your blond hair all golden and sunlight; this scoffing poppy is your blood-red mouth.

And these cornflowers, lovely mystery! Azure points impervious to change, these cornflowers are your eyes, so blue that they are like two fragments of fallen sky.

REVERIE

The sweet-breathed breeze opens the wild roses and makes fertile everything on mountain and plain.

The lily and the red verveine fall flowering from its fingers, everything comes into full bloom and quivers at its voice.

But one frail plant draws back and flees trembling the kiss that will kill it.

I know plaintive souls who are like sensitive plants, and who die from happiness.

NOTES FOR *RÊVERIE*

Date: c. 1880
Source: Théodore de Banville, *Les Cariatides*, Livre Deuxième, Amours d'Elise, feuillets détachés—no. V. G. Charpentier, Paris 1879, p. 79.
Manuscript: in a private collection in France
On the title page: "Musique de   On n'a jamais su"
(Music by   No one knows who)
[1] The poem has no title.
[2] Entrouvre *les roses* des bois (Debussy)
Entr'ouvre *la rose* des bois (Banville)
[3] Tout s'*entrouvre* à sa coupe pleine (Debussy)
Tout s'*enivre* à sa coupe pleine (Banville)
Comment: The song is unpublished.

SOUHAIT[1]

— *Théodore de Banville*

Oh! quand la Mort, que rien ne saurait apaiser,
Nous prendra tous les deux dans un dernier baiser
Et jettera sur nous le manteau de ses ailes,
Puissions-nous reposer sous deux pierres jumelles!
Puissent les fleurs de rose aux parfums embaumés
Sortir de nos deux corps qui se sont tant aimés,
Et nos âmes fleurir ensemble, et sur nos tombes
Se regarder longtemps d'amoureuses colombes![2]

ZÉPHYR[1]

— *Théodore de Banville*

Si j'étais le Zéphyr ailé,
J'irais mourir sur votre bouche.
Ces voiles, j'en aurais la clé,
Si j'étais le Zéphyr ailé.
Près des seins, pour qui je brûlais,
Je me glisserais dans la couche.
Si j'étais le Zéphyr ailé,
J'irais mourir sur votre bouche.

HOPE

Ah! when Death whom none can appease takes us both in one final
kiss and covers us with the cloak of its wings, may we rest beneath
twin stones! May roses with their balmy perfume emerge from our bod-
ies which so loved each other, may our souls flower together, and may
amorous doves look long at each other on our tombs!

ZEPHYR

Were I the winged Zephyr, I would go to expire on your mouth. I
would possess the key to these veils, were I the winged Zephyr. I
would slide into bed next to those breasts for which I yearned. Were I
the winged Zephyr, I would go to expire on your mouth.

NOTES FOR *SOUHAIT*

Date: Florence, 1881
Source: Théodore de Banville, *Les Cariatides,* Les Stalactites. G. Charpentier,
Paris 1879, p. 222.
Manuscript: in a private collection in France
[1] The poem has no title.
[2] Se *regarder* longtemps d'amoureuses colombes (Debussy)
Se *becqueter* longtemps d'amoureuses colombes (Banville)
First performance: Claire Croiza at the Salle Gaveau, 29 June 1938.
Comment: The song is unpublished.

NOTES FOR *ZÉPHYR*

Date: Rome, November 1881
Source: Théodore de Banville, *Les Cariatides,* Livre Troisième—En habit zin-
zolin—no. II. G. Charpentier, Paris 1879, p. 200.
Manuscript: in a private collection in France
[1] The title of the poem is *Triolet à Philis*
Publisher: B. Schott's Söhne, Mainz 1932
Comment: The title was added by the publisher.

LES ROSES

— Théodore de Banville

Lorsque le ciel de saphir est de feu,[1]
Lorsque l'été de son haleine touche
La folle Nymphe amoureuse, et par jeu
Met un charbon rougissant sur sa bouche;
Quand sa chaleur dédaigneuse et farouche
Fait tréssaillir le myrte et le cyprès,
On sent brûler sous ses magiques traits
Les fronts blêmis et les lèvres mi-closes[2]
Et le riant feuillage des forêts,
Et vous aussi, coeurs enflammés des Roses.

———————

ROSES

When the sapphire sky is afire, when summer touches with its breath the mad Nymph in love and playfully places a glowing ember on her lips; when its disdainful and untamed heat makes the myrtle and cypress quiver, one can feel its magical touch burning pale foreheads and half-closed lips, and the laughing forest leaves, and you too, you Roses with flaming hearts.

NOTES FOR *LES ROSES*

Date: c. 1881
Source: Théodore de Banville, *Les Cariatides*, Livre Troisième—Les Caprices, en dixains à la manière de Clément Marot—no. XV. G. Charpentier, Paris 1879, p. 186.
Manuscript: in a private collection in France
Dedication: "à Madame Vasnier"
[1] Lorsque le ciel est *de* feu (Debussy)
Lorsque le ciel est *en* feu (Banville)
[2] Les fronts blêmis et les lèvres *mi-closes* (Debussy)
Les fronts blêmis et les lèvres *décloses* (Banville)
First performance: Madame Vasnier accompanied by Achille de Bussy at the Salons Flaxland, 12 May 1882
Comment: The song is unpublished.

SÉGUIDILLE

— Théophile Gautier

Un jupon serré sur les hanches,
Un peigne énorme sur son chignon,[1]
Jambe nerveuse et pied mignon,
Oeil de feu, teint pâle et dents blanches;
    Alza! olà
    Voilà
La véritable Manola.

Gestes hardis, libre parole,
Sel et piment à pleine mains,
Oubli parfait du lendemain,
Amour fantasque et grâce folle.

Chanter, danser aux son des castagnettes,[2]
Et, dans les courses de taureaux,
Juger les coups des toréros,
Tout en fumant des cigarettes.

[Amour fantasque.][3]

————————

SEGUIDILLA

Skirt drawn tight across the hips, enormous comb in her chignon, nervous leg and charming foot, fiery eye, pale skin, white teeth—Alza O la, behold Manola herself.

Bold gestures, bold words, handfuls of salt and pimento, perfect forgetfulness of the morrow, temperamental love and mad grace.

Singing, dancing to the sound of castanets and, at the bullfights, analyzing the toreadors' feats while smoking cigarettes.

[Temperamental love.]

NOTES FOR *SÉGUIDILLE*

Date: c. 1881
Source: Théophile Gautier, *Poésies complètes,* Tome second, Espana 1845. Charpentier et Cie, Paris 1876, p. 113.
Manuscript: in a private collection in the United States
Dedication: "à Madame Vasnier"
[1] Un peigne énorme *sur* son chignon (Debussy)
Un peigne énorme *à* son chignon (Gautier)
[2] Chanter, danser *au son des* castagnettes (Debussy)
Chanter, danser *aux* castagnettes (Gautier)
[3] Line added by Debussy
Comments: The refrain is omitted after the second and the third stanzas. The song is unpublished.

PIERROT

— Théodore de Banville

Le bon Pierrot, que la foule contemple,
Ayant fini les noces d'Arlequin,
Suit en songeant le boulevard du Temple.
Une fillette au souple casaquin
En vain l'agace de son oeil coquin;
Et cependant mystérieuse et lisse
Faisant de lui sa plus chère délice,
La blanche lune aux cornes de taureaux
Jette un regard de son oeil en coulisse
À son ami Jean Gaspard Debureau.[1]

_____

PIERROT

Good Pierrot, watched by the crowd, having done with Harlequin's wedding, wanders dreamily along the Boulevard du Temple. A girl with a clinging blouse vainly importunes him with her mocking glance; and meanwhile, mysterious and polished, cherishing him above all things, the white moon with horns like a bull peers into the wings at his friend Jean Gaspard Debureau.

NOTES FOR *PIERROT*

Date: c. 1881
Source: Théodore de Banville, *Les Cariatides*, Livre Troisième—Les Caprices, en dixains à la manière de Clément Marot—no. VI. G. Charpentier, Paris 1879, pp. 181–182.
Manuscript: in The Library of Congress, Washington, D.C.
Dedication: "à Madame Vasnier"
On the title page: Musique sur l'air de (Music to the tune of . . .)

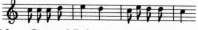

[1] Jean Gaspard Debureau (1796–1848), French mîme who created the role of Pierrot
Publisher: *La Revue musicale*, 1 May 1926, Supplément musical, *Quatre mélodies inédites de Claude Debussy. Quatre Chansons de jeunesse*, Éditions Jobert, Paris 1969
Comment: The tune, on the title page, is *Au clair de la lune*, a folksong, the opening words of which are: "Au clair de la lune, mon ami Pierrot."

AIMONS-NOUS ET DORMONS[1]

— *Théodore de Banville*

Aimons-nous et dormons
Sans songer au reste du monde;
Ni le flot de la mer, ni l'ouragan des monts,
Tant que nous nous aimons
N'effleurera ta tête blonde,[2]
Car l'amour est plus fort
Que les Dieux et la mort!

Le soleil s'éteindrait
Pour laisser ta blancheur plus pure.
Le vent, qui jusqu'à terre incline la forêt,
En passant n'oserait
Jouer avec ta chevelure,
Tant que tu cacheras
Ta tête entre mes bras!

Et lorsque nos deux coeurs
S'en iront aux sphères heureuses
Où les célestes lys écloront sous nos pleurs,
Alors, comme deux fleurs,
Joignons nos lèvres amoureuses,
Et tâchons d'épuiser
La mort dans un baiser!

———————

LET US LOVE AND SLEEP

Let us love and sleep without dreaming of the rest of the world; neither the sea swell nor the mountain storm, so long as we love each other, shall touch your blond head, for love is stronger than either the Gods or death!

The sun would cease to burn in order to leave your pallor more pure. The wind, which bows the forest to the ground, would not dare to play with your hair as it passes, so long as you hide your head in my arms!

And when our hearts depart for the blessed spheres where celestial lilies will open beneath our tears, then like two flowers let us join our loving lips, and let us try to wear death out with a kiss!

NOTES FOR *AIMONS-NOUS ET DORMONS*

Date: c. 1881
Source: Théodore de Banville, *Les Exilés*, Odelettes. G. Charpentier, Paris 1878, pp. 184–185.
Manuscript: in a private collection in France
Dedication: "à mon ami Paul Vidal"
[1] The poem has no title.
[2] *N'effleurera* ta tête blonde (Debussy)
Ne courbera ta tête blonde (Banville)
Publisher: *The Etude*, February 1933, pp. 110–111. Theodore Presser Company, Bryn Mawr, Pa., 1933

RONDEL CHINOIS

— Author unknown

Sur le lac bordé d'azalée
De nénuphar et de bambou
Passe une jonque d'acajou
À la pointe éffilée.

Une chinoise dort voilée
D'un flot de crèpe jusqu'au cou.
Sur le lac bordé d'azalée
De nénuphar et de bambou.

Sous sa véranda dentelée
Un mandarin se tient debout
Fixant de ses yeux de hibou
La dame qui passe isolée
Sur le lac bordé d'azalée.

———————

CHINESE RONDEL

On the lake, bordered with azaleas, waterlilies and bamboo, a mahogany junk with pointed bow passes.

A Chinese girl is asleep, veiled in a swath of crepe up to her neck, on the lake bordered with azaleas, waterlilies and bamboo.

On his lacy veranda, a mandarin stands watching with his owl's eyes the lady passing alone on the lake bordered with azaleas.

———————

NOTES FOR *RONDEL CHINOIS*

Date: c. 1881
Source: unknown
Manuscript: in The Library of Congress, Washington, D.C.
Dedication: "À Madame Vasnier la seule qui peut chanter et faire oublier tout ce que cette musique à d'inchantable et de chinois. Ach. Debussy"
(To Madame Vasnier, the only one who can sing and cause to be forgotten all this music possesses of the unsingable and Chinese)
On the title page: "Musique chinoise (d'après des manuscrits du temps)"
(Chinese music [based on contemporary manuscripts])
Comments: The song is unpublished.

TRAGÉDIE

— Léon Valade

Les petites fleurs n'ont pu vivre.
Une nuit d'avril a surpris
Leurs calices bleus: sous le givre
Ils sont morts, ils sont flétris.

Deux enfants s'aimaient d'amour tendre.
Un beau jour le couple est parti;
Parti du pays! sans attendre
Que père ou mère eût consenti...

Partout leur fuite vagabonde
S'est butté à de mauvais sorts;
Ils ont eu nul bonheur au monde,
Ils se sont flétris, ils sont morts.

———————

TRAGEDY

The tiny flowers could not live, an April night took their blue chalices by surprise: they are dead beneath the frost, they have withered.

Two children fell tenderly in love. One fine day they went away, left the country! without awaiting their fathers' or mothers' consent...

They met with misadventures in the course of their vagabond flight; they found no happiness in the world, they withered and they died.

NOTES FOR *TRAGÉDIE*

Date: c. 1881
Source: Léon Valade, *Nocturnes, poèmes imités de Henri Heine.* A. Patay, Paris 1880, p. 35.
Manuscript: in a private collection in Germany
Dedication: "À Madame Vasnier la seule muse qui m'ait jamais inspiré quelque chose ressemblant à un sentiment musical (pour ne parler que de celui-là)"
(To Madame Vasnier, the sole Muse who has ever inspired in me anything resembling musical feeling [to mention only that one])
Comment: The song is unpublished.

JANE

— Leconte de Lisle

Je pâlis et tombe en langueur:
Deux beaux yeux m'ont blessé le coeur.

Rose pourprée et tout humide,
Ce n'était pas sa lèvre en feu;
C'étaient ses yeux d'un si beau bleu
Sous l'or de sa tresse fluide.

Je pâlis et tombe en langueur:
Deux beaux yeux m'ont brisé le coeur.[1]

Toute mon âme fut ravie,
Doux étaient son rire et sa voix;
Mais ses deux yeux bleus, je le vois
Ont pris mes forces et ma vie.

Je pâlis et tombe en langueur:
Deux beaux yeux m'ont brisé le coeur.[1]

Hélas, la chose est bien certaine:
Si Jane repousse mon voeu,
Dans ses deux yeux d'un si beau bleu
J'irai puisé ma mort prochaine.[2]

Je pâlis et tombe en langueur:
Deux beaux yeux m'ont brisé le coeur.[1]

———

JANE

I grow pale and listless: my heart has been wounded by two lovely eyes.

It was not her fiery lip, moist crimson rose; it was her eyes of such a lovely blue beneath the gold of her flowing tresses.

I grow pale and listless: my heart has been broken by two lovely eyes.

All my soul was enraptured, her laugh and her voice were sweet; but her two blue eyes, I see, have sapped my strength and my life.

I grow pale and listless: my heart has been broken by two lovely eyes.

Alas, it's all too true: if Jane rejects my suit, I will die from her two beautiful blue eyes.

I grow pale and listless: my heart has been broken by two lovely eyes.

NOTES FOR *JANE*

Date: c. 1881
Source: Leconte de Lisle, *Poèmes antiques*, Chansons écossaises—no. I. Alphonse Lemerre, Paris 1874, pp. 290–291.
Manuscript: in a private collection in Belgium
Dedication: "à Madame Vasnier"
[1] Deux beaux yeux m'ont *brisé* le coeur (Debussy)
Deux beaux yeux m'ont *blessé* le coeur (Leconte de Lisle)
[2] *J'irai* puisé ma mort prochaine (Debussy)
J'aurai puisé ma mort prochaine (Leconte de Lisle)
Publisher: Theodore Presser, Bryn Mawr, Pa., 1982
First performance: Claire Croiza at the Salle Gaveau, 29 June 1938.
Comment: This song appeared in a doctoral dissertation: Peter Ruschenburg, "Stilkritische Untersuchungen zu den Liedern Claude Debussy," Hamburg 1966, pp. 169–170.

FANTOCHES

— *Paul Verlaine*

Scaramouche et Pulcinella
Qu'un mauvais dessein rassembla
Gesticulent, noirs sous la lune.

Cependant l'excellent docteur
Bolonais cueille avec lenteur
Des simples parmi l'herbe brune.

Lors sa fille, piquant minois,
Sous la charmille, en tapinois,
Se glisse demi-nue, en quête

De son beau pirate espagnole,
Dont un langoureux rossignol
Clame la détresse à tue-tête.

————————

MARIONETTES

Scaramouche and Pulcinella, brought together by some evil scheme, gesticulate, black beneath the moon.

In the meantime, the good Bolognese doctor slowly picks simples in the twilit grass.

While his daughter, a saucy minx, steals slyly half-naked, seeking

Her handsome Spanish pirate, whose distress is loudly proclaimed by a languorous nightingale.

NOTES FOR *FANTOCHES*

Date: 8 January 1882
Source: Paul Verlaine, *Fêtes galantes.* Alphonse Lemerre, Paris 1869, pp. 25–26.
Manuscripts: (1) dated, in the Toscanini Memorial Archives, New York Public Library, Lincoln Center, New York; (2) undated, in the Bibliothèque Nationale, Paris
Dedication: "à Madame Vasnier" (fifth in the "Vasnier Songbook")
Comments: This version is unpublished. A second slightly different version, composed in 1891, is no. II of *Fêtes galantes,* first series.

O FLORAISON DIVINE DES LILAS[1]

— *Théodore de Banville*

O floraison divine des Lilas,[2]
Je te bénis, pour si peu que tu dures!
Nos pauvres coeurs de souffrir étaient las;
Enfin l'oubli guérit nos peines dures.
Enivrez-vous, fleurs, horizons, verdures!
Le clair réveil du matin gracieux
Charme l'azur irradié des cieux;
Mai fleurissant cache les blanches tombes,
Tout éclairé de feux délicieux,
Et l'air frémit, blanc des vols de colombes.

———————

AH, DIVINE LILAC BLOOMING

Ah, divine lilac blooming, I bless you, however little time you last! Our poor hearts are tired of suffering; forgetfulness, at last, heals our harsh sorrows. Flowers, horizons, greenery, drink deep! The graceful morning's clear awakening charms the radiant blue of the sky; flowering May conceals the white tombs, everything is illuminated by delightful fires, and the air trembles, white with the flight of doves.

———————

NOTES FOR *O FLORAISON DIVINE DES LILAS*

Date: 12 April 1882
Source: Théodore de Banville, *Les Cariatides*, Livre Troisième—Les Caprices, en dixains à la manière de Clément Marot—no. XVII. G. Charpentier, Paris 1879, p. 187.
Manuscript: in a private collection in France
[1] The title of the poem is *Le Lilas*
[2] O floraison divine *des* lilas (Debussy)
O floraison divine *du* lilas (Banville)
First performance: Claire Croiza at the Salle Gaveau, 29 June 1938
Comment: The song is unpublished.

FÊTE GALANTE

— Théodore de Banville

Voilà Silvandre et Lycas et Myrtil,
Car c'est ce soir fête chez Cydalise,
Partout dans l'air court un parfum subtil;
Dans le grand parc où tout s'idéalise
Avec la rose Aminthe rivalise.
Philis, Eglé, qui suivent leurs amants,
Cherchent l'ombrage en mille endroits charmants;[1]
Dans le soleil qui s'irrite et qui joue,
Luttant d'orgueil avec les diamants,
Sur leur chemin le Paon blanc fait la roue.

FÊTE GALANTE

Behold Silvandre and Lycas and Myrtil, for tonight there's a celebration at the home of Cydalise, a subtle perfume fills the air; in the vast park, where all is perfection, Aminta rivals the rose. Phyllis and Eglia, who pursue their lovers, seek the shadows in a thousand charming spots; beneath the sun that excites and plays, proudly emulating diamonds, the white peacock spreads its tail on their path.

NOTES FOR *FÊTE GALANTE*

Date: 1882
Source: Théodore de Banville, *Les Cariatides,* Livre Troisième—Les Caprices, en dixains à la manière de Clément Marot—no. III. G. Charpentier, Paris 1879, p. 180.
Manuscripts: (1) dated manuscript, with the dedication, in a private collection in France; (2) undated manuscript in the Bibliothèque musicale François-Lang, Abbaye de Royaumont, France
Dedication: "à Madame Vasnier"
On the title page: "Musique Louis IXV avec formules 1882"
[1] Cherchent l'ombrage *en mille endroits* charmants (Debussy)
Cherchent l'ombrage *et les abris* charmants (Banville)
First performance: Madame Vasnier accompanied by Achille de Bussy at the Salons Flaxland, 12 May 1882
Comment: The song is unpublished.

FLOTS, PALMES, SABLES

— Armand Renaud

Loin des yeux du monde,
La mer est profonde,
Les palmiers sont hauts,
Les sables sont chauds.

S'il te faut les endroits calmes
Où tout chante et tout bénit,
Viens au fond du bois des palmes,
Avec moi, choisir un nid,
Un nid où, mort pour la foule,
Nous vivrons pour l'eau qui coule,
Pour le ramier qui roucoule
À l'heure où le jour finit.

Loin des yeux du monde,
La mer est profonde,
Les palmiers sont hauts,
Les sables sont chauds.

S'il te faut les endroits mornes
Où le corps est châtié,
Allons au désert sans bornes,
Sous le soleil sans pitié;
T'ayant là, je serai forte,
Mourir! mourir! que m'importe,
Si je partage, étant morte,
Ton sépulcre par moitié!

Loin des yeux du monde,
La mer est profonde,
Les palmiers sont hauts,
Les sables sont chauds.

———————

WAVES, PALMS, SANDS

Far from anyone's eyes, the sea is deep, the palm trees are high, the sands are hot.

If you desire calm places where everything sings and showers down blessings, come into the palm forest with me, choose a nest, a nest where, dead to the world, we will live for the running water, for the wood dove cooing at the hour when day falls.

Far from anyone's eyes, the sea is deep, the palm trees are high, the sands are hot.

If you desire dismal places where the body is punished, let us go to the trackless desert beneath the pitiless sun; with you there, I would be strong, dying! dying! what would it matter if when dead I shared half your tomb!

Far from anyone's eyes, the sea is deep, the palm trees are high, the sands are hot.

NOTES FOR *FLOTS, PALMES, SABLES*

Date: 2 June 1882
Source: Armand Renaud, *Poésies de Armand Renaud*, Les Nuits persanes—Idylles japonaises—Orient. Alphonse Lemerre, Paris 1870, pp. 88–89.
Manuscript: in a private collection in the United States
Dedication: "à Madame Vasnier"
Comments: The second stanza is omitted. The first stanza is repeated, as a refrain, between the third and the fourth stanzas.
The song is unpublished.

EN SOURDINE

— *Paul Verlaine*

Calmes dans le demi-jour
Que les branches hautes font,
Pénétrons bien notre amour
De ce silence profond.

Fondons nos âmes, nos coeurs
Et nos sens extasiés,
Parmi les vagues langueurs[1]
Des pins et des arbousiers.

Ferme tes yeux à demi,
Croise tes bras sur ton sein,
Et de ton coeur endormi
Chasse à jamais tout dessein.

Laissons-nous persuader
Au souffle berceur et doux,
Qui vient à tes pieds rider
Les ondes de gazon roux.

Et quand, solennel, le soir
Des chênes tombera,[2]
Voix de notre désespoir,
Le rossignol chantera.

[Voix de notre désespoir,
Le rossignol chantera.][3]

———————

MUTED

Calm in the half light made by the lofty branches, let us permeate our love with this deep silence.

Let us mingle our souls, our hearts, our senses in ecstasy among the vague murmurings of the pines and arbutus trees.

Half close your eyes, fold your arms across your bosom, and let your sleeping heart empty itself of all thought forever.

Let us be wooed by the lulling and gentle breeze that wrinkles the russet grass at your feet.

And when evening descends solemnly from the oaks, the nightingale will sing, the voice of our despair.

NOTES FOR *EN SOURDINE*

Date: Vienna, 16 September 1882
Source: Paul Verlaine, *Fêtes galantes*. Alphonse Lemerre, Paris 1869, pp. 49–50.
Manuscripts: (1) dated, in the Bibliothèque Nationale, Paris; (2) dated, in a private collection in the United States (version published in 1944); (3) undated, in a private collection in the United States
Dedication: "à Madame Vasnier" (on Paris manuscript only) (second in the "Vasnier Songbook")
[1] Parmi les *molles* langueurs (Debussy, undated manuscript)
Parmi les *vagues* langueurs (Verlaine)
[2] Des chênes tombera (Debussy, dated manuscript, published 1944)
Des chênes *noirs* tombera (Verlaine)
[3] Lines added by Debussy
Publisher: Elkan-Vogel, Philadelphia, Pa., 1944. The title: *Calmes dans le Demi-jour (En sourdine) In Undertones*
First performance: G. Jean-Aubry presented this song at a concert given by *La Revue musicale*, 14 March 1938, with Madame Blanc-Audra.
Comments: These three manuscripts all show slight differences. On the back of the last page of the undated manuscript are the first nine bars of an early version of *Mandoline*.
An entirely different version of this song, composed in 1891, is no. I of *Fêtes galantes*, first series.

MANDOLINE

— *Paul Verlaine*

Les donneurs de sérénades
Et les belles écouteuses
Échangent des propos fades
Sous les ramures chanteuses.

C'est Tircis et c'est Aminte,[1]
Et c'est l'éternel Clitandre,
Et c'est Damis qui pour mainte
Cruelle fait maint vers tendre.

Leurs courtes vestes de soie,
Leurs longues robes à queues,
Leur élégance, leur joie
Et leurs molles ombres bleues

Tourbillonnent dans l'extase
D'une lune rose et grise,[2]
Et la mandoline jase
Parmi les frissons de brise.

———————

MANDOLINE

The serenaders and the lovely listeners exchange idle banter beneath the singing branches.

There is Tircis, and Aminte, and the eternal Clitandre, and there is Damis who made so many tender verses for so many cruel women.

Their short silken jackets and their long trailing gowns, their elegance, their joy, and their soft blue shadows

Twirl in the ecstasy of a pink and gray moon, and the mandoline chatters on amidst the trembling breezes.

NOTES FOR *MANDOLINE*

Date: Vienna, 25 November 1882

Source: Paul Verlaine, *Fêtes galantes*. Alphonse Lemerre, Paris 1869, pp. 33–34.

Manuscripts: (1) dated manuscript, with the dedication, in the Bibliothèque Nationale, Paris; (2) undated manuscript in the Houghton Library, Harvard University, Cambridge, Mass.

Dedication: "à Madame Vasnier" (third in the "Vasnier Songbook")

[1] C'est Tircis et c'est *Lycandre* (Debussy, undated manuscript)

C'est Tircis et c'est *Aminte* (Verlaine)

[2] D'une lune *grise et rose* (Debussy, undated manuscript)

D'une lune *rose et grise* (Verlaine)

Publisher: *La Revue illustrée*, 1 September 1890, pp. 185–188, with illustrations by Willette. Durand et Schoenewerk, Paris 1890

Comments: On the back of the last page of the undated manuscript are found the first sixteen bars of an early version of *En sourdine*, without the words.

RONDEAU

— *Alfred de Musset*

Fut-il jamais douceur de coeur pareille
À voir Manon dans mes bras, sommeiller.
Son front coquet parfume l'oreiller,
Dans son beau sein, j'entends son coeur qui veille.
Un songe passe et s'en vient l'égayer.

Ainsi s'endort la fleur d'églantier[1]
Dans son calice enfermant une abeille.
Moi, je la berce, un plus charmant métier,
        Fut-il jamais?

Mais le jour vient, et l'aurore vermeille
Effeuille au vent son printemps virginal,[2]
Le peigne en main et la perle à l'oreille
À son miroir, Manon va m'oublier.[3]
Hélas! l'amour sans lendemain ni veille
        Fut-il jamais?

———————

RONDEAU

Was anything ever sweeter to my heart than to see Manon sleeping in my arms. Her lovely forehead perfumes the pillow, and within her fair bosom I can hear her heart keeping watch. A dream passes and its passing makes her happy.

Thus sleeps the eglantine with a bee enclosed in its chalice. And I rock her in my arms—was there ever a more charming occupation?

But day comes and the vermillion dawn scatters her virginal springtime to the winds. With her comb in hand and a pearl in each ear, Manon will look into her mirror and forget me. Alas, was there ever such a love, knowing no yesterday and no tomorrow?

NOTES FOR *RONDEAU*

Date: 1882
Source: Alfred de Musset, *Poésies nouvelles*. Alphonse Lemerre, Paris 1876, p. 243.
Manuscript: once owned by the publisher, now lost
Dedication: "Pour mon ami Alexandre de Meck souvenir bien affectueux" (For my friend Alexandre de Meck, this affectionate souvenir)
    [1] Ainsi s'endort *la* fleur d'églantier (Debussy)
Ainsi s'endort *une* fleur d'églantier (Musset)
    [2] Effeuille au vent son *printemps virginal* (Debussy)
Effeuille au vent son *bouquet printanier* (Musset)
    [3] À son miroir, Manon *va* m'oublier (Debussy)
À son miroir, Manon *court* m'oublier (Musset)
Publisher: B. Schott's Söhne, Mainz 1932

PANTOMIME

— *Paul Verlaine*

Pierrot, qui n'a rien d'un Clitandre,
Vide un flacon sans plus attendre,
Et, pratique, entame un pâté.
[Pierrot, qui n'a rien d'un Clitandre,
Vide un flacon sans plus attendre.][1]

Cassandre, au fond de l'avenue,
Verse une larme méconnue
Sur son neveu déshérité.

Ce faquin d'Arlequin combine
L'enlèvement de Colombine
Et pirouette quatre fois.
[Et pirouette quatre fois.][1]

Colombine rêve, surprise
De sentir un coeur dans la brise
Et d'entendre en son coeur des voix.
[Et d'entendre en son coeur des voix.
Ah.][1]

PANTOMIME

Pierrot, who is nothing like Clitandre, empties a flagon at one gulp and, practical as he is, cuts into a pâté.

Cassandre, at the end of the allée, sheds a silent tear for her disinherited nephew.

Harlequin, the cad, plots to kidnap Columbine and twirls around four times.

Columbine is dreaming, surprised at feeling a heart on the breeze and at hearing voices in her heart.

NOTES FOR *PANTOMIME*

Date: 1882
Source: Paul Verlaine, *Fêtes galantes*. Alphonse Lemerre, Paris 1869, pp. 3–4.
Manuscript: in the Bibliothèque Nationale, Paris
Dedication: "à Madame Vasnier" (first in the "Vasnier Songbook")
[1] Added by Debussy
Publisher: *La Revue musicale*, 1 May 1926. Supplément musical, *Quatre mélodies inédites de Claude Debussy. Quatre Chansons de jeunesse*, Editions Jobert, Paris 1969

CLAIR DE LUNE

— Paul Verlaine

Votre âme est un paysage choisi
Que vont charmant masques et bergamasques
Jouant du luth et dansant et quasi
Tristes sous leurs déguisements fantasques.

Tout en chantant sur le mode mineur
L'amour vainqueur et la vie opportune,
Ils n'ont pas l'air de croire à leur bonheur
Et leur chanson se mêle au clair de lune,
[Et leur chanson se mêle au clair de lune,]¹

Au calme clair de lune triste et beau,
Qui fait rêver les oiseaux dans les arbres
Et sangloter d'extase les jets d'eau,
Les grands jets d'eau sveltes parmi les marbres.
[Ah—
Au calme clair de lune triste et beau.]¹

MOONLIGHT

Your soul is a choice landscape where charming masqueraders and ber-
gamaskers pass to and fro playing the lute and dancing almost sadly in
their fantastic disguises.

They sing the while in the minor mode of conquering love and the easy
life, they do not seem to believe in their happiness and their song min-
gles with the moonlight,

With the calm moonlight, sad and lovely, that makes the birds dream in
the trees and the fountains sob with ecstasy, those tall, svelte fountains
among the marbles.

———————

NOTES FOR *CLAIR DE LUNE*

Date: 1882
Source: Paul Verlaine, *Fêtes galantes*. Alphonse Lemerre, Paris 1869, pp. 1–2.
Manuscripts: (1) in the Bibliothèque Nationale, Paris; (2) in the Newberry
Library, Chicago, Ill.
Dedication: "à Madame Vasnier" (fourth in the "Vasnier Songbook")
[1] Added by Debussy
Publisher: *La Revue musicale,* 1 May 1926, Supplément musical, *Quatre
mélodies inédites de Claude Debussy. Quatre Chansons de jeunesse*, Editions Jobert,
Paris 1969
Comments: An entirely different version of this song, composed in 1891, is
no. III of *Fêtes galantes,* first series.

LA FILLE AUX CHEVEUX DE LIN

— *Leconte de Lisle*

Sur la luzerne en fleur assise,
Qui chante dans le frais matin?[1]
C'est la fille aux cheveux de lin,
La belle aux lèvres de cerise.

L'amour, au clair soleil d'été,
Avec l'alouette a chanté.

Ta bouche a des couleurs divines,
Ma chère, et tente le baiser!
Sur l'herbe en fleur veux-tu causer,
Fille aux cils longs, aux boucles fines?

L'amour, au clair soleil d'été,
Avec l'alouette a chanté.

Ne dis pas non, fille cruelle!
Ne dis pas oui! J'entendrai mieux
Le long regard de tes grands yeux
Et ta bouche fine, ô ma belle![2]

Adieu les daims, adieu les lièvres
Et les rouges perdrix! Je veux
Baiser le blond de tes cheveux,[3]
Presser la pourpre de tes lèvres!

L'amour, au clair soleil d'été,
Avec l'alouette a chanté.

———————————

THE GIRL WITH THE FLAXEN HAIR

Seated among the flowering alfalfa, who is singing in the cool morning? It is the girl with the flaxen hair, the beauty with the cherry lips.

Love, with the clear sun of summertime, has sung with the lark.

Your mouth, my dear, has divine hues and tempts kisses! Would you like to chat here on the flowering grass, you with the long eyelashes and delicate curls?

Love, with the clear sun of summertime, has sung with the lark.

Do not say no, cruel girl! Do not say yes! I would rather listen to the long look of your wide-open eyes and your delicate mouth, my lovely one!

Farewell deer, farewell hares and russet partridges! I want to kiss the blond of your hair and press the purple of your lips!

Love, with the clear sun of summertime, has sung with the lark.

————

NOTES FOR *LA FILLE AUX CHEVEUX DE LIN*

Date: c. 1882
Source: Leconte de Lisle, *Poèmes antiques,* Chansons écossaises—no. IV. Alphonse Lemerre, Paris 1874, pp. 293–294.
Manuscript: in a private collection in Austria
Dedication: "À Madame Vasnier qui a realisé ce problème que, ce n'est pas la musique qui fait la beauté du chant, mais le chant qui fait la beauté de la musique. (Surtout [pour] la mienne) l'auteur humble et reconnaissant"
(To Madame Vasnier, who is aware of the problem that the music doesn't make beautiful singing, but that singing makes the music beautiful [above all mine], from the humble and grateful author)
On the last page: "Tout ce que je peux avoir de bon dans le cerveau est là dedans   Voyez et jugez   Ach. Debussy"
(Everything in my brain that is good is herein   See and judge)
[1] Qui chante *dans* le frais matin (Debussy)
Qui chante *dés* le frais matin (Leconte de Lisle)
[2] Et ta *bouche fine,* ô ma belle (Debussy)
Et ta *lèvre rose,* ô ma belle (Leconte de Lisle)
[3] Baiser le *blond* de tes cheveux (Debussy)
Baiser le *lin* de tes cheveux (Leconte de Lisle)
Comments: The refrain is omitted between the third and the fourth stanzas. The song is unpublished.
La Fille aux cheveux de lin is the title of Prelude no. VIII, from Book I, composed between 1909 and 1910.

SÉRÉNADE

— *Théodore de Banville*

Las! Colombine a fermé le volet,
Et vainement le chasseur tend ses toiles,
Car la fillette au doux esprit follet,
De ses rideaux laissant tomber les voiles,
S'est dérobée, ainsi que les étoiles.
Bien qu'elle cache à l'amant indigent
Son casaquin pareil au ciel changeant,
C'est pour charmer cette beauté barbare
Que remuant comme du vif-argent,
Arlequin chante et gratte sa guitare.

———————

SERENADE

Ah! Columbine has closed the shutter, and the hunter vainly spreads his toils, for the little girl, sweet and fanciful, has drawn her curtains like a veil and concealed herself like the stars. Although she hides from her deprived lover her blouse that is like the changing sky, Harlequin, to charm this wild beauty, moves like quicksilver, sings and plucks his guitar.

NOTES FOR *SÉRÉNADE*

Date: c. 1882
Source: Théodore de Banville, *Les Cariatides*, Livre Troisième—Les Caprices, en dixains à la manière de Clément Marot—no. VII. G. Charpentier, Paris 1879, p. 182.
Manuscript: in a private collection in France
Dedication: "à Madame Vasnier"
First performance: Claire Croiza at the Salle Gaveau, 29 June 1938.
Comment: The song is unfinished and unpublished.

COQUETTERIE POSTHUME

— *Théophile Gautier*

Quand je mourrai, que l'on me mette,
Avant de clouer mon cercueil,
Un peu de rouge à la pommette,
Un peu de noir au bord de l'oeil.

Car je veux, dans ma bière close,
Comme le soir de son aveu,
Rester éternellement rose
Avec du kh'ol sous mon oeil bleu.

Posez-moi, sans jaune immortelle,
Sans coussin de larmes brodé,
Sur mon oreiller de dentelle
De ma chevelure inondé.

Cet oreiller, dans les nuits folles,
A vu dormir nos fronts unis,
Et sous le drap noir des gondoles
Compté nos baisers infinis.

Entre mes mains de cire pâle,
Que la prière réunit,
Tournez ce chapelet d'opale,
Par le Pape à Rome bénit:

Je l'égrènerai dans la couche
D'où nul encor ne s'est levé;
Sa bouche en a dit sur ma bouche
Chaque *Pater* et chaque *Ave*.

Quand je mourrai, que l'on me mette,[1]
Avant de clouer mon cercueil,
Un peu de rouge à la pommette,
Un peu de noir au bord de l'oeil.

———

POSTHUMOUS COQUETTRY

When I die, let me—before my coffin is nailed shut—be given a touch of red on my cheeks and a touch of black at the edges of my eyes.

For in my closed coffin I want to be as I was on the evening he made his vows to me, eternally pink, with kohl beneath my blue eyes.

Without yellow immortelles or a cushion embroidered with tears, lay me on my lace pillow with my hair flowing about me.

That pillow has on passionate nights witnessed us asleep, our foreheads touching, and the black sheet still bears the forms of our endless embraces.

Between my pale waxen hands joined in prayer, slip this opal rosary blessed by the Pope in Rome:

I shall tell it on the couch from which no one has yet ever arisen; his mouth against mine has said each *Pater* and *Ave.*

When I die, let me—before my coffin is nailed shut—be given a touch of red on my cheeks and a touch of black at the edges of my eyes.

———————

NOTES FOR *COQUETTERIE POSTHUME*

Date: 31 March 1883
Source: Théophile Gautier, *Emaux et camées.* Charpentier et Cie, Paris 1872, pp. 39–41.
Manuscript: in the Bibliothèque Nationale, Paris
Dedication: "à Madame Vasnier" (sixth in the "Vasnier Songbook")
[1] Stanza added by Debussy
First performance: G. Jean-Aubry presented this song, sung by Madame Blanc-Audra, at a concert given by *La Revue musicale,* 14 March 1938.
Comments: The third and the fourth stanzas are omitted.
The song is unpublished.

CHANSON ESPAGNOLE[1]

— *Alfred de Musset*

Nous venions de voir le taureau,
   Trois garçons, trois filles,[2]
Sur la pelouse il faisait beau,
Et nous dansions un boléro
   Au son des castagnettes:
      Dites moi, voisin,
      Si j'ai bonne mine,
      Et si ma basquine
      Va bien ce matin,
Vous me trouvez la taille fine?
Les filles de Cadix aiment assez cela.

Et nous dansions un boléro,
   Un soir, c'était dimanche,
Vers nous s'ent vint un hidalgo,
Cousu d'or, la plume au chapeau,
   Et le poing sur la hanche:
      Si tu veux de moi,
      Brune au doux sourire,
      Tu n'as qu'a le dire,
      Cet or est à toi.
—Passez votre chemin, beau sire,
Les filles de Cadix n'entendent pas cela!

———————

SPANISH SONG

We have just seen the bull, three boys, three girls; it was a lovely day
on the lawn, and we danced a bolero to the sound of castanets.
"Tell me, neighbor, do I look well, does my basquine suit me this
morning, don't you find I have a fine figure? The girls of Cadiz enjoy
that."

And we danced a bolero one Sunday evening, and a hidalgo ap-
proached us dressed all in gold embroidery with a feather in his cap
and his hand on his hip. "If you like me, smiling, dark-haired beauty,
you have but to say it and this gold is yours!" "On your way, handsome gentleman. . . ." The girls of Cadiz don't listen to that sort
of thing.

NOTES FOR *CHANSON ESPAGNOLE*

Date: 1883
Source: Alfred de Musset, *Oeuvres posthumes, Poésies diverses*. Alphonse
Lemerre, Paris 1876, p. 18.
Manuscript: in the Bibliothèque Nationale, Paris
Dedication: "à Madame Vasnier" (seventh in the "Vasnier Songbook")
[1] The title of the poem is *Chanson*
[2] Trois garçons, trois *filles* (Debussy)
Trois garçons, trois *fillettes* (de Musset)
Comments: The last stanza of the poem is omitted. The song, written for
two equal voices, is unpublished.
On the back of the last page of the manuscript of *Diane au bois*, Debussy
copied out in pencil the three stanzas of this poem.

BEAU SOIR

— *Paul Bourget*

Lorsque au soleil couchant les rivières sont roses,
Et qu'un tiède frisson court sur les champs de blé,
Un conseil d'être heureux semble sortir des choses
    Et monter vers le coeur troublé;

Un conseil de goûter le charme d'être au monde
Cependant qu'on est jeune et que le soir est beau,
Car nous nous en allons, comme s'en va cette onde:
    Elle à la mer,—nous au tombeau!

———————

BEAUTIFUL EVENING

When in the setting sun the rivers are rose and a warm breeze passes over the wheat fields, a command to be happy seems to emanate from all things and mount to the unquiet heart;

A command to enjoy the charm of being alive while one is young and the evening is beautiful, for we are departing as this wave departs: it to the sea—we to the tomb!

———

NOTES FOR *BEAU SOIR*

Date: 1883
Source: Paul Bourget, *Les Aveux*, Livre Second, Dilettantisme, *En voyage*—no. VII. Alphonse Lemerre, Paris 1882, p. 105.
Manuscript: not found
Publisher: Vve Girod, Éditeur, Paris 1891
Comment: This song has been variously dated between 1878 and 1880. Because *Les Aveux*, first published in 1882, contains the group of poems *En voyage*, the title of which bears the note: "Irlande, Ecosse (1881)," these early dates cannot be justified. We suggest 1883 as the more likely date for this song.

ROMANCE

— Paul Bourget

Silence ineffable de l'heure
Où le coeur aimant sur un coeur
Se laisse en aller et s'endort,
— Sur un coeur aimant qui l'adore!...[1]

Musique tendre des paroles,
Comme un sanglot de rossignols,
Si tendre qu'on voudrait mourir,
— Sur la bouche qui la soupire!...[2]

L'ivresse ardente de la vie
Fait défaillir l'amant ravi,
Et l'on n'entend battre qu'un coeur,
— Musique et silence de l'heure!...

ROMANCE

Ineffable silence of the hour when the heart in love allows itself to relax upon another heart and sleep—on a loving heart that adores it!...

Tender music of words like the sobbing of nightingales, so tender one wants to expire—upon the mouth that emits it like a sigh!...

Ardent intoxication of life that weakens the enraptured lover, and one hears the beating of only one heart—music, and the silence of the hour!...

NOTES FOR *ROMANCE*

Date: September 1883
Source: Paul Bourget, *Les Aveux*, Livre Premier—Amour. Alphonse Lemerre, Paris 1882, p. 16.
Manuscript: in the Bibliothèque Nationale, Paris
Dedication: "à Madame Vasnier" (eighth in the "Vasnier Songbook")
[1] Sur un coeur *qui l'adore* (Debussy)
Sur un coeur *qu'il adore* (Bourget)
[2] Sur la bouche qui *la* soupire (Debussy)
Sur la bouche qui *les* soupire (Bourget)
First performance: G. Jean-Aubry presented this song, sung by Madame Blanc-Audra, at a concert given by *La Revue musicale*, 14 March 1938.
Comment: The song is unpublished.

MUSIQUE

— *Paul Bourget*

La lune se levait, pure, mais plus glacée
Que le ressouvenir de quelque amour passé.
Les étoiles, au fond du ciel silencieux,
Brillaient, mais d'un éclat changeant, comme des yeux
Où flotte une pensée insaisissable à l'âme.
Et le violon, tendre et doux, comme une femme
Dont la voix s'affaiblit dans l'ardente langueur,
Chantait: "Encore un soir perdu pour le bonheur."

—————————

PAYSAGE SENTIMENTAL

— *Paul Bourget*

Le ciel d'hiver, si doux, si triste, si dormant,
Où le soleil errait parmi des vapeurs blanches,
Était pareil au doux, au profond sentiment
Qui nous rendait heureux mélancoliquement,
Par cet après-midi de baisers sous les branches.

Branches mortes qu'aucun souffle ne remuait,
Branches noires avec quelque feuille fanée,
Ah! que ta bouche s'est à ma bouche donnée
Plus tendrement encore dans ce grand bois muet,
Et dans cette langueur de la mort de l'année!

MUSIC

The moon rose, pure but icier than the distant memory of some past love. The stars against the silent sky glittered, but changeably—like eyes reflecting the unknowable thoughts of the soul. And the violin, tender and soft, like a woman's voice weak with ardent languor, sang: "Another evening lost for happiness."

THE LANDSCAPE OF FEELING

The winter sky, so soft, so sad, so dormant, through which the sun wandered in the white mists, was like that soft and profound emotion that made us melancholically happy one afternoon when we kissed beneath the branches.

Dead branches, stirred by no breath, black branches with here and there a faded leaf, Ah! how your mouth gave itself up to mine more tenderly than ever in that vast, silent woods, in that languor of the death of the year!

NOTES FOR *MUSIQUE*

Date: 1883
Source: Paul Bourget, *Les Aveux*, Livre Premier—Amour. Alphonse Lemerre, Paris 1882, p. 50.
Manuscript: in the Bibliothèque Nationale, Paris
Dedication: "à Madame Vasnier" (ninth in the "Vasnier Songbook")
Comment: The song is unpublished.

NOTES FOR *PAYSAGE SENTIMENTAL*

Date: November 1883
Source: Paul Bourget, *Les Aveux*, Livre Premier—Amour. Alphonse Lemerre, Paris 1882, p. 17.
Manuscript: in the Bibliothèque Nationale, Paris
Dedication: "à Madame Vasnier" (tenth in the "Vasnier Songbook")
Publisher: *La Revue illustrée,* 15 April 1891, p. 342. Société Nouvelle d'Éditions Musicales (Anc. maison Paul Dupont), Paris 1907

La mort de tout, sinon de toi que j'aime tant,
Et sinon du bonheur dont mon âme est comblée,
Bonheur qui dort au fond de cette âme isolée,
Mystérieux, paisible et frais comme l'étang
Qui pâlissait au fond de la pâle vallée.[1]

————————

L'ARCHET

— *Charles Cros*

Elle avait de beaux cheveux blonds
Comme une moisson d'août, si longs
Qu'ils lui tombaient jusqu'aux talons.

Elle avait une voix étrange,
Musicale, de fée ou d'ange,
Des yeux verts sous leur noire frange.

Lui, ne craignait pas de rival,
Quand il traversait mont ou val,
En l'emportant sur son cheval.

Mais l'amour la prit fort au coeur,[1]
Que pour un sourir moqueur,
Il lui vint un mal de langueur.

Et dans ses dernières caresses:

————————

The death of everything, if not of you whom I so love, and if not of the happiness that overflows my soul, a happiness sleeping deep within that solitary soul, mysterious, peaceful and fresh as the spring that palely flows there below in the pale valley.

––––––––––

THE BOW

She had lovely blond hair like an autumn harvest, so long that it fell to her heels.

She had a strange voice, musical, like that of a sprite or an angel, and green eyes beneath their black fringe.

He feared no rival as he crossed the mountain or valley, bearing her on his steed.

But love had so touched her heart that for a mocking smile she fell ill of languishing.

And in her last caresses:

––––––––––

NOTES FOR *PAYSAGE SENTIMENTAL*

[1] *Qui pâlissait* au fond de la pâle vallée (Debussy song and second edition of poem)
Que nous vîmes au fond de la pâle vallée (Debussy manuscript and first edition of poem)

NOTES FOR *L'ARCHET*

Date: c. 1883
Source: Charles Cros, *Le Coffret de santal,* Divinations—no. 10. Alphonse Lemerre, Paris 1873, p. 27.
Manuscript: in a private collection in France
[1] *Mais* l'amour la prit fort au coeur (Debussy)
L'amour la prit *si* fort au coeur (Cros)
Comments: The following stanzas are omitted: the fourth, the last two lines of the sixth, and the seventh to the thirteenth (the last).
The song is incomplete and unpublished.

CHANSON TRISTE[1]

— *Maurice Bouchor*

On entend un chant sur l'eau
   Dans la brume;
Ce doit être un matelot
Qui veut se jeter à l'eau
   Pour la lune.

La lune entr'ouvre le flot
   Qui sanglote,
Le matelot tombe à l'eau...
On entend traîner sur l'eau
   Quelques notes.

FLEUR DES EAUX[1]

— *Maurice Bouchor*

Non, les baisers d'amour n'éveillent point les morts!
Baise l'amour vivant de ta lèvre divine;
Et le dernier soupir que rendra ta poitrine
Ne sera point chargé d'inutiles remords.

Non, les baisers d'amour n'éveillent point les morts.
N'en crois pas là-dessus les ballades anciennes!
Chantez, chantez toujours, lèvres musiciennes,
La chanson des amours qui vivent sans remords.

On ne fait point l'amour dans le lit froid des morts!
On ne cherche pas des yeux dans la nuit noire.
N'en crois pas là-dessus quelque ancienne histoire;
Sous terre on n'a pas plus d'amour que de remords.

SAD SONG

There is a singing on the water through the mist; it must be a sailor longing to throw himself into the water for the moon.

The moon cleaves the sobbing waves, the sailor falls into the water... a few notes drift back across the water.

FLOWER OF THE WATERS

No, love's kisses do not wake the dead! Kiss a living love with your divine lips; and the last sigh from your bosom will never be laden with futile regrets.

No, love's kisses do not wake the dead. Don't believe what the romantic ballads say about it! Sing, sing always, musical lips, the song of loves that live without regrets.

There is no lovemaking in death's cold bed! One does not seek out someone's eyes in the black night. Don't believe some old story when it comes to that; beneath the earth there is no love, just as there is no regret.

NOTES FOR *CHANSON TRISTE*

Date: c. 1883
Source: Maurice Bouchor, *Les Poèmes de l'Amour et de la Mer*, La Fleur des eaux—no. III. Charpentier & Cie, Paris 1876, p. 14.
Manuscript: in a private collection in France
[1] The sketches have no title.
Comment: Sketches only are found in a small notebook.

NOTES FOR *FLEUR DES EAUX*

Date: c. 1883
Source: Maurice Bouchor, *Les Poèmes de l'Amour et de la Mer*, La Fleur des eaux—no. XXXVI. Charpentier & Cie, Paris 1876, pp. 77–78.
Manuscript: in a private collection in France
[1] The fragment has no title.
Comment: The words in italics are all that is found in a small notebook.

Viens, aime-moi d'amour, ne pensons pas aux morts!
Ne montre pas le ciel de ta belle main blanche.
Cueilles-en les beaux fruits de l'amour, *sur la branche*
Où ne s'est pas glissé l'affreux ver de remords.

ÉGLOGUE

— *Leconte de Lisle*

Gallus
Chanteurs mélodieux, habitants des buissons,
Le ciel pâlit, Vénus à l'horizon s'éveille;
Cynthia vous écoute, enivrez son oreille
Des flots d'or de vos belles chansons.[1]

Cynthia
La nuit sereine monte, et roule sans secousse
Le choeur éblouissant des astres au ciel bleu;
Moi, de mon bien-aimé, jeune et beau comme un Dieu,
J'ai l'image en mon âme et j'entends la voix douce.

Gallus
O Cynthia, sais-tu mon rêve et mon désir?
Phoebé laisse tomber sa lueur la plus belle,
Et l'amoureux ramier gémit et bat de l'aile,
Et dans les bois songeurs passe un divin soupir.

Cynthia
La source s'assoupit et murmure apaisée,
Et de molles clartés baignent les noirs gazons.
Qu'ils sont doux à mes yeux, vos calmes horizons,
O bois chers à Gallus, tout brillants de rosée!

Gallus
Que ton sommeil soit pur, fleur du beau sol latin,
Oh! bien mieux que ce myrte et bien mieux que ces roses,
Puissé-je parfumer ton seuil et tes pieds roses
De nocturnes baisers, jusqu'au frais matin!

Come, make love to me, let us not think of the dead! Don't point heavenward with your lovely white hand. Gather the fine fruits of love *on the branch, where the fearful worm of remorse has not yet crawled.*

ECLOGUE

Gallus: Melodious songsters, denizens of the copses, the sky grows pale, Venus awakens on the horizon; Cynthia is listening, intoxicate her ears with the golden flood of your lovely songs.

Cynthia: The serene night deepens and smoothly unrolls the dazzling choir of stars in the blue sky; I have in my soul the image of my beloved, young and handsome as a God, and I hear his sweet voice.

Gallus: O Cynthia, do you know what my love and desire are? Phoebus sends down his loveliest gleams and the lovestruck wood dove quivers and flutters its wings, and a divine sigh gusts through the dreaming woods.

Cynthia: The spring drowses and, lulled, murmurs, and the dark sward is bathed in soft shafts of light. How sweet they are to my eyes, these woods dear to Gallus, glittering with dew!

Gallus: May your sleep be pure, flower of the fine Latin earth! Oh, more than this myrtle or these roses, may I perfume your threshold and your rosy feet with nocturnal kisses until the cool morning!

NOTES FOR *ÉGLOGUE*

Date: c. 1883
Source: Leconte de Lisle, *Poèmes antiques*. Alphonse Lemerre, Paris 1874, pp. 242–244.
Manuscript: in the Bibliothèque Nationale, Paris
[1] *Des flots* d'or de vos belles chansons (Debussy)
Versez lui le flot d'or de vos belles chansons (Leconte de Lisle)
Comments: The poem has ten stanzas, the sixth to the ninth are omitted. The song, written for soprano and tenor, is unpublished.

Cynthia
Vénus! ralentis donc les heures infinies!
Ne sois pas, ô bonheur, quelque jour regretté!
Dure à jamais, nuit chère! et porte, ô volupté,
Dans l'Olympe éternel nos âmes réunies!

VOICI QUE LE PRINTEMPS . . .[1]

— *Paul Bourget*

Voici que le printemps, ce fils léger d'Avril,
Beau page en pourpoint vert brodé de roses blanches,
Paraît leste, fringant et les poings sur les hanches,
Comme un prince acclamé revient d'un long exil.

Les branches des buissons verdis rendent étroite
La route qu'il poursuit en dansant comme un fol;
Sur son épaule gauche il porte un rossignol,
Un merle s'est posé sur son épaule droite.

Et les fleurs qui dormaient sous les mousses des bois
Ouvrent leurs yeux où flotte une ombre vague et tendre;
Et sur leurs petits pieds se dressent pour entendre
Les deux oiseaux siffler et chanter à la fois.

Car le merle sifflote et le rossignol chante;
Le merle siffle ceux qui ne sont pas aimés,
Et pour les amoureux languissants et charmés
Le rossignol prolonge une chanson touchante.

Cynthia: Venus! stay the infinite hours! O happiness, be not one day regretted! Last forever, dear night, and you, Pleasure, bear our joined souls to eternal Olympus!

BEHOLD THE SPRING . . .

Behold the spring, that light son of April, a handsome page in green velvet embroidered with white roses, and see how nimble he is, how dashing, his hands on his hips like a prince being hailed on his return from long exile.

The greening twigs of the hedgerows make a straight path along which he advances, dancing like a jester; on his left shoulder he sports a nightingale and a blackbird has lit on his right shoulder.

And the flowers that were asleep beneath the forest moss open their eyes that reflect a vague, tender shadow, and stand on tiptoe to hear the two birds whistling and singing together.

For the blackbird whistles and the nightingale sings; the blackbird whistles for those who are not loved, and for languishing and enchanted lovers the nightingale pours out a touching song.

NOTES FOR *VOICI QUE LE PRINTEMPS* . . .

Date: January 1884
Source: Paul Bourget, *Les Aveux*, Livre Second—Dilettantisme. Alphonse Lemerre, Paris 1882, pp. 71–72.
Manuscript: in the Bibliothèque Nationale, Paris
Dedication: "à Madame Vasnier" (eleventh in the "Vasnier Songbook")
[1] The title of the poem is *Romance*. The "Vasnier Songbook" gives: *Romance. Musique pour éventail*.
Publisher: under the title *Romance*, Société Nouvelle d'Editions Musicales (Anc. maison Paul Dupont), Paris 1907

APPARITION

— *Stéphane Mallarmé*

La lune s'attristait. Des séraphins en pleurs
Rêvant, l'archet aux doigts, dans le calme des fleurs
Vaporeuses, tiraient de mourantes violes
De blancs sanglots glissant sur l'azur des corolles.
— C'était le jour béni de ton premier baiser.
Ma songerie aimant à me martyriser[1]
S'enivrait savamment du parfum de tristesse
Que même sans regret et sans déboire laisse
La cueillaison d'un Rêve au coeur qui l'a cueilli.
J'errais donc, l'oeil rivé sur le pavé vieilli,
Quand avec du soleil aux cheveux, dans la rue
Et dans le soir, tu m'es en riant apparue
Et j'ai cru voir la fée au chapeau de clarté
Qui jadis sur mes beaux sommeils d'enfant gâté
Passait, laissant toujours de ses mains mal fermées
Neiger de blancs bouquets d'étoiles parfumées.
[d'étoiles parfumées.][2]

APPARITION

The moon grew sad. Dreaming seraphim in tears, their bows in hand,
drew from dying white viols in the calm of misty flowers sobs that
slipped across the blue corollas. — That was the blessed day of your
first kiss. My dreaming, fond of making me a martyr, purposefully in-
toxicated itself with the odor of sadness that—without any regret or
rebuff—allows the harvesting of a Dream to the heart that has gathered
it. Thus I wandered, my eyes fixed on the aged paving stones, when
with sun-touched hair you appeared in the street, in the evening,
laughing before me, and I seemed to see that fairy with the halo of light
who long ago in my lovely spoiled-child's dreams passed by, leaving to
snow down ever from her half-opened hands white bouquets of scented
stars.

NOTES FOR *APPARITION*

> Date: Ville d'Avray, 8 February 1884
> Source: Stéphane Mallarmé, in *Lutèce*, 24–30 November 1883, p. 2.
> Manuscript: in The Library of Congress, Washington, D.C.
> Dedication: "à Madame Vasnier"
> [1] Ma songerie aimant à *se* martyriser (Debussy manuscript)
> Ma songerie aimant à *me* martyriser (Mallarmé)
> [2] Added by Debussy
> Publisher: *La Revue musicale*, 1 May 1926, Supplément musical, *Quatre
> mélodies inédites de Claude Debussy. Quatre Chansons de jeunesse*, Editions Jobert,
> Paris 1969
> Comments: A small notebook entitled "Musical Notes," whose location is
> now unknown, contains several pages of sketches for a new version of this song.
> The only words given are those of lines 1, 3, 4, and 9. Because this notebook
> also includes sketches for *Soupir* (the first of the *Trois Poèmes de Stéphane Mal-
> larmé*) and for *La Boîte à joujoux*, both composed in 1913, the sketches for *Appari-
> tion* can be presumed to have also been made at the same time. This supposition
> is borne out by quotations from this song in two letters of this period. (We have
> found no earlier quotation to this song nor to any other song that Debussy did
> not publish himself.)
> First performance: Jane Bathori, 17 May 1926

LA ROMANCE D'ARIEL

— *Paul Bourget*

Au long de ces montagnes douces,
Dis! viendras-tu pas à l'appel
De ton délicat Ariel
Qui veloute à tes pieds les mousses?

Suave Miranda, je veux
Qu'il fasse juste assez de brise
Pour que ce souffle tiéde frise
Les pointes d'or de tes cheveux!

Les clochettes des digitales
Sur ton passage tinteront;
Les églantines sur ton front
Effeuilleront leurs blancs pétales.

Sous le feuillage du bouleau
Blondira ta tête bouclée;
Et dans le creux de la vallée
Tu regarderas bleuir l'eau,

L'eau du lac lumineux ou sombre,
Miroir changeant du ciel d'été,
Qui sourit avec sa gaîté
Et qui s'attriste avec son ombre;

Symbole, hélas! du coeur aimant,
Où le chagrin, où le sourire
De l'être trop aimé, se mire
Gaîment ou douloureusement...

———————

ARIEL'S SONG

Come, will you not come over these fair mountains when summoned
by your delicate Ariel, he who makes the moss like velvet to your feet?

Sweet Miranda, I should wish for just enough breeze that its warm
breath might ruffle the golden tips of your hair!

The foxglove bells will chime as you pass; the eglantine will shed its
white petals on your forehead.

Your curly head will become more blond beneath the birch leaves, and
in the depth of the valley you will see the water turn to blue,

The water of the luminous dark lake, a changing mirror of the summer
sky, smiling gaily and growing sad in its shadow;

Alas, a symbol of the loving heart in which the sorrow or smile of
someone too well loved is reflected, gaily or sadly...

NOTES FOR *LA ROMANCE D'ARIEL*

Date: February 1884
Source: Paul Bourget, *Les Aveux*, Livre Second—Dilettantisme: En voyage—
no. V. Alphonse Lemerre, Paris 1882, pp. 101–102.
Manuscript: in the Bibliothèque Nationale, Paris
Dedication: "à Madame Vasnier" (twelfth in the "Vasnier Songbook")
Comments: The first and second stanzas are omitted.
The song is unpublished.

REGRET

— Paul Bourget

Devant le ciel d'été, tiède et calmé,
Je me souviens de toi, comme d'un songe,
Et mon regret fidèle, aime et prolonge
    Les heures où j'étais aimé.

Les astres brilleront, dans la nuit noire;
Le soleil brillera, dans le jour clair;
Quelque chose de toi, flotte dans l'air,
    Qui me pénètre la mémoire.

Quelque chose de toi, qui fut à moi:
Car j'ai possédé tout, de ta pensée,
Et mon âme, trahie et délaissée,
    Est encor tout entière à toi.

[Devant le ciel d'été, tiède et calmé,
Je me souviens de toi, comme d'un songe.][1]

REGRET

Under the summer sky, warm and becalmed, I remember you as in a dream, and my constant regret relishes and draws out the hours when I was loved.

The stars will shine in the black night; the sun will shine in the clear day; something of you is suspended in the air that penetrates into my memory.

Something of you that was mine: for I filled your sweet thoughts, and my betrayed and abandoned soul is still completely yours.

[Under the summer sky, warm and becalmed, I remember you as in a dream.]

NOTES FOR *REGRET*

Date: February 1884
Source: Paul Bourget, *Les Aveux,* Livre Premier—Amour. Alphonse Lemerre, Paris 1882, p. 44.
Manuscript: in the Bibliothèque Nationale, Paris
Dedication: "à Madame Vasnier" (thirteenth, and last, in the "Vasnier Songbook")
[1] Lines added by Debussy
First performance: G. Jean-Aubry presented this song, sung by Madame Blanc-Audra, at a concert given by *La Revue musicale,* 14 March 1938.
Comment: This is the last song Debussy included in the book which he entitled "Chansons" and gave to Madame Vasnier before leaving for the Villa Medici in early 1885.
The song is unpublished.

BARCAROLLE

— Edouard Guinand

Viens! l'heure est propice:
Notre barque glisse
Sur le flot calmé.
L'odeur des mélèzes
Couvrant les falaises
Rend l'air embaumé.

Sous les grands bois sombres
Voltigent les ombres
Des oiseaux de nuit.
Dans notre sillage,
Tremblotante image,
La lune nous suit...

Viens! tout est silence!
Nul bruit ne s'élance
Des eaux ni des monts.
Loin des yeux des hommes,
Seuls ici nous sommes,
Et nous nous aimons!...

———————

BARCAROLLE

Come! the time is ripe: our boat glides over the calm waters. The scent of the larch trees covering the banks perfumes the air.

Beneath the tall, somber trees the shadows of night-birds flit. The trembling image of the moon follows in our wake...

Come! All is quiet! No sound comes from the water or the hills. Far from the eyes of men, here we are alone and in love!...

NOTES FOR *BARCAROLLE*

Date: c. 1885
Source: Edouard Guinand, *Au courant de la vie.* Stances—Sonnets—Poèmes par Ed. Guinand. Paul Ollendorff, Paris 1885, p. 286.
Manuscript: not found
Comments: The only known reference to this song appeared in a dealer's catalogue in 1931.
The song is unpublished.

CHEVAUX DE BOIS

— *Paul Verlaine*

Tournez, tournez, bons chevaux de bois,
Tournez cent tours, tournez mille tours,
Tournez souvent et tournez toujours,
Tournez, tournez au son des haut-bois.

L'enfant tout rouge et la mère blanche,[1]
Le gars en noir en la fille en rose,
L'une à la chose et l'autre à la pose,
Chacun se paie un sou de dimanche.

Tournez, tournez chevaux de leur coeur,
Tandis qu'autour de tous vos tournois
Clignote l'oeil du filou sournois,
Tournez au son du piston vainqueur.

C'est ravissant comme ça vous soûle
D'aller ainsi dans ce cirque bête!
Bien dans le ventre et mal dans la tête,
Du mal en masse et du bien en foule.

Tournez, tournez sans qu'il soit besoin
D'user jamais de nuls éperons,
Pour commander à vos galops ronds,
Tournez, tournez, sans espoir de foin.

Et dépêchez, chevaux de leur âme,
Déjà, voici la nuit qui tombe
Va réunir pigeon et colombe,
Loin de la foire et loin de madame.

Tournez, tournez! le ciel en velours
D'astres en or se vêt lentement.
Voici partir l'amante et l'amant.
Tournez au son joyeux des tambours.
[tournez.][2]

———

WOODEN HORSES

Turn, turn, fine wooden horses, a hundred times, a thousand times, often and forever, turn, turn to the oboes' sound.

The ruddy child and pale mother, the fellow in black and the girl in pink, one eager, the other hesitant, each pays his sou on Sunday.

Turn, turn, horses of their hearts, while as you revolve the clever pickpocket winks; turn to the sound of the conquering trumpet!

It's astonishing how intoxicating it is, going round and round in this giddy ring! The stomach replete, the head aching, masses of unhappiness, and hordes of good feeling.

Turn, turn, without ever having to use spurs to control your circular gallop, turn, turn, without hope of fodder.

And hurry, horses of their souls. See, night is already falling, it will reunite the pigeon and the dove, far from the fair, far from my lady.

Turn, turn, the velvet sky slowly dons its golden stars. The lover and his lass are going off. Turn to the joyous noise of the drums.

———————

NOTES FOR *CHEVAUX DE BOIS*

Date: Paris 1885
Source: Paul Verlaine, *Romances sans paroles,* Paysages belges IV. Imprimerie de M. Lhermitte, Sens 1874, pp. 26–27.
Manuscript: in the Bibliothèque Nationale, Paris
Dedication: "Souvenir amico musical à mon ami Bachelet"
(An amical-musical souvenir for my friend Bachelet)
    [1] This stanza was taken from a later version of the poem.
    [2] Added by Debussy
Comment: This version of the song is unpublished.

(DEUX ROMANCES)

— Paul Bourget

(I)   ROMANCE

L'âme évaporée et souffrante,
L'âme douce, l'âme odorante
Des lys divins que j'ai cueillis
Dans le jardin de ta pensée,
Où donc les vents l'ont-ils chassée,
Cette âme adorable des lys?

N'est-il plus un parfum qui reste
De la suavité céleste
Des jours où tu m'enveloppais
D'une vapeur surnaturelle,
Faite d'espoir, d'amour fidéle,
De béatitude et de paix?

————————

(TWO ROMANCES)

(I) ROMANCE

The spent and suffering soul, the sweet soul, the soul redolent with the lilies I picked in the garden of your thoughts, where have the winds dispersed this adorable soul of the lilies?

Does nothing but a scent remain of the celestial softness of the days when you enclosed me in an otherworldly vapor of hope, of steadfast love, beatitude, and peace?

NOTES FOR *(I) ROMANCE*

Date: 1886
Source: Paul Bourget, *Les Aveux*, Livre Second—Amour. Alphonse Lemerre, Paris 1882, p. 51.
Manuscript: in the Bibliothèque Nationale, Paris
Publisher: A. Durand & Fils, Paris, 1891
Comment: The manuscript shows no title. It was added by the publisher.

(II) LES CLOCHES[1]

Les feuilles s'ouvraient sur le bord des branches,
Délicatement,
Les cloches tintaient, légères et franches,
Dans le ciel clément.

Rythmique et fervent comme une antienne,
Ce lointain appel
Me remémorait la blancheur chrétienne
Des fleurs de l'autel.

Ces cloches parlaient d'heureuses années,
Et, dans le grand bois,
Semblaient reverdir les feuilles fanées
Des jours d'autrefois.

————

(II)   THE BELLS

The leaves opened at the tips of the branches, delicately, the bells rang out lightly, frankly, in the clement sky.

Rhythmic and fervent as an antiphon, that distant call brought back to me the Christian pallor of altar flowers.

Those bells spoke of happy years, and seemed to turn the faded leaves in the thick woods of bygone yesterdays green once again.

―――――――

NOTES FOR *(II) LES CLOCHES*

Date: 1886
Source: Paul Bourget, *Les Aveux*, Livre Second—Dilettantisme. Alphonse Lemerre, Paris 1882, p. 79.
Manuscript: in the Bibliothèque Nationale, Paris
[1] The title of the poem is *Romance*.
Publisher: A. Durand & Fils, Paris, 1891
Comment: The manuscript shows no title. It was added by the publisher.

NOTES FOR *(DEUX ROMANCES)*

Comments: The title *Deux Romances* does not appear in the published edition of these two songs, which have always been issued separately.

Because all but two of the nine Bourget settings can be dated before 1885, we suggest that these songs are the "mélodies de Bourget" Debussy mentions in a letter to Monsieur Vasnier of 19 October 1886 (see *La Revue musicale*, 1 May 1926, p. 39). Koechlin (idem, p. 118), Vallas (*Claude Debussy et son temps*, p. 128), and Bernac (*The Interpretation of French Song*, p. 160) all agree that these songs were composed before 1891. The date given on the manuscript, 1891, is the date of publication.

ARIETTES OUBLIÉES

— Paul Verlaine

I (C'est l'extase langoureuse)

Le vent dans la plaine
Suspend son haleine.
(Favart)

C'est l'extase langoureuse,
C'est la fatigue amoureuse,
C'est tous les frissons des bois
Parmi l'étreinte des brises,
C'est, vers les ramures grises,
Le choeur des petites voix.

O le frêle et frais murmure,
Cela gazouille et susurre!
Cela ressemble au cri doux
Que l'herbe agitée expire...
Tu dirais, sous l'eau qui vire,
Le roulie sourd des cailloux.

Cette âme qui se lamente
En cette plainte dormante,
C'est la nôtre, n'est-ce pas?
La mienne, dis, et la tienne,
Dont s'exhale l'humbre antienne
Par ce tiède soir, tout bas?

FORGOTTEN AIRS

I (This is the languorous ecstasy)

> *The wind in the plain*
> *Holds its breath.*
> (Favart)

This is the languorous ecstasy, this is the fatigue of love, this is all the woods' trembling as the breezes embrace them, this is the choir of tiny voices in the gray branches.

O frail fresh murmuring, it burbles and whispers! It is like the soft cry the ruffled grass emits... You would say, like the soundless movement of pebbles beneath swirling water.

This soul that laments itself with such sleepy strain, isn't it ours? It is mine, isn't it, and yours, being breathed out in a humble antiphon on this warm evening, so softly?

NOTES FOR *I (C'est l'extase langoureuse)*

    Date: March 1887
    Source: Paul Verlaine, *Romances sans paroles*, Ariettes oubliées—no. I. Imprimerie de M. Lhermitte, Sens 1874, p. 7.
    Manuscripts: (1) dated, in a private collection in France; (2) undated, in the Bibliothèque musicale François-Lang, Abbaye de Royaumont, France.
    Comment: Debussy used the first line of the epigraph of this poem: "Le vent dans la plaine," for the title of Prelude no. III from Book I, composed between 1909 and 1910.

II   (*Il pleure dans mon coeur*)

Il pleut doucement sur la ville.
(A. Rimbaud)

Il pleure dans mon coeur
Comme il pleut sur la ville,
Quelle est cette langueur
Qui pénètre mon coeur?

O bruit doux de la pluie
Par terre et sur les toits!
Pour un coeur qui s'ennuie,
O le bruit de la pluie![1]

Il pleure sans raison
Dans ce coeur qui s'écoeure.
Quoi! nulle trahison?
Ce deuil est sans raison.

C'est bien la pire peine
De ne savoir pourquoi,
Sans amour et sans haine,
Mon coeur a tant de peine.

———————

II   (It weeps in my heart)

It is raining softly on the town.
(A. Rimbaud)

It weeps in my heart as it rains on the town, what is this languor that pierces my heart?

O soft sound of the rain on the ground and on the roofs! For a forlorn heart, oh, the sound of the rain!

In this sickened heart, there is unreasoned weeping. What, no betrayal? This mourning has no motive.

It is the worst sorrow, not knowing why—without love and without hatred—my heart is so sad.

NOTES FOR *II* (*Il pleure dans mon coeur*)

Date: 1885–1887
Source: Paul Verlaine, *Romances sans paroles*, Ariettes oubliées—no. III. Imprimerie de M. Lhermitte, Sens 1874, p. 9.
Manuscript: in a private collection in France
[1] O le *bruit* de la pluie (Debussy)
O le *chant* de la pluie (Verlaine)
Comments: Debussy used "c'est bien la pire peine," from stanza 4, line 1 of this poem, in a letter to P.-J. Toulet, 20 June 1917. See also the letter to Alexander Charpentier, 27 September 1908.

III   (L'ombre des arbres . . .)

> Le rossignol qui du haut d'une
> branche se regarde dedans, croit
> être tombé dans la rivière. Il est
> au sommet d'un chêne et toute fois
> il a peur de se noyer.
> (Cyrano de Bergerac)

L'ombre des arbres dans la rivière embrumée
    Meurt comme de la fumée,
Tandis qu'en l'air, parmi les ramures réelles
    Se plaignent les tourterelles.

Combien, ô voyageur, ce paysage blême
    Te mira blême toi-même,
Et que tristes pleuraient dans les hautes feuillées
    Tes espérances noyées.

———————

III   *(The shadow of the trees . . .)*

> *The nightingale that sees itself*
> *in the river below from its high*
> *branch thinks it has fallen into*
> *the water. It is at the very top*
> *of an oak tree and yet it is afraid*
> *of drowning.*
> (Cyrano de Bergerac)

The shadow of the trees in the misted river fades like smoke, while in the air among the real branches the turtledoves mourn.

And how this pallid landscape reflected your pallor, O voyager, and how sadly your drowned expectations wept among the high branches.

———————

NOTES FOR *III (L'ombre des arbres . . .)*

Date: Paris, 6 January 1885
Source: Paul Verlaine, *Romances sans paroles*, Ariettes oubliées—no. IX. Imprimerie de M. Lhermitte, Sens 1874, p. 17.
Manuscript: location unknown
Comment: Debussy wrote "toutes mes *espérances* en sont *noyées*" (all my *expectations* were *drowned*), stanza 4, line 4 of this poem, in a letter to André Caplet, 3 June 1913.

Paysages belges   CHEVAUX DE BOIS[1]

Par saint Gille,
Viens-nous-en,
Mon agile
Alezan!
(V. Hugo)[2]

Tournez, tournez, bons chevaux de bois,
Tournez cent tours, tournez mille tours,
Tournez souvent et tournez toujours,
Tournez, tournez au son des hautbois.

L'enfant tout rouge et la mère blanche,
Le gars en noir et la fille en rose,
L'une à la chose et l'autre à la pose,
Chacun se paie un sou de dimanche.

Tournez, tournez chevaux de leur coeur,
Tandis qu'autour de tous vos tournois
Clignote l'oeil du filou sournois,
Tournez au son du piston vainqueur!

C'est étonnant comme ça vous soûle
D'aller ainsi dans ce cirque bête!
Rien dans le ventre et mal dans la tête[3]
Du mal en masse et du bien en foule.

Tournez, dadas, sans qu'il soit besoin
D'user jamais de nuls éperons,
Pour commander à vos galops ronds,
Tournez, tournez, sans espoir de foin.

Et dépêchez, chevaux de leur âme,
Déjà, voici que sonne à la soupe
La nuit qui tombe et chasse la troupe
De gais buveurs que leur soif affame.

Belgian Landscapes   WOODEN HORSES

By Saint Giles, let us go,
my nimble sorrel steed!
(V. Hugo)

Turn, turn, fine wooden horses, a hundred times, a thousand times, often and forever, turn, turn to the oboes' sound.

The ruddy child and pale mother, the fellow in black and the girl in pink, one eager, the other hesitant, each pays his sou on Sunday.

Turn, turn, horses of their hearts, while as you revolve, the clever pickpocket winks; turn to the sound of the conquering trumpet!

It's astounding how intoxicating it is, going round and round in this giddy ring: the stomach queasy, the head aching, masses of unhappiness and hordes of good feeling.

Turn, without ever having to use spurs to control your circular gallop, turn, turn, with no hope of fodder.

And hurry, horses of their souls. The bell has already rung for supper, night is falling and dispersing the troop of merry drinkers made hungry by their thirst.

NOTES FOR *Paysages belges*   CHEVAUX DE BOIS

Date: 1885–1887
Source: Paul Verlaine, *Sagesse*, III—no. XVII. Société générale de Librairie catholique (Ancienne maison Victor Palmé), Paris 1881, pp. 100–101.
Manuscript: in the Bibliothèque musicale François-Lang, Abbaye de Royaumont, France
[1] The poem has no title.
[2] The epigraph, taken from the early version of the poem, was added in the 1903 edition of the song.
[3] *Rien* dans le ventre et mal dans la tête (published song)
Bien dans le ventre et mal dans la tête (Debussy manuscript and Verlaine)
Comment: The poem has eight stanzas, the fifth and sixth are omitted.

Tournez, tournez! le ciel en velours
D'astres en or se vêt lentement.
L'église tinte un glas tristement.
Tournez au son joyeux des tambours!
[Tournez.]⁴

—————

Aquarelles   I. GREEN

Voici des fruits, des fleurs, des feuilles et des branches,
Et puis voici mon coeur qui ne bat que pour vous.
Ne le déchirez pas avec vos deux mains blanches,
Et qu'à vos yeux si beaux l'humble présent soit doux.

J'arrive tout couvert encore de rosée
Que le vent du matin vient glacer à mon front.
Souffrez que ma fatigue, à vos pieds reposée,
Rêve des chers instants qui la délasseront.

Sur votre jeune sein, laissez rouler ma tête
Toute sonore encore de vos derniers baisers;¹
Laissez-la s'apaiser de la bonne tempête,
Et que je dorme un peu puisque vous reposez.

—————

Turn, turn, the velvet sky slowly dons its golden stars. The church
sadly tolls the knell. Turn to the joyous noise of the drums!

_____

Watercolors I. GREEN

Here are fruits, flowers, leaves and branches, and here is my heart that
beats only for you. Do not tear it with your two white hands, and may
the humble offering find favor in your lovely eyes.

I arrive still covered with the dew that the morning wind has just fro-
zen on my forehead. Let me lay my fatigue at your feet and dream of
the dear moments that will soothe it.

Let my head, still resounding from your last kisses, repose on your
young breast; let it calm itself after the storm, and let me sleep a bit,
since you too are resting.

_____

NOTE FOR *Paysages belges*   CHEVAUX DE BOIS

   [4] Added by Debussy

NOTES FOR *Aquarelles I. GREEN*

   Date: Rome, January 1886
   Source: Paul Verlaine, *Romances sans paroles*, Aquarelles. Imprimerie de M.
Lhermitte, Sens 1874, p. 41.
   Manuscripts: (1) dated, location unknown; (2) undated, in the Bibliothèque
musicale François-Lang, Abbaye de Royaumont, France.
   [1] Toute sonore encore de vos derniers baisers (Debussy)
   Toute sonore encor de vos derniers baisers (Verlaine)

Aquarelles   *II. SPLEEN*

Les roses étaient toutes rouges,
Et les lierres étaient tout noirs.

Chère, pour peu que tu te bouges,
Renaissent tous mes désespoirs.

Le ciel était trop bleu, trop tendre,
La mer trop verte et l'air trop doux.

Je crains toujours,—ce qu'est d'attendre!—
Quelque fuite atroce de vous.

Du houx à la feuille vernie
Et du luisant buis je suis las,

Et de la campagne infinie
Et de tout, fors de vous, hélas!

———————

Watercolors   II. SPLEEN

The roses were all red, the ivy all black.

Dear, you need only move for all my despair to be reborn.

The sky was too blue, too tender, the sea too green and the air too mild.

I am still afraid—it was to be expected!—of the awful thought that you might run away.

I am tired of holly with burnished leaves and of shiny boxwood,

And of the infinite landscape and of everything—save of you, alas!

———————

NOTES FOR *Aquarelles II. SPLEEN*

Date: 1885–1887
Source: Paul Verlaine, *Romances sans paroles*, Aquarelles. Imprimerie de M. Lhermitte, Sens 1874, p. 42.
Manuscript: in the Bibliothèque musicale François-Lang, Abbaye de Royaumont, France.

NOTES FOR *ARIETTES OUBLIÉES*

Date: January 1885–March 1887 and 1903
Dedication: (on 1903 edition only) "à Miss Mary Garden, inoubliable Mélisande, cette musique (déjà un peu vieille) en affectueux et reconnaissant hommage."
(For Miss Mary Garden, unforgettable Mélisande, this music [already somewhat old-fashioned] in affectionate and grateful homage.)
Publisher: Vve Girod, Éditeur, Paris 1888, separately as *Ariettes*: I, II, III, IV, *Chevaux de bois*, V *Green*, VI *Spleen*. E. Fromont, Paris 1903, *Ariettes oubliées. C'est l'extase langoureuse*, in a supplement to the *Courrier musical*, 15 November 1903.
First performance: Maurice Bagès (tenor), accompanied by Debussy, sang two of the *Ariettes* at a concert of the Société Nationale, 2 February 1889.
Comments: Debussy made various changes for the 1903 edition of these songs.
André Caplet, with Debussy's permission, orchestrated *C'est l'extase langoureuse* and *Green*. The scores were never published.
The first performance of the orchestral version was given by Jane Bathori at the Concerts Colonne, with Gabriel Pierné conducting, 12 March 1921, at the Théâtre du Châtelet.

CINQ POÈMES DE CHARLES BAUDELAIRE

(I)   LE BALCON

Mère des souvenirs, maîtresse des maîtresses,
O toi, tous mes plaisirs! ô toi tous mes devoirs!
Tu te rappelleras la beauté des caresses,
La douceur du foyer et le charme des soirs,
Mère des souvenirs, maîtresse des maîtresses!

Les soirs illuminés par l'ardeur du charbon,
Et les soirs au balcon, voilés de vapeurs roses.
Que ton sein m'était doux! que ton coeur m'était bon!
Nous avons dit souvent d'impérissables choses,
Les soirs illuminés par l'ardeur du charbon.

Que les soleils sont beaux par les chaudes soirées!
Que l'espace est profond! que le coeur est puissant!
En me penchant vers toi, reine des adorées,
Je croyais respirer le parfum de ton sang.
Que les soleils sont beaux par les chaudes soirées!

La nuit s'épaississait ainsi qu'une cloison,
Et mes yeux dans le noir devinait tes prunelles,
Et je buvais ton souffle, ô douceur, ô poison!
Et tes pieds s'endormaient dans mes mains fraternelles.
La nuit s'épaississait ainsi qu'une cloison.

Je sais l'art d'évoquer les minutes heureuses,
Et revis mon passé blotti dans tes genoux.
Car à quoi bon chercher tes beautés langoureuses
Ailleurs qu'en ton cher corps et qu'en ton coeur si doux?
Je sais l'art d'évoquer les minutes heureuses!

FIVE POEMS OF CHARLES BAUDELAIRE

(1)   THE BALCONY

Mother of memories, mistress of mistresses, O thou all my pleasures, all my duties! You will recall the beauty of caresses, the sweetness of the hearth and the charm of evenings, mother of memories, mistress of mistresses!

Evenings lit with the glow of the coals, and evenings on the balcony, veiled in pink mists. How sweet your bosom was, how good your heart! We often said imperishable things, on evenings lit with the glow of the coals.

How beautiful suns are on hot evenings! How deep space is, how powerful the heart! Leaning toward you, the queen of all I adore, I seemed to breathe in the odor of your blood. How beautiful suns are on hot evenings!

The night thickened like a wall, and in the darkness my eyes divined yours, and I drank in your breath, O sweetness, O poison! And your feet lay dormant in my fraternal hands. The night thickened like a wall.

I know the art of invoking happy moments, and I again saw my past buried in your lap. For what good is it to seek your languorous beauties elsewhere than in your own cherished body and in your tender heart? I know the art of invoking happy moments.

NOTES FOR *(1) LE BALCON*

Date: January 1888
Source: Charles Baudelaire, *Les Fleurs du mal,* Spleen et idéal—no. XXXVII. Michel Lévy, Paris 1868, pp. 137–138.
Comments: The phrase "l'art d'évoquer les minutes heureuses," from stanza 5, line 1, was used by Debussy in an article he wrote for *La Revue blanche,* 15 April 1901. See also the letters to Emma Debussy, 29 November 1910, and to Georges Hartmann, 18 December 1899.

Ces serments, ces parfums, ces baisers infinis,
Renaîtront-ils d'un gouffre interdit à nos sondes,
Comme montent au ciel les soleils rajeunis
Après s'être lavés au fond des mers profondes?
— O serment! ô parfums! ô baisers infinis!

———————

(II) HARMONIE DU SOIR

Voici venir le temps où vibrant sur sa tige
Chaque fleur s'évapore ainsi qu'un encensoir;
Les sons et les parfums tournent dans l'air du soir;
Valse mélancolique et langoureux vertige!

Chaque fleur s'évapore ainsi qu'un encensoir;
Le violon frémit comme un coeur qu'on afflige;
Valse mélancolique et langoureux vertige!
Le ciel est triste et beau comme un grand reposoir.

Le violon frémit comme un coeur qu'on afflige,
Un coeur tendre, qui hait le néant vaste et noir!
Le ciel est triste et beau comme un grand reposoir;
Le soleil s'est noyé dans son sang qui se fige.

Un coeur tendre, qui hait le néant vaste et noir,
Du passé lumineux recueille tout vestige!
Le soleil s'est noyé dans son sang qui se fige...
Ton souvenir en moi luit comme un ostensoir!

———————

These pledges, these odors, these endless kisses, will they be reborn from a gulf we are forbidden to plumb, as the renewed suns mount into heaven after having been cleansed in the depths of deep seas? O pledges! O odors! O endless kisses!

(II) EVENING HARMONY

Now is the time when each flower, trembling on its stalk, emits its perfume like a censer; the sounds and perfumes turn in the evening air; melancholy waltz, languorous vertigo!

Each flower emits its perfume like a censer; the violin throbs like an afflicted heart; melancholy waltz, languorous vertigo! The sky is sad and beautiful as an immense altar.

The violin throbs like an afflicted heart, a tender heart aghast at the vast dark void! The sky is sad and beautiful as an immense altar; the sun is drowned in its own congealing blood.

A tender heart aghast at the vast dark void gathers to itself all traces of the luminous past! The sun is drowned in its own congealing blood... Within me, your memory glitters like a monstrance!

NOTES FOR *(II) HARMONIE DU SOIR*

Date: January 1889
Source: Charles Baudelaire, *Les Fleurs du mal*, Spleen et idéal—no. XLVIII. Michel Lévy, Paris 1868, p. 185.
Comment: Debussy used the third line of the first stanza of this song, "Les sons et les parfums tournent dans l'air du soir," for the title of Prelude no. IV from Book I, composed between 1909 and 1910.

(III) LE JET D'EAU

Tes beaux yeux sont las, pauvre amante
Reste longtemps sans les rouvrir,
Dans cette pose nonchalante
Où t'a surprise le plaisir.
Dans la cour le jet d'eau qui jase
Et ne se tait ni nuit ni jour,
Entretient doucement l'extase
Où ce soir m'a plongé l'amour.

 La gerbe d'eau qui berce[1]
  Ses mille fleurs,
 Que la lune traverse
  De ses pâleurs,[2]
 Tombe comme une averse
  De larges pleurs.

Ainsi ton âme qu'incendie
L'éclair brûlant des voluptés
S'élance, rapide et hardie,
Vers les vastes cieux enchantés.
Puis elle s'épanche, mourante,
En un flot de triste langueur,
Qui par une invisible pente
Descend jusqu'au fond de mon coeur.

 La gerbe d'eau qui berce
  Ses mille fleurs,
 Que la lune traverse
  De ses pâleurs,
 Tombe comme une averse
  De larges pleurs.

(III)   THE FOUNTAIN

Your lovely eyes are tired; poor beloved, keep them closed and remain for a time in that casual pose you took when pleasure gripped you. In the courtyard the splatter of the fountain that plays night and day softly prolongs the ecstasy into which love plunged me this evening.

The spray of water that cradles its thousand flowers, through which the moon's pallors gleam, falls like a shower of huge tears.

Thus your soul, ignited by the burning flash of love's pleasures, springs up, rapid and daring, to vast enchanted skies. Thus it falls back dying in a flood of sad languour down the invisible slope into the depths of my heart.

The spray of water that cradles its thousand flowers, through which the moon's pallors gleam, falls like a shower of huge tears.

NOTES FOR *(III) LE JET D'EAU*

Date: March 1889
Source: Charles Baudelaire, *Les Fleurs du mal*, Spleen et idéal—no. XCVII. Michel Lévy, Paris 1868, pp. 231–232.
[1] The refrain is a variant found in *La Petite Revue*, 8 July 1865, p. 108n.
[2] De ses *pâleurs* (Debussy)
De ses *lueurs* (Baudelaire)
Comments: Debussy orchestrated this song in 1907, and published it the same year. After his death, André Caplet revised the orchestration. The manuscript of Caplet's version is in the Bibliothèque Nationale, Paris.
The first performance of the orchestral version took place at the Concert Colonne, 24 February 1907, with Hélène Demellier as the soloist.

O toi, que la nuit rend si belle,
Qu'il m'est doux, penché vers tes seins,
D'écouter la plainte éternelle
Qui sanglote dans les bassins!
Lune, eau sonore, nuit bénie,
Arbres qui frissonnez autour,
Votre pure mélancolie
Est le miroir de mon amour.

La gerbe d'eau qui berce
   Ses mille fleurs,
Que la lune traverse
   De ses pâleurs,
Tombe comme une averse
   De larges pleurs.

———

(IV) RECUEILLEMENT

Sois sage, ô ma Douleur, et tiens-toi plus tranquille,
Tu réclamais le Soir; il descend; le voici:
Une atmosphère obscure enveloppe la ville,
Aux uns portant la paix, aux autres le souci.

Pendant que des mortels la multitude vile,
Sous le fouet du Plaisir, ce bourreau sans merci,
Va cueillir des remords dans la fête servile,
Ma Douleur, donne-moi la main; viens par ici,

Loin d'eux. Vois se pencher les défuntes Années,
Sur les balcons du ciel, en robe surannées;
Surgir du fond des eaux le Regret souriant;

Le Soleil moribond s'endormir sous une arche,
Et, comme un long linceul traînant à l'Orient,
Entends, ma chère, entends la douce Nuit qui marche.

———

O thou, made so lovely by the night, how sweet I find it to bend toward thy breasts, hearing the eternal plaint that weeps into the basin!
Moon, sounding water, blessed night, trees that tremble, your pure
melancholy is the mirror of my love.

The spray of water that cradles its thousand flowers, through which the
moon's pallors gleam, falls like a shower of huge tears.

(IV)   RECOLLECTION

Be prudent, O my Sorrow, and more calm. You asked for the Evening;
it is falling; it is here: a shadowy atmosphere envelops the city, bringing
peace to some, to others care.

While the base multitude of men, goaded by Pleasure, that merciless
torturer, reap remorse from the slavish festival, give me your hand, my
Sorrow; come this way,

Far from them. See the dead Years leaning over the balustrades of
heaven in their outmoded costumes; see smiling Regret emerge from
the waters' depths; see

the dying Sun fall asleep in an archway and, in its long winding-sheet
drawn up from the East, listen, my Beloved, to the footsteps of the soft
Night.

NOTES FOR *(IV) RECUEILLEMENT*

Date: 1889
Source: Charles Baudelaire, *Les Fleurs du mal*, Spleen et idéal—no. CIV.
Michel Lévy, Paris 1868, p. 139.
Manuscripts: two in the Bibliothèque Nationale, Paris
Comment: The manuscripts show slight variations.

(V) *LA MORT DES AMANTS*

Nous aurons des lits pleins d'odeurs légères,
Des divans profonds comme des tombeaux,
Et d'étranges fleurs sur des étagères,
Écloses pour nous sous des cieux plus beaux.

Usant à l'envi leurs chaleurs dernières,
Nos deux coeurs seront deux vastes flambeaux,
Qui réfléchiront leurs doubles lumières
Dans nos deux esprits, ces miroirs jumeaux.

Un soir fait de rose et de bleu mystique,
Nous échangerons un éclair unique,
Comme un long sanglot, tout chargé d'adieux;

Et plus tard un Ange, entr'ouvrant les portes,
Viendra ranimer, fidèle et joyeux,
Les miroirs ternis et les flammes mortes.

———————

(V) THE DEATH OF LOVERS

We shall have beds filled with light scents, divans deep as tombs, and strange flowers on pedestals will bloom for us beneath lovelier skies.

Spending their final passions at will, our two hearts will be two immense torches reflecting their twin lights in our two souls, twin mirrors.

On an evening of pink and mystic blue, we will exchange one single flash of light like a long sob laden with parting;

And later, an Angel, opening the portals, will come to bring back to life, faithful and joyous, the faded mirrors and the dead flames.

———————

NOTES FOR *(V) LA MORT DES AMANTS*

Date: December 1887
Source: Charles Baudelaire, *Les Fleurs du mal,* La Mort—no. CXLVI. Michel Lévy, Paris 1868, p. 339.

NOTES FOR *CINQ POÈMES DE CHARLES BAUDELAIRE*

Date: December 1887–March 1889
Manuscripts: in the Bibliothèque Nationale, Paris
Dedication: "à Etienne Dupin"
Publisher: Librairie de L'Art Indépendant, Paris 1890
Comments: The first edition, issued by subscription and limited to 150 copies, was underwritten by Etienne Dupin and Ernest Chausson.

LA BELLE AU BOIS DORMANT

— *E. Vincent Hyspa*

Des trous à son pourpoint vermeil,
Un chevalier va par la brune,
Les cheveux tout pleins de soleil,
Sous un casque couleur de lune.
Dormez toujours, dormez au bois,
L'anneau, la Belle, à votre doigt.

Dans la poussière des batailles
Il a tué loyal et droit,
En frappant d'estoc et de taille,
Ainsi que frapperait un roi.
Dormez au bois, où la verveine,
Fleurit avec la marjolaine.

Et par les monts et par la plaine,
Monté sur son grand destrier,
Il court, il court à perdre haleine,[1]
Et tout droit sur ses étriers.[2]
Dormez la Belle au Bois, rêvez
Qu'un prince vous épouserez.

Dans la fôret des lilas blancs,
Sous l'éperons d'or qui l'excite,
Son destrier perle de sang
Les lilas blancs, et va plus vite.[3]
Dormez au bois, dormez la Belle
Sous vos courtines de dentelle.

Mais il a pris l'anneau vermeil,
Le chevalier qui par la brune,
A des cheveux pleins de soleil,
Sous un casque couleur de lune.
Ne dormez plus, la Belle au Bois,
L'anneau n'est plus à votre doigt.

———————

THE SLEEPING BEAUTY

A knight with holes in his vermillion doublet travels through the darkness, his hair the color of sunlight beneath his moonlit helmet. Sleep on, sleep in the wood, Beauty, the ring upon your finger.

In the dust of battles he has killed loyally, steadfast, thrusting about him like a king. Sleep in the wood, where the verbena flowers with the marjoram.

Over mountains and through valleys, astride his great steed he speeds breathlessly, standing straight in the stirrups. Sleep, Sleeping Beauty, dream of a Prince who will wed you.

In the white-lilac forest his steed, prodded by golden spurs, spatters drops of blood on the white lilac and gallops more swiftly. Sleep in the wood, sleep, Beauty under your lace bed curtains.

But he has taken the vermillion ring, the knight with his sun-touched hair riding through the darkness in his moon-tinted helmet. Sleep no more, Sleeping Beauty, the ring is gone from your finger.

NOTES FOR *LA BELLE AU BOIS DORMANT*

Date: July 1890
Source: É. Vincent Hyspa. Place and date of publication unknown
Manuscript: in a private collection in the United States
[1] Il court *galoppe* à perdre haleine (manuscript)
Il court, *il court* à perdre haleine (published song)
[2] *Ayant perdu selle,* estries (manuscript)
Et tout droit sur ses étriers (published song)
[3] Les lilas blancs *mais* va plus vite (manuscript)
Les lilas blancs, *et* va plus vite (published song)
Publisher: Société Nouvelle d'Éditions Musicales, Paris 1902

LES ANGÉLUS

— *Grégoire Le Roy*

Cloches chrétiennes pour les matines,
Sonnant au coeur d'espérer encore!
Angélus angélisés d'aurore!
Las! où sont vos prières câlines?

Vous étiez de si douces folies!
Et chanterelles d'amours prochaines!
Aujourd'hui souveraine est ma peine,
Et toutes matines abolies.

Je ne vis plus que d'ombre et de soir;
Les las angélus pleurent la mort,
Et là, dans mon coeur résigné, dort
La seule veuve de tout espoir.

———————

THE ANGELUS

Christian matin bells ring, signaling the heart to continue to hope. Angelus bells made angelic by the dawn! Alas, where are your soothing prayers?

You sang of such sweet follies! Harbingers of future loves! Today, my sorrow is sovereign and the matins sound no more.

I see nothing but shadow and evening; the weary angelus mourns the dead and there, in my resigned heart, sleeps the lone widow of all hope.

NOTES FOR *LES ANGÉLUS*

Date: 1891
Source: Grégoire Le Roy, *La Chanson du Pauvre*, Société du Mercure de France, Paris 1907, p. 161. (An earlier source has not been found.)
Manuscript: in a private collection in the United States
Publisher: J. Hamelle, Paris 1891

FÊTES GALANTES—1er Recueil

— Paul Verlaine

(I)   EN SOURDINE

Calmes dans le demi-jour
Que les branches hautes font,
Pénétrons bien notre amour
De ce silence profond.

Fondons nos âmes, nos coeurs
Et nos sens extasiés,
Parmi les vagues langueurs
Des pins et des arbousiers.

Ferme tes yeux à demi,
Croise tes bras sur ton sein,
Et de ton coeur endormi
Chasse à jamais tout dessein.

Laissons-nous persuader
Au souffle berceur et doux,
Qui vient à tes pieds rider
Les ondes de gazon roux.

Et quand, solennel, le soir
Des chênes noirs tombera,
Voix de notre désespoir,
Le rossignol chantera.

———————

FÊTES GALANTES—First series

(1)   MUTED

Calm in the half-light made by the lofty branches, let us permeate our love with this deep silence.

Let us mingle our souls, our hearts, our senses in ecstasy among the vague murmurings of the pines and arbutus trees.

Half close your eyes, fold your arms across your bosom, and let your sleeping heart empty itself of all thought forever.

Let us be wooed by the lulling and gentle breeze that wrinkles the russet grass at your feet.

And when evening descends solemnly from the dark oaks, the nightingale will sing, the voice of our despair.

NOTES FOR *(1) EN SOURDINE*

Dedication: "à Madame Robert Godet"

Manuscripts: (1) (in D major), dated 1891, in a private collection in France; (2) (in B major), dated "May 1892," in the Humanities Research Center, The University of Texas at Austin, Austin, Texas

Comments: The 1891 manuscript was reproduced in *Collections Comoedia-Charpentier,* 1942, pp. 36–38. The word *roux* is omitted at the end of stanza 4, line 4. This version is unlike either the early version or the published version.

The 1892 manuscript bears the dedication: "à Mademoiselle Catherine Stevens en hommage et pour marquer un peu de ma joie d'être son affectueusement dévoué Claude Debussy"

(For Mademoiselle Catherine Stevens, in homage and as a small mark of my joy at being her affectionately devoted Claude Debussy)

This manuscript shows slight differences from the published version.

This version of the song is entirely different from the early version composed in 1882.

(II) FANTOCHES

Scaramouche et Pulcinella
Qu'un mauvais dessein rassembla
Gesticulent, noirs sous la lune.

Cependant l'excellent docteur
Bolonais cueille avec lenteur
Des simples parmi l'herbe brune.

Lors sa fille, piquant minois,
Sous sa charmille, en tapinois,
Se glisse demi-nue, en quête

De son beau pirate espagnol,
Dont un amoureux rossignol[1]
Clame la détresse à tue-tête.

(II) MARIONETTES

Scaramouche and Pulcinella, brought together by some evil scheme, gesticulate, black beneath the moon.

In the meantime, the good Bolognese doctor slowly picks simples in the twilit grass.

While his daughter, a saucy minx, under her bower steals slyly half-naked, seeking

Her handsome Spanish pirate, whose distress is loudly proclaimed by a love-struck nightingale.

NOTES FOR *(II) FANTOCHES*

Dedication: "à Madame Lucien Fontaine"
[1] Dont un *amoureux* rossignol (Debussy)
Dont un *langoureux* rossignol (Verlaine)
Comment: This second version of the song differs only slightly from the first version composed in 1882.

(III)   CLAIR DE LUNE

Votre âme est un paysage choisi
Que vont charmant masques et bergamasques
Jouant du luth et dansant et quasi
Tristes sous leurs déguisements fantasques.

Tout en chantant sur le mode mineur
L'amour vainqueur et la vie opportune,
Ils n'ont pas l'air de croire à leur bonheur
Et leur chanson se mêle au clair de lune,

Au calme clair de lune triste et beau,
Qui fait rêver les oiseaux dans les arbres
Et sangloter d'extase les jets d'eau,
Les grands jets d'eau sveltes parmi les marbres.

———————

(III) MOONLIGHT

Your soul is a choice landscape where charming masqueraders and ber-
gamaskers pass to and fro playing the lute and dancing almost sadly in
their fantastic costumes.

They sing the while in the minor mode of conquering love and the easy
life, they do not seem to believe in their happiness and their song min-
gles with the moonlight.

With the calm moonlight, sad and lovely, that makes the birds dream in
the trees and the fountains sob with ecstasy, those tall, svelte fountains
among the marbles.

NOTES FOR *(III) CLAIR DE LUNE*

Dedication: "à Madame Arthur Fontaine"
Comment: This second version of the song is entirely different from the
first version composed in 1882.
Clair de lune is the title of no. III of the *Suite bergamasque,* composed between
1890 and 1905.

NOTES FOR *FÊTES GALANTES—1ᵉʳ Recueil*

Date: 1891
Source: Paul Verlaine, *Fêtes galantes.* Alphonse Lemerre, Paris 1869, pp. 49–
50, 25–26, 1–2.
Manuscript: in the Bibliothèque Nationale, Paris
Publisher: E. Fromont, Paris 1903
Comments: On the title page of the manuscript, the songs are numbered as
follows: 1. *En sourdine.* 2. *Clair de lune.* 3. *Fantoches.* The first is dedicated to
"Mademoiselle C. Stevens," the second is dedicated to "Madame A. Fontaine."
In the published edition, the songs are slightly altered, the order of the second
and the third songs is reversed, and the dedications do not appear.

(TROIS MÉLODIES)

— *Paul Verlaine*

(I) La mer est plus belle

La mer est plus belle
Que les cathédrales,
Nourrice fidèle,
Berceuse de râles,
La mer sur qui prie
La Vierge Marie!

Elle a tous les dons
Terribles et doux.
J'entends ses pardons
Gronder ses courroux.
Cette immensité
N'a rien d'entêté.

Oh! si patiente,
Même quand méchante!
Un souffle ami hante
La vague, et nous chante:
"Vous sans espérance,
Mourez sans souffrance!"

Et puis, sous les cieux
Qui s'y rient plus clairs,
Elle a des airs bleus,
Roses, gris et verts...
Plus belle que tous,
Meilleure que nous!

———————

(THREE MELODIES)

(I) *The sea is more beautiful*

The sea is more beautiful than cathedrals, a faithful nurse, cradling the ouzels, the sea over which the Virgin Mary prays!

It has all the qualities, terrible and sweet: I hear its pardons as they rage... its vastness is without determination.

Oh, so patient, even when wicked! A friendly breath haunts the wave and sings to us: "You without hope, die without suffering!"

And then, beneath the clear, smiling skies, it takes on blue tints, pink, gray, green... Lovelier than anything, better than are we!

NOTES FOR *(I) La mer est plus belle*

Dedication: "à Ernest Chausson"
First performance: Marthe Legrand at a concert in the salon of the Princesse Cystria, 16 January 1904

(II)   Le son du cor s'afflige . . .

Le son du cor s'afflige vers les bois
D'une douleur on veut croire orpheline
Qui vient mourir au bas de la colline
Parmi la bise errant en courts abois.

L'âme du loup pleure dans cette voix
Qui monte avec le soleil qui décline
D'une agonie on veut croire câline
Et qui ravit et qui navre à la fois.

Pour faire mieux cette plainte assoupie,
La neige tombe à longs traits de charpie
A travers le couchant sanguinolent,

Et l'air a l'air d'être un soupir d'automne,
Tant il fait doux par ce soir monotone
Où se dorlote un paysage lent.

———————

(II)   The sound of the horn grieves . . .

The sound of the horn grieves through the woods with an almost or-phan silence that dies at the foot of the hill in the gusting north wind.

The soul of the wolf weeps in this voice that rises with the setting sun, in an agony almost soothing that both enraptures and disturbs us.

To set off this sighing plaint, the snow falls like cottonwool across the blood-red sunset,

And the air has the air of being an autumnal sigh, so mild is this dulled evening that tenderly enfolds the slow landscape.

NOTES FOR *(II) Le son du cor s'afflige* . . .

Dedication: "à Robert Godet"
Comment: Reference to this song and to *L'échelonnement des haies* is found in a letter to Robert Godet, 30 January 1892:

Entre temps, j'ai écrit deux mélodies avec ce qu'il me reste de plumes! Cela vous est dédié, et n'est pas pour vous plaire mais pour vous donner une preuve de pensée amicale, vous en pardonnerez l'apparente futilité parce que j'y ai mis de mon coeur.

(In the meantime, I've written two songs with my remaining pens! They are dedicated to you, not to give you pleasure, but rather as a proof of friendly thoughts, so you will forgive their trifling appearance because I've put my heart into them.)

Debussy writes of "d'un silence qu'on voudrait *croire orphelin*" (a silence one might think orphaned), certainly a reference to stanza 1, line 2, in a letter to Pierre Louÿs of July 1903.

(III)   L'échelonnement des haies

L'échelonnement des haies
Moutonne à l'infini, mer
Claire dans le brouillard clair
Qui sent bon les jeunes baies.

Des arbres et des moulins
Sont légers sur le vert tendre
Où vient s'ébattre et s'étendre
L'agilité des poulains.

Dans ce vague d'un Dimanche
Voici se jouer aussi
De grandes brebis aussi
Douces que leur laine blanche.

Tout à l'heure déferlait
L'onde, roulée en volutes,
De cloches comme des flûtes
Dans le ciel comme du lait.

———————

(III)   The hedgerows stretch out

The hedgerows stretch out, smooth and infinite, the sea clear through the mist redolent of young berries.

Trees and mills stand lightly on the tender strand where colts frisk and gambol.

In this Sunday idleness, the grown lambs play too, soft as their white wool.

A while ago, the vaulted waves of the bells, like flutes, rolled out into the milky sky.

NOTES FOR *(III) L'échelonnement des haies*

Dedication: "à Robert Godet"
Comment: A second manuscript of this song, in a private collection in Germany, bears the dedication: "Ce manuscrit illisible mais rehaussé de bleu, à Lucien Fontaine en toute sympathie.   C.D.   Avril 95"
(This unreadable manuscript, but touched up with blue, to Lucien Fontaine with kindest regards.   C.D.   April 95)

NOTES FOR *(TROIS MÉLODIES)*

Date: December 1891
Source: Paul Verlaine, *Sagesse*, III—nos. XV, IX, XIII. L. Vanier, Paris 1889, pp. 119, 108, 116.
Manuscripts: in a private collection in France
Publisher: J. Hamelle, Paris 1901
Comments: Pierre Louÿs, in a letter to Debussy, called these songs: "verlainiennes jusqu'au bout des croches" (Verlainian down to the last eighth note).

PROSES LYRIQUES

— Claude Debussy

(I)   DE RÊVE[1]

La nuit a des douceurs de femmes!
Et les vieux arbres sous la lune d'or, songent
À celle qui vient de passer la tête emperlée,
Maintenant navrée!
À jamais navrée!
Ils n'ont pas su lui faire signe...

Toutes! Elles ont passé
Les Frêles,
Les Folles,
Semant leur rire au gazon grêle,
Aux brises frôleuses
La caresse charmeuse
Des hanches fleurissantes!
Hélas! de tout ceci, plus rien qu'un blanc frisson.

Les vieux arbres sous la lune d'or, pleurent
Leurs belles feuilles d'or
Nul ne leur dédiera plus la fiérte des casques d'or
Maintenant ternis!
À jamais ternis!
Les chevaliers sont morts sur le chemin du Grâal!

La nuit a des douceurs de femmes!
Des mains semblent frôler les âmes
Mains si folles, si frêles,[2]
Au temps où les épées chantaient pour Elles!...
D'étranges soupirs s'élèvent sous les arbres.
Mon âme! c'est du rêve ancien qui t'étreint!

LYRICS IN PROSE

(I) OF DREAMS

The night has a woman's softness, and the ancient trees beneath the golden moon dream of Her who has just gone by, her head dressed with pearls. Heartbroken now, heartbroken forever, they were unable to make a sign to her...

All, all have gone by: the Frail, the Foolish, sowing their laughter on the sparse grass, the caress of their florid hips on the glancing breezes. Alas! nothing remains of it but a pale shudder.

The old trees beneath the golden moon weep their lovely golden leaves! No one will now give them the pride of golden helmets, tarnished now, tarnished forever. The knights are dead on the quest for the Grail!

The night has a woman's softness, hands seem to touch lightly upon souls, hands so foolish, so frail, in the days when swords sang out on their behalf!... Strange sighs emanate from beneath the trees. My soul, you are caught up in ancient dreams!

NOTES FOR *(I) DE RÊVE*

Date: 1892
Source: Claude Debussy, in *Entretiens politiques et littéraires*, December 1892, pp. 269–270.
Manuscript: in a private collection in France
Dedication: "à V. Hocquet"
[1] The poem had no title.
[2] The *Entretiens* gives:
Mains si folles,
Mains si frêles,

(II)   DE GRÈVE[1]

Sur la mer les crépuscules tombent,
Soie blanche effilée!
Les vagues comme de petites folles,
Jasent, petites filles sortant de l'école,
Parmi les froufrous de leur robe,
Soie verte irisée!

Les nuages, graves voyageurs,
Se concertent sur le prochain orage,
Et, c'est un fond vraiment trop grave
À cette anglaise aquarelle.
Les vagues, les petites vagues,
Ne savent plus où se mettre,
Car voici la méchante averse,
Froufrous de jupes envolées,
Soie verte affolée!

Mais la lune, compatissante à tous,
Vient apaiser ce gris conflit,
Et caresse lentement ses petites amies,
Qui s'offrent, comme lèvres aimantes
À ce tiède et blanc baiser.
Puis, plus rien!
Plus que les cloches attardées
Des flottantes églises
Angélus des vagues,
Soie blanche apaisée!

_____

(II) OF STRANDS

Twilights fall over the sea, white raveled silk. Waves like foolish girls, girls coming from school among the rustling of their dresses, chatter away, green iridescent silk!

Clouds, sober travelers, plot the coming storm, and it is indeed too sober a background for this English watercolor. Waves, the little waves, do not know which way to turn, for behold the mischievous shower, the rustlings of flying skirts, panicked green silk.

Yet the moon, with pity for all, comes to calm this gray struggle, and it slowly soothes its little friends who offer themselves to this moist white kiss like loving lips. Then nothing! Nothing but the belated bells of the floating churches, Angelus of the waves, smoothed white silk!

NOTES FOR *(II) DE GRÈVE*

Date: 1892
Source: Claude Debussy, in *Entretiens politiques et littéraires,* December 1892, pp. 270–271.
Manuscript: not located
Dedication: "à Raymond Bonheur"
[1] The poem had no title.
Comment: Debussy uses *"toute soie"* in quotation marks, certainly a reference to this poem, in a letter to Pierre Louÿs of July 1903. See also the letter to René Peter, undated (1893?).

(III) DE FLEURS

Dans l'ennui si désolément vert
De la serre de douleur,
Les Fleurs enlacent mon coeur
De leurs tiges méchantes.
Ah! quand reviendront autour de ma tête
Les chères mains si tendrement désenlaceuses?

Les grands Iris violets
Violèrent méchamment tes yeux,
En semblant les refléter,
Eux, qui furent l'eau du songe
Où plongèrent mes rêves si doucement
Enclos en leur couleur;
Et les lys, blancs jets d'eau de pistils embaumés,
Ont perdu leur grâce blanche
Et ne sont plus que pauvres malades sans soleil!

Soleil! ami des fleurs mauvaises,
Tueur de rêves! Tueur d'illusions
Ce pain béni des âmes misérables!
Venez! Venez! Les mains salvatrices!
Brisez les vitres de mensonge,
Brisez les vitres de maléfice,
Mon âme meurt de trop de soleil!

Mirages! Plus ne refleurira la joie de mes yeux,
Et mes mains sont lasses de prier,
Mes yeux sont las de pleurer!
Eternellement ce bruit fou
Des pétales noirs de l'ennui,
Tombant goutte à goutte sur ma tête
Dans le vert de la serre de douleur!

(III)   OF FLOWERS

In the boredom of sorrow's hothouse, so desolately green, the flowers entwine my heart in their cruel tendrils. Ah! when will the hands that so tenderly disentwine be placed again about my head?

The huge violet irises mischievously ravish your eyes while pretending to reflect them, they who were the water of the dream into which my dreams sank, enveloped so softly in their color; and the lilies, white pistil-scented fountains, have lost their pale grace and are no more than poor invalids without the sun!

Sun! friend of evil flowers, killer of dreams! Killer of illusions, blessed bread of unhappy souls! Come! Come! redeeming hands, shatter the panes of falsehood, shatter the panes of evil, my soul expires from too much sun!

Mirages! the joy of my eyes will never bloom again, and my hands are tired of praying, my eyes tired of weeping! Forever this insane sound of boredom's black petals falling like drops upon my head in the green of sorrow's hothouse!

NOTES FOR *(III) DE FLEURS*

   Date: June 1893
   Source: Claude Debussy
   Manuscripts: (1) dated, in a private collection in Austria; (2) undated, entitled "Ier Cahier de Proses Lyriques. Proses 3–4," in the Bibliothèque Nationale, Paris
   Dedication: "à Madame E. Chausson"
   Comments: The dated manuscript bears the inscription: "à Madame E. Chausson pour sa fête, et pour rendre respectueusement hommage au charme qu'elle met à être Madame Chausson"
   (To Madame E. Chausson on her saint's day, and to pay respectful homage to the charming way in which she is Madame Chausson)
   The undated manuscript bears the inscription: "à Madame M. A. Fontaine en hommage à sa voix si délicieusement musicienne"
   (To Madame M. A. Fontaine, in homage to her delightfully musical voice)

(IV)   DE SOIR

Dimanche sur les villes,
Dimanche dans les coeurs!
Dimanche chez les petites filles
Chantant d'une voix informée
Des rondes obstinées
Où de bonnes Tours
N'en ont plus que pour quelques jours!

Dimanche, les gares sont folles!
Tout le monde appareille
Pour des banlieues d'aventure
En se disant adieu
Avec des gestes éperdus!

Dimanche les trains vont vite,
Dévorés par d'insatiables tunnels;
Et les bons signaux des routes
Echangent d'un oeil unique
Des impressions mécaniques.

Dimanche, dans le bleu de mes rêves
Où mes pensées tristes
De feux d'artifices manqués
Ne veulent plus quitter
Le deuil de vieux Dimanches trépassés.

Et la nuit à pas de velours
Vient endormir le beau ciel fatigué,
Et c'est Dimanche dans les avenues d'étoiles;
La Vierge or sur argent
Laisse tomber les fleurs de sommeil!

(IV)   OF EVENING

Sunday over towns, Sunday in hearts! Sunday for little girls who in their childish voices sing persistent rounds in which fine Towers are given but a few more days!

Sunday, the train stations are madness! Everyone packs up for the suburbs of adventure, saying farewell with frantic gestures!

Sunday the trains go swiftly, devoured by insatiable tunnels; and the kindly signal lights trade mechanical impressions with their single eye.

Sunday, in the blue of my dreams where my sad thoughts of fizzled fireworks are loath to abandon mourning for former Sundays dead and gone.

And the night with its velvet footfall comes to put the lovely, tired day to sleep, and it is Sunday on the avenues of the stars; the gold-on-silver Virgin lets fall the flowers of slumber!

NOTES FOR *(IV) DE SOIR*

> Date: July 1893
> Source: Claude Debussy
> Manuscripts: (1) undated, entitled "Ier Cahier de Proses Lyriques. Proses 3–4," in the Bibliothèque Nationale, Paris; (2) dated sketch in the Bibliothèque Nationale, Paris
> Dedication: "à Henry Lerolle"
> Comments: The undated manuscript bears the inscription: "à Madame M. A. Fontaine en hommage à sa voix si délicieusement musicienne"
> (To Madame M. A. Fontaine, in homage to her delightfully musical voice)
> The dated sketch shows many corrections and only the words: "Vieux Dimanches trépassés" and "Vite les petits anges." The melody is unlike the published version.

NOTES FOR *PROSES LYRIQUES*

> Date: 1892–July 1893
> Publisher: E. Fromont, Paris 1895
> First performance: *De fleurs* and *De soir* sung by Thérèse Roger accompanied by Debussy at a concert of the Société Nationale, 17 February 1894.
> Comment: In a letter to Pierre de Bréville, 24 March 1898, Debussy writes:

> Quant aux "Proses," j'ai changé d'avis, et il m'apparait très inutile de les augmenter d'un fracas orchestral quelconque.

> (As for the "Proses," I've changed my mind and I think it would be useless to augment them with any kind of orchestral din.)

Vite, les petits anges
Dépassez les hirondelles
Afin de vous coucher
Forts d'absolution!
Prenez pitié des villes,
Prenez pitié des coeurs,
Vous, la Vierge or sur argent!

———————

CHANSONS DE BILITIS
— Pierre Louÿs

I   LA FLÛTE DE PAN[1]

Pour le jour des Hyacinthies, il m'a donné une syrinx faite de roseaux bien taillés, unis avec la blanche cire qui est douce à mes lèvres comme le miel.

Il m'apprend à jouer, assise sur ses genoux; mais je suis un peu tremblante. Il en joue après moi, si doucement que je l'entends à peine.

Nous n'avons rien à nous dire, tant nous sommes près l'un de l'autre; mais nos chansons veulent se répondre, et tour à tour nos bouches s'unissent sur la flûte.

Il est tard; voici le chant des grenouilles vertes qui commence avec la nuit. Ma mère ne croira jamais que je suis restée si longtemps à chercher ma ceinture perdue.

———————

Quick! you tiny angels, overtake the swallows that you may rest with absolution! Take pity on towns, take pity on hearts, You, gold-on-silver Virgin!

THE SONGS OF BILITIS

I PAN'S FLUTE

For Hyacinthus' day he gave me a flute made of neatly cut reeds joined together with white wax as sweet as honey to my lips.

He teaches me to play, sitting on his lap; but I tremble a bit. He plays it after me, so softly that I can barely hear him.

We have nothing to say to each other, so close are we to each other; but our songs try to answer each other, and by turns our mouths meet on the flute.

It is late; there is the song of the green frogs that starts up at nightfall. My mother will never believe that I have spent so long a time in searching for my lost sash.

NOTES FOR *I LA FLÛTE DE PAN*

Date: 22 June 1897
Source: Pierre Louÿs, *Les Chansons de Bilitis*—traduites du grec pour la première fois par P. L., Bucoliques en Pamphylie, No. 20. Librairie de l'Art indépendant, Paris 1895, p. 47.
Manuscripts: (1) dated, in a private collection in France; (2) undated, in the Bibliothèque Nationale, Paris
    [1] The title of the poem is *La Syrinx*.

II   *LA CHEVELURE*

Il m'a dit: "Cette nuit, j'ai rêvé. J'avais ta chevelure autour de mon cou. J'avais tes cheveux comme un collier noir autour de ma nuque et sur ma poitrine.

"Je les caressais, et c'étaient les miens; et nous étions liés pour toujours ainsi, par la même chevelure la bouche sur la bouche, ainsi que deux lauriers n'ont souvent qu'une racine.

"Et peu à peu, il m'a semblé, tant nos membres étaient confondus, que je devenais toi-même ou que tu entrais en moi comme mon songe."

Quand il eu achevé, il mit doucement ses mains sur mes épaules, et il me regarda d'un regard si tendre, que je baissai les yeux avec un frisson.

———————

II   THE HAIR

He told me: "Last night I had a dream. Your hair was around my neck. Your hair was like a black collar around my neck and upon my chest.

"I caressed it and it was mine; and we were bound together thus forever, by the same hair, mouth against mouth, as two laurels often have but one root.

"And gradually, so intertwined were our members, it seemed to me that I was becoming you, or that you were entering into me like a dream."

When he had finished, he gently placed his hands on my shoulders, and he looked at me with so tender a look that I lowered my eyes with a shiver.

NOTES FOR *II LA CHEVELURE*

Date: 1897
Source: Pierre Louÿs, *Les Chansons de Bilitis*—traduites du grec par Pierre Louÿs, Bucoliques en Pamphylie, No. 31. Société du Mercure de France, Paris 1898, p. 85.
Manuscript: in the Bibliothèque Nationale, Paris
Publisher: *L'Image*, no. 11, October 1897, p. 339, with illustrations by Van Dongen
Comments: This poem was not included in the first edition of *Les Chansons de Bilitis*, in 1895. Pierre Louÿs gave Debussy a copy of the final version before it was published.
The song as it appeared in *L'Image* showed the following variants:
The title: *Chansons de Bilitis*
Dedication: "À madame A. Peter"
First line: Il *me* dit: "Cette nuit. . . ."

III LE TOMBEAU DES NAÏADES

Le long du bois couvert de givre, je marchais; mes cheveux devant ma bouche se fleurissaient de petits glaçons, et mes sandales étaient lourdes de neige fangeuse et tassée.

Il me dit: "Que cherches-tu!" — "Je suis la trace du satyre. Ses petits pas fourchus alternent comme des trous dans un manteau blanc." Il me dit: "Les satyres sont morts.

"Les satyres et les nymphes aussi. Depuis trente ans il n'a pas fait un hiver aussi terrible. La trace que tu vois est celle d'un boùc. Mais restons ici, où est leur tombeau."

Et avec le fer de sa houe il cassa la glace de la source où jadis riaient les Naïades. Il prenait de grands morceaux froids, et les soulevant vers le ciel pâle, il regardait au travers.

———————

III   THE TOMB OF THE NAIADS

I walked through the frost-covered woods; my hair across my mouth blossomed with tiny icicles, and my sandals were heavy and caked with muddy snow.

He spoke to me: "What are you seeking?" "I am following the track of a satyr, his tiny cloven footprints are laid out like holes in a white mantle." He said: "The satyrs are dead.

"The satyrs and the nymphs too. For thirty years, there has not been so terrible a winter. The tracks you see are those of a stag. But let us stay here, where their tomb is."

And with the blade of his hoe he broke the ice of the springs where the Naiads had once laughed. He picked up the huge cold fragments and, raising them to the pale sky, he peered through them.

NOTES FOR *III LE TOMBEAU DES NAÏADES*

Date: Merçin, 23 August 1898
Source: Pierre Louÿs, *Les Chansons de Bilitis*—traduites du grec pour la première fois par P. L., Bucoliques en Pamphylie, No. 31. Librairie de l'Art indépendant, Paris 1895, p. 57.
Manuscript: in a private collection in France
Dedication: "Ce manuscrit à Madame Lucien Fontaine pour sa fête et l'assurer une fois de plus de ma particulière sympathie et de ma joie d'être son très fidèle Claude Debussy"
(This manuscript to Madame Lucien Fontaine for her saint's day and to assure her once again of my special regard and my pleasure at being her very faithful Claude Debussy)
Comment: Debussy wrote to Pierre Louÿs, 24 December 1897:
"La troisième Chansons de Bilitis s'orne de toute la musique dont je suis redevable à ma nature bien organisée."
(The third Chansons de Bilitis contains all the music for which I am beholden to my well-organized nature.)

NOTES FOR *CHANSONS DE BILITIS*

Date: June 1897–August 1898
Publisher: E. Fromont, Paris 1899
First performance: Blanche Marot accompanied by Debussy at a concert of the Société Nationale in the Salle Pleyel, 17 March 1900

TROIS CHANSONS DE CHARLES D'ORLÉANS

I   Dieu! qu'il la fait bon regarder!

Dieu! qu'il la fait bon regarder,
La gracieuse bonne et belle;
Pour les grans biens que sont en elle,
Chascun est prest de la louer.
Qui se pourroit d'elle lasser?
Tousjours sa beauté renouvelle.

Dieu! qu'il la fait bon regarder,
La gracieuse bonne et belle!
Par de ça, ne de là, la mer
Ne sçay dame ne damoiselle
Qui soit en tous biens parfais telle.
C'est ung songe que d'i penser;
Dieu! qu'il la fait bon regarder!

———————

THREE SONGS BY CHARLES D'ORLÉANS

I   Lord! how good it is to look at her!

Lord! how good it is to look at her, a buxom and lovely gracious lady;
for her high qualities, all are eager to praise her. Who could ever tire of
her? Her beauty constantly increases.

Lord! how good it is to look at her, a buxom and lovely gracious lady!
Nowhere does the sea touch any woman, married or single, who is in
any way more perfect than she. It is folly even to think it! Lord! how
good it is to look upon her!

NOTE FOR *I Dieu! qu'il la fait bon regarder!*

The early unpublished version of this song and *Yver, vous n'estes qu'un villain* was written for the amateur choral group organized by Lucien Fontaine
which Debussy conducted from 1893 to 1904. These songs, particularly the second, differ from the 1908 versions.

II   *Quant j'ai ouy le tabourin*

Quant j'ai ouy le tabourin
Sonner, pour s'en aller au may,
En mon lit n'en ay fait affray
Ne levé mon chief du coissin;

En disant: il est trop matin
Ung peu je me rendormiray:
Quant j'ai ouy le tabourin
Sonner pour s'en aller au may.

Jeunes gens partent leur butin
De nonchaloir m'accointeray
A lui je m'abutineray
Trouvé l'ay plus prouchain voisin;
Quant j'ai ouy le tabourin
Sonner, pour s'en aller au may,[1]
En mon lit n'en ay fait affray
Ne levé mon chief du coissin.

———

II   *When I heard the drum*

When I heard the drum beat summoning us to the maying, I did not leap from my bed or lift my head from my pillow;

Saying: it is too early in the morning. I will sleep a bit longer—when I heard the drum beat summoning us to the maying.

Let the young folk divide up their spoils, I shall be content to remain indifferent; I will share my spoils with him, for he was my nearest neighbor, when I heard the drum beat.

NOTES FOR *II Quant j'ai ouy le tabourin*

¹ Debussy added the last three lines.

In a letter to Louis Laloy, 16 June 1908, Debussy asks him for the "sens exact" of the words he underlined in this poem, which he copied out in full. The words are: *affray, partent, m'acointeray, m'abutineray,* and *l'ay.* He then continues:

"Je trouve cette petite pièce si pleine de douce musique intérieure que— naturellement—je ne peux me retenir de 'l'extérioriser'—comme dirait notre ami Victor Segalen. Que le gentil Charles d'Orléans veuille bien m'en absoudre.

"J'aime mieux vous dire tout de suite que j'attends votre réponse pour fixer mes couleurs."

(I find this piece so full of soft inner music that—naturally—I cannot refrain from "exteriorizing" it—as our friend Victor Segalen would say. I trust the noble Charles d'Orléans will absolve me.

I prefer to let you know right away that I'm awaiting your reply to decide my colors.)

III   Yver, vous n'estes qu'un villain;

Yver, vous n'estes qu'un villain;
Esté est plaisant et gentil,
En témoing de may et d'avril
Qui l'accompaignent soir et main.

Esté revet champs, bois et fleurs
De sa livrée de verdure
Et de maintes autres couleurs
Par l'ordonnance de nature.

Mais vous, Yver trop estes plein
De nége, vent, pluye et grézil.
On vous deust banir en éxil.[1]
Yver, vous n'estes qu'un villain.

_____

III   *Winter, you are no better than a rascal;*

Winter, you are no better than a rascal; Summer is pleasant and kind, as May and April can testify, accompanying it evening and morning.

Summer covers the fields, woods, and flowers with his verdant livery, and many other colors too, according to nature.

But you, Winter, are too full of snow, wind, rain and hail. You ought to be exiled. Winter, you are no better than a rascal.

NOTES FOR *III Yver, vous n'estes qu'un villain*

Comments: The title of this song is used as the epigraph of Part III of *En blanc et noir*, composed in 1915.
[1] The penultimate line is omitted:
Sans point flater, je parle plain.

NOTES FOR *TROIS CHANSONS DE CHARLES D'ORLÉANS*

Date: April 1898 (I and III)–1908 (II)
Source: Charles d'Orléans, *Poésies complètes de Charles d'Orléans,* Tome II: *Chanson VI, Rondeau LXXVII, Chanson LXXXII.* Alphonse Lemerre, Paris 1874, pp. 8, 122, 48–49.
Manuscripts: (1) undated 1908 version of I, II, and III and single copy of no. I, in Bibliothèque Nationale, Paris; (2) early version of nos. I and III (numbered I and II), dated "April 1898," dedicated to Lucien Fontaine, in a private collection in Germany
Publisher: A. Durand & Fils, Paris, 1908
First performance: Debussy conducted at the Concerts Colonne, 9 April 1909
Comments: The songs are for four voices without accompaniment. They were undoubtedly written for the amateur choral group organized by Lucien Fontaine which Debussy conducted.

* BERCEUSE pour "La Tragédie de la Mort"
sur une vieille chanson poitevine[1]

— René Peter

Il était un' fois une fée
qui avait un beau sceptre blanc,
il était un' plaintive enfant
qui pleurait pour des fleurs fanées.

La fée en la voyant pleurer
détacha des fleurs de son sceptre
et les laissa douc'ment tomber;
l'enfant les noua dans ses tresses
et lui dit: "—En as-tu encore?"

Il en tomba mille et mille autres,
le long d'ses yeux, le long d'sa bouche,
des mauv's, des jaunes et des rouges;
l'enfant en couvrit ses épaules
et lui dit: "—En as-tu encore?"

Il en tomba tout autour d'elle,
autant de parures nouvelles,
des colliers clairs, des ceintur's d'or,
d'autres couraient le long d'ses jambes,
cachant ses pieds sous des guirlandes
"—En as-tu? En as-tu encore?"

La blanch' fée enfin descendit
elle ôta des ch'veux d'la p'tit' fille
les fleurs répandues les premier's
et qui étaient déjà flétries.

Mais l'enfant les lui prit des mains
et les jeta sur le chemin
avec de légers cris de colère.

Et la fée, la blanche fée dit:
"—Pourquoi j'ter ces fleurs sur le ch'min?
Tandis qu'elles passent d'autres naissent;
c'est ton bonheur, c'est ton bonheur que tu laisses."

LULLABYE, for "The Tragedy of Death"
on an old song from Poitiers

Once upon a time there was a fairy with a lovely white wand, there was a sad child who cried because the flowers were faded.

Seeing her cry, the fairy plucked the flowers from her wand and gently let them fall. The child braided them into her hair and said, "Have you more of them?"

And thousands more fell down across her eyes, her mouth, her hands, yellow and red; the child covered her shoulders with them and said: "Have you more of them?"

And more fell all about her like new jewels, bright necklaces, golden sashes, others fell about her legs, concealing her feet beneath garlands. "Have you any more, more?"

Finally, the white fairy came down and removed from the child's hair those flowers that had fallen first and that were already withered.

But the child took them from her and threw them down upon the path with soft angry cries.

And the white fairy said, "Why throw the flowers upon the path? When they fade, others will grow; you are throwing away your own happiness."

NOTES FOR *BERCEUSE*

Date: April 1899
Source: René Peter, *La Tragédie de la Mort*. Mercure de France, Paris 1899, p. 16 (with Preface by Pierre Louÿs).
Manuscript: in The Library of Congress, Washington, D.C.
Dedication: "Cher René, excuse moi de prendre momentanément l'accent poitevin' pour t'assurer une fois de plus de ma sincère amitié! Claude Debussy"
(Dear René, forgive me for momentarily assuming a "Poitevin" accent to assure you once again of my sincere friendship!)
[1] The song has no title.
Comments: The song is unpublished. It is for voice alone, for the so-called *chanson de la mère* (the mother's song) in the first act of the play.
* The original version of the song is given in Appendix A.

NUITS BLANCHES

— *Claude Debussy*

Tout à l'heure ses mains plus délicates que des
fleurs, se poseront sur mes yeux...[1]

Ce soir, il m'a semblé que le mensonge[2]
Traînait dans les plis de sa jupe,
Et ses petits pieds ont foulé
Mon coeur sans merci.

Dans le lourd silence de la nuit
Il y a quelqu'un derrière moi,
Quelqu'un venu à travers mes songes
Dont mon coeur rompu,
La Fièvre de mon sang
Rythment le doux nom.
Voici qu'une main s'est posé sur mon épaule
Petite main qui noue et denoue à son gré
Le fil de ma destinée.
Lorsqu'elle est entrée il m'a semblé
Que le mensonge traînait aux plis de sa jupe;
La lueur de ses grands yeux mentait
Et dans la musique de sa voix
Quelque chose d'étrange vibrait.

————————

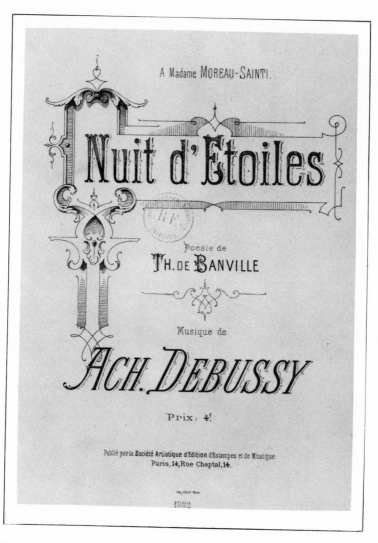

1. Debussy's first pub-
lished composition, a song
composed in 1880

2. A rare example of the manuscript of three song texts. Two are mislabeled: *Pantomime* should read *Fantoches* and *Pierrot* should read *Pantomime*

3. An early manuscript of *Mandoline*, a song included in the "Vasnier Songbook"

SOIRÉE MUSICALE

donnée par le Violoniste

MAURICE THIEBERG

Avec le gracieux concours de

Mme VASNIER et de Mr ACHILLE de BUSSY

Vendredi 12 Mai 1882, à 8 heures 1/2 très-précises

PROGRAMME :

1. A. **Allegro de la Sonate**, Mi bemol majeur... BEETHOVEN
   B. **Pensées fugitives**, pour Piano et Violon... St-HELLER & H. W. ERNST
   Andante con Variazoni et Intermezzo (Presto) par
   MM. de BUSSY et THIEBERG.
2. **Air d'Actéon**.................................. AUBER
   Chanté par Mme VASNIE
3. **Concerto** en Mi majeur....................... VIEUXTEMPS
   Adagio et Rondo, par M. THIEBERG.
4. A. **Nocturno,** } pour Piano et Violon........... Ach. de BUSSY
   B. **Scherzo,** }
   par l'auteur et M. THIEBERG.
5. A. **Adagio du Concerto Militaire** .... LIPINSKI
   B. **Polonaise brillante**...................... WIENIAWSKI
   par M. THIEBERG.
6. A. **Fête galante** .... } Ach. de BUSSY
   B. **Les Roses**............................... }
   Chanté par Mme VASNIE
7. A. **Berceuse**................................ RÉBER
   B. **Rhapsodie Hongroise**..................... MISZKA HAUSER
   par M. THIEBERG.

Prix du Billet : 6 francs

4. The first performance of
Fête galante and *Les Roses,*
sung by Mme Vasnier ac-
companied by Achille de
Bussy

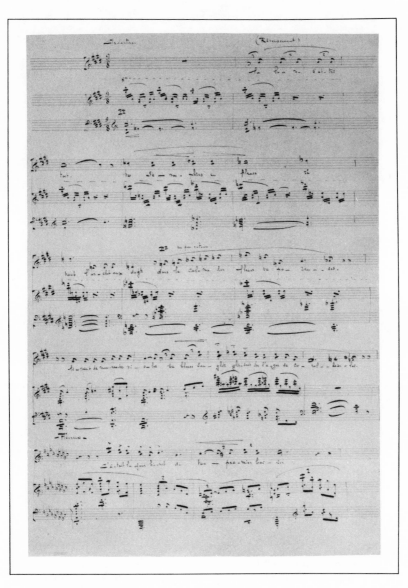

5. *Apparition*, the song
Debussy composed in 1884
at Ville d'Avray, where he
was visiting M. and Mme
Vasnier

6.   The early unpublished
version of *Chevaux de bois*

7. Debussy sent a copy of this first edition to Pierre Louÿs inscribed: "Où courent-ils? / Chez Pierre Louÿs / 1, rue Grétry / Paris. Claude Debussy. Mai 1895"

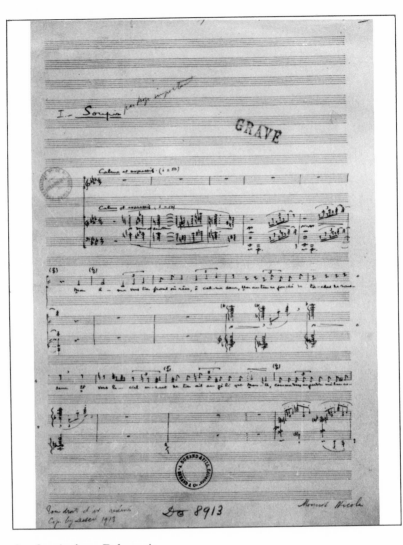

8.   *Soupir*, from Debussy's
last songs, the *Trois Poèmes
de Stéphane Mallarmé*, was
composed in 1913. This
manuscript shows variations
with the final version.

Le Samedi 21 Mars, à 9 heures

——— NOUVELLE ———

Société Philharmonique
de Paris   *(13ᵉ Année)*

SALLE DES CONCERTS	Directeur : Mᵛ E. REY
45, rue La Boëtie ✹	✹ ✹ 9 rue de l'Isly
PARIS *(Salle Gaveau)*	*(Agence Musicale de Paris)*
Tél. : Wagram 28-20	Tél. : Central 11-52

ONZIÈME SÉANCE

Le ▮▮▮▮▮▮▮ 1914, *à 9 heures du soir*

Claude DEBUSSY
Mᵐᵉ E. VALLIN-PARDO
Le Quatuor HAYOT

═══ PROGRAMME ═══

1. **Quatuor** *en Sol majeur* .... MOZART
   Le QUATUOR HAYOT
2. **3 Poèmes** de STÉPHANE MALLARMÉ (1ʳᵉ audition) .... DEBUSSY
   Mᵐᵉ VALLIN-PARDO et l'AUTEUR
3. **Childrens Corner** (suite pour piano) .... DEBUSSY
   Mʳ CLAUDE DEBUSSY
4. **Le Promenoir des déux Amants** .... DEBUSSY
   Mᵐᵉ VALLIN-PARDO et l'AUTEUR
5. *a)* **La Soirée dans Grenade** ....⎫
   b) **La Fille aux cheveux de Lin** (1ᵉʳ Cahier des Préludes) ...⎬ DEBUSSY
   c) **Général Lavine** *(excentric)* ....⎭
   Mʳ CLAUDE DEBUSSY
6. **Quatuor** à cordes .... DEBUSSY
   Le QUATUOR HAYOT

PIANO GAVEAU

PRIX DES PLACES :

Fauteuils d'Orchestre, 12 fr. – Loge *(la place)*, 12 fr. – Pourtour d'Orchestre, 6 fr. Premier Balcon (1ᵉʳ rang), 8 fr. — Premier Balcon (autres rangs, *face*), 7 fr. — Premier Balcon (autres rangs), 6 fr. — Premier Balcon-Pourtour, 5 fr. — Deuxième Balcon, (1ᵉʳ rang), 5 fr. — Deuxième Balcon (2ᵐᵉ rang), 4 fr. — Deuxième Balcon-Pourtour, 4 fr. — Entrée, 3 fr.

Billets à l'avance : à la SALLE GAVEAU et chez les Éditeurs de Musique : Mᵐᵉˢ DURAND, 4, place de la Madeleine; ESCHIG, 13, rue Laffitte et 48, rue de Rome; MATHOT, 15, rue Bergère; VIEUX, 51, rue de Rome.

9.   The first performance of
*Trois Poèmes de Stéphane Mal-
larmé,* sung by Mme Vallin
accompanied by Debussy

10.   In this letter to Gustave
Doret, 5 June 1896, Debussy
lists his six principal works
and adds that he has just
finished *Pelléas et Mélisande*

11. Debussy ends this
letter to the conductor
D.-E. Inghelbrecht with:
"Laissez nous tous sous le
patronnage de Charles
d'Orléans, doux prince aimé
des muses et si gentil
français."

19 mai

1 9 1 7

[handwritten letter from Debussy to Paul Dukas]

12. In this letter to Paul
Dukas, 19 May 1917, De-
bussy opens with the quotation from Laforgue he has so
frequently used: "Je croupis
dans les usines du Néant."

SLEEPLESS NIGHTS

A while ago, her hands, more delicate than flowers, were placed upon my eyes...

That evening, I felt that falsehood was caught in the folds of her skirt, and her tiny feet mercilessly trampled my heart.

In the pregnant silence of the night, someone follows me, someone who has entered through my dreams and whose sweet name beats on my broken heart and in my fevered blood. And now a hand is laid upon my shoulder, a tiny hand that knots or unknots as it will the thread of my fate. When she entered, it seemed to me that falsehood was caught in the folds of her skirt; the glow of her huge eyes lied, and something strange vibrated in the music of her voice.

NOTES FOR *NUITS BLANCHES*

Date: 1899–1902
Source: Claude Debussy
Manuscript: in the Bibliothèque de l'Opéra, Paris
[1] A single page with nine measures of music and these two lines are all that remains of what Debussy entitled: *2ᵐᵉ Cahier de "Proses lyriques."* The last three measures were published by Octave Séré in *Musicien français d'aujourd'hui,* Paris 1911, p. 130.
[2] These lines are all that Vallas remembers of what he saw in a small notebook (now lost) that had belonged to Debussy's wife Lilly. (See *Les Nouvelles littéraires,* 15 April 1933.)
Comments: In a letter to Georges Hartmann, dated 20 August 1899, Debussy mentions: "Nuits blanches, 5 poèmes pour une voix avec accompagnement de piano."
(Sleepless nights, 5 poems for single voice with piano accompaniment.)
The songs, announced by the publisher Fromont in 1900, were never published.

DANS LE JARDIN

— Paul Gravollet

Je regardais dans le jardin,
Furtif, au travers de la haie;
Je t'ai vue, enfant! et soudain,
Mon coeur tressaillit: je t'aimais!

Je m'égratignais aux épines,
Mes doigts saignaient avec les mûres,
Et ma souffrance était divine:
Je voyais ton front de gamine,
Tes cheveux d'or et ton front pur!

Grandette et pourtant puérile,
Coquette d'instinct seulement,
Les yeux bleus ombrés de longs cils,
Qui regardent tout gentiment,
Un corps un peu frêle et charmant,
Une voix de mai, des gestes d'avril!

Je regardais dans le jardin,
Furtif, au travers de la haie;
Je t'ai vue, enfant! et soudain,
Mon coeur tressaillit: je t'aimais.

IN THE GARDEN

I peered furtively into the garden through the hedge and saw you, child! and suddenly my heart leaped: I loved you!

I scratched myself on the thorns, my fingers bled from the bramble-berries and my suffering was divine: I saw your childlike face, your golden hair, your pure forehead!

A young girl and yet boyish, a flirt by instinct alone, your blue eyes shadowed with long lashes looked with kindness, your body somehow frail and charming, the voice of May, the gestures of April!

I peered furtively into the garden through the hedge and saw you, child! and suddenly my heart leaped: I loved you!

NOTES FOR *DANS LE JARDIN*

Date: May 1903
Source: Paul Gravollet, *Les Frissons,* No. 5. J. Hamelle, Paris 1905.
Manuscript: in a private collection in the United States
Publisher: J. Hamelle, Paris 1905
Comment: The date is given on the title page of the manuscript. Vallas gives the date 1891 but offers no proof. Both d'Indy's *Mirage* and Ravel's *Manteau de fleurs,* their respective contributions to *Les Frissons,* a collection of twenty-two songs, were composed in 1903.

TROIS CHANSONS DE FRANCE

(I)   RONDEL: *Le temps a laissié son manteau*
— *Charles d'Orléans*

Le temps a laissié son manteau
De vent, de froidure et de pluye,
Et s'est vestu de broderye,
De soleil raiant, cler et beau.[1]

Il n'y a beste ne oiseau
Qui en son jargon ne chante ou crye:[2]
Le temps a laissié son manteau.[3]

Rivière, fontaine et ruisseau
Portent, en livrée jolye,
Goultes d'argent d'orfaverie.
Chascun s'abille de nouveau,
Le temps a laissié son manteau.

(II)   LA GROTTE[1]
— *Tristan Lhermite*

Auprès de cette grotte sombre
Où l'on respire un air si doux,
L'onde lutte avec les cailloux,
Et la lumière avecque l'ombre.

Ces flots, lassés de l'exercise
Qu'ils ont fait dessus ce gravier,
Se reposent dans ce vivier
Où mourut autrefois Narcisse…

THREE SONGS OF FRANCE

(I)   RONDEL: *The weather has shed its cloak*

The weather has shed its cloak of wind, cold and rain, and has donned an embroidered garment of radiant, clear, and lovely sunshine.

No beast or bird that does not sing or shout in its own tongue—the weather has shed its cloak.

Rivers, fountains, brooks all wear with jolly abandon liveries of silver and gold droplets. Each thing wears a new dress—the weather has shed its cloak.

(II)   THE GROTTO

Near this dark grotto where the air is so soft, the current struggles against the pebbles, the light against the shadow.

These waves, tired of moving over the gravel, come to rest in the pond where Narcissus once died...

NOTES FOR *(I) RONDEL: Le temps a laissié son manteau*

> Date: 1904
> Source: Charles d'Orléans, *Poésies complètes de Charles d'Orléans*, Tome II, *Rondeau LXIII*. Alphonse Lemerre, Paris 1874, p. 115.
> [1] "raiant," a variant of "luyant," is found in some editions of the poem
> [2] *Qui en* son jargon ne chante ou crye (Debussy)
> *Qu'en* son jargon ne chante ou crye (Charles d'Orléans)
> [3] The following line is omitted here, as in some editions of the poem:
> De vent de froidure et de pluye

NOTES FOR *(II) LA GROTTE*

> Source: Tristan Lhermite, *Collection des plus belles pages*, Les Amours—Odes—*Le Promenoir des deux amants*: verses 1, 2, and 4. Mercure de France, Paris 1909, pp. 51–52.
> [1] The title of the poem is *Le Promenoir des deux amants*.
> Comment: This song is repeated, under the title *Auprès de cette grotte sombre*, as no. I of *Le Promenoir des deux amants*, 1910.

L'ombre de cette fleur vermeille
Et celle de ces joncs pendant
Paraissent estre là-dedans
Les songes de l'eau qui sommeille.

(III)   RONDEL: Pour ce que Plaisance est morte
— *Charles d'Orléans*

Pour ce que Plaisance est morte
Ce may, suis vestu de noir;
C'est grand pitié de véoir
Mon coeur qui s'en desconforte.

Je m'abille de la sorte
Que doy, pour faire devoir;
Pour ce que Plaisance est morte,
Ce may, suis vestu de noir.

Le temps ces nouvelles porte
Qui ne veut déduit avoir;
Mais par force du plouvoir
Fais des champs clore la porte,
Pour ce que Plaisance est morte.

The shadow of that vermillion flower and of the bending reeds seem to be part of the dreams of the sleeping water.

(III)   RONDEL: *Because Plaisance is dead*

Because Plaisance is dead this May, I am dressed in black; it is a great pity to see my heart so unhappy.

I dress in this fitting manner out of duty: because Plaisance is dead this May, I am dressed in black

The weather brings us news we do not want to hear; but because it rains it makes the fields shut their door, because Plaisance is dead.

NOTES FOR *(III) RONDEL: Pour ce que Plaisance est morte*

Source: Charles d'Orleans, *Poésies complètes de Charles d'Orléans*, Tome II, Rondeau LIX. Alphonse Lemerre, Paris 1874, p. 113.
Comment: Debussy writes that "mes heures sont plutôt vêtues de noir" (my days are more or less clothed in black), taken from stanza 1, line 2, in a letter to his publisher Georges Hartmann, 6 July 1898. See also the letter to Jacques Durand, 22 July 1915.

NOTES FOR *TROIS CHANSONS DE FRANCE*

Date: 1904
Manuscripts: in the Bibliothèque Nationale, Paris
Dedication: "à Madame S. Bardac"
Publisher: A. Durand & Fils, Paris 1904

FÊTES GALANTES—2ᵉ Recueil
— *Paul Verlaine*

(I) *LES INGÉNUS*

Les hauts talons luttaient avec les longues jupes,
En sorte que, selon le terrain et le vent,
Parfois luisaient des bas de jambes, trop souvent
Interceptés!—et nous aimions ce jeu de dupes.

Parfois aussi le dard d'un insecte jaloux
Inquiétait le col des belles sous les branches,
Et c'étaient des éclairs soudains de nuques blanches
Et ce régal comblait nos jeunes yeux de fous.

Le soir tombait, un soir équivoque d'automne:
Les belles, se pendant rêveuses à nos bras,
Dirent alors des mots si spécieux, tout bas,
Que notre âme depuis ce temps tremble et s'étonne.

———————

(II) *LE FAUNE*

Un vieux faune de terre cuite
Rit au centre des boulingrins,
Présageant sans doute une suite
Mauvaise à ces instants sereins

Qui m'ont conduit et t'ont conduite,
—Mélancoliques pélerins,—
Jusqu'à cette heure dont la fuite
Tournoie au son des tambourins.

———————

FÊTES GALANTES—Second series

(I) THE INGENUOUS

High heels struggled with long skirts in such a way that, depending on the terrain and the wind, a glittering ankle was sometimes revealed— too often intercepted! and we enjoyed this silly game.

Sometimes too the sting of a jealous insect disturbed the collars of the beauties beneath the branches, and then there were lightning glimpses of white necks, and this feast sated our foolish young eyes.

The evening fell, an equivocal autumn evening: the beauties, leaning dreamily on our arms, would then utter such fair-seeming words, their voices low, that ever since our souls have trembled and been astonished.

———————

(II) THE FAUN

An old terra-cotta faun laughs in the center of the grassy plots, undoubtedly predicting a bad outcome to these serene moments

That have brought you and me—melancholy pilgrims—to this hour that passes to the sound of tambourins.

———————

(III)   COLLOQUE SENTIMENTAL

Dans le vieux parc solitaire et glacé,
Deux formes ont tout à l'heure passé.

Leurs yeux sont morts et leurs lèvres sont molles,
Et l'on entend à peine leurs paroles.

Dans le vieux parc solitaire et glacé,
Deux spectres ont évoqué le passé.

— Te souvient-il de notre extase ancienne?
— Pourquoi voulez-vous donc qu'il m'en souvienne?

— Ton coeur bat-il toujours à mon seul nom?
Toujours vois-tu mon âme en rêve? — Non.

— Ah! Les beaux jours de bonheur indicible
Où nous joignions nos bouches! — C'est possible.

— Qu'il était bleu, le ciel, et grand l'espoir!
— L'espoir a fui, vaincu, vers le ciel noir.

Tels ils marchaient dans las avoines folles,
Et la nuit seule entendit leurs paroles.

———————

(III)   SENTIMENTAL CONVERSATION

In the old park, deserted and ice covered, two figures passed by a while ago.

Their eyes are dead and their lips are slack, and their words can barely be heard.

In the old park, deserted and ice covered, two specters evoked the past.

"Do you remember our old ecstasy?" "Why do you want me to remember it?"

"Does your heart still beat at my name? Do you still see my soul in your dreams?" "No."

"Ah! the lovely days of unutterable happiness when our lips were joined!" "It's possible."

"How blue the sky was, and how vast our hope!" "Hope has fled, vanquished, into the black sky."

Thus they walked through the wild oats, and only the night heard their words.

NOTES FOR *FÊTES GALANTES—2ᵉ Recueil*

Date: 1904
Source: Paul Verlaine, *Fêtes galantes.* L. Vanier, Paris 1891, pp. 17–18, 35–36, 55–56.
Manuscripts: (1) two sets in the Bibliothèque Nationale, Paris; (2) early, totally different, version of *Colloque sentimental* in a private collection in Germany.
Dedication: "pour remercier le mois de juin 1904   A.l.p.M."
(to thank the month of June 1904   A.l.p.M.)
Publisher: A. Durand & Fils, Paris, 1904
First performance: Debussy was the accompanist at Madame Edouard Colonne's last "Jeudi musical," 23 June 1904.
Comment: In a letter to Jacques Durand, dated July 1904, Debussy writes:

À propos des "Fêtes galantes," je vous supplie de ne pas oublier la dédicace ainsi conçue: "Pour remercier le moi de Juin 1904, suivie des lettres: A.l.p.M." C'est un peu mysterieux, mais il faut bien faire quelque chose pour la légende.

(With regard to the "Fêtes galantes," please don't forget the following dedication: "To thank the month of June 1904, followed by the letters: A.l.p.M." It's a bit mystifying, but something has to be done for the legend.) The initials stand for "A la petite Mienne"—for my own little dear.

LE PROMENOIR DES DEUX AMANTS

— Tristan Lhermite

I Auprès de cette grotte sombre

Auprès de cette grotte sombre
Où l'on respire un air si doux,
L'onde lutte avec les cailloux,
Et la lumière avecque l'ombre.

Ces flots, lassés de l'exercice
Qu'ils ont fait dessus ce gravier,
Se reposent dans ce vivier
Où mourut autrefois Narcisse...

L'ombre de cette fleur vermeille
Et celle de ces joncs pendants
Paraissent estre là-dedans
Les songes de l'eau qui sommeille.

———

II Crois mon conseil, chère Climène

Crois mon conseil, chère Climène;
Pour laisser arriver le soir,
Je te prie, allons nous asseoir
Sur le bord de cette fontaine.

N'ouïs-tu pas soupirer Zéphire,
De merveille et d'amour atteint,
Voyant des roses sur ton teint,
Qui ne sont pas de son empire?

Sa bouche d'odeur toute pleine,
A soufflé sur notre chemin,
Mêlant un esprit de jasmin
A l'ombre de ta douce haleine.

———

THE TWO LOVERS' PROMENADE

I   Near this dark grotto

Near this dark grotto where the air is so soft, the current struggles against the pebbles, the light against the shadow.

These waves, tired of moving over the gravel, come to rest in the pond where Narcissus once died...

The shadow of that vermillion flower and of the bending reeds seem to be part of the dreams of the sleeping water.

II   Take my advice, dear Climene

Take my advice, dear Climene; as the evening falls, I beg you, let us sit at the edge of this fountain.

Do you not hear Zephyr sighing of marvels and requited love, at seeing the roses of your complexion over which he has no control?

His mouth, full of perfume, has breathed upon our path, mingling a touch of jasmine with the shadow of your sweet breath.

NOTE FOR *I Auprès de cette grotte sombre*

This song appeared as no. II—*La Grotte* in *Trois Chansons de France*, in 1904.

III   Je tremble en voyant ton visage

Je tremble en voyant ton visage
Flotter avecque mes désirs,
Tant j'ai de peur que mes soupirs
Ne lui fassent faire naufrage.

De crainte de cette aventure
Ne commets pas si librement
A cet infidéle élément
Tous les trésors de la Nature.

Veux-tu, par un doux privilège,
Me mettre au-dessus des humains?
Fais-moi boire au creux de tes mains,
Si l'eau n'en dissout point la neige.

––––––––––

III   I tremble at seeing thy face

I tremble at seeing thy face floating with my desires, so afraid am I that my sighs will shipwreck it.

For fear that this adventure will not so freely endow that faithless element with all the treasures of Nature.

Do you want to grant me the sweet privilege of rising above all other humans? Let me drink from your hands, if water will not melt their snow.

———————

NOTES FOR *LE PROMENOIR DES DEUX AMANTS*

   Date: 1904 (I)–1910 (II & III)
   Source: Tristan Lhermite, *Collection des plus belles pages*, 2ème édition, Les Amours—Odes—*Le Promenoir des deux amants*, verses 1, 2, 4; 14–16; 22–24. Mercure de France, Paris 1909, pp. 51–52, 54, 55.
   Manuscripts: in the Bibliothèque Nationale, Paris
   Dedication: "à Emma Claude Debussy...p.m. son mari C.D."
(for Emma Claude Debussy...p.m. her husband C.D.) The initials stand for "petite mienne"—my own little dear.
   Publisher: Durand & Cie, Paris 1910
   First performance: Jane Bathori accompanied by Ricardo Viñes 14 January 1911 at a concert of the Société nationale de musique in the Salle Erard

TROIS BALLADES DE FRANÇOIS VILLON

I BALLADE DE VILLON A S'AMYE

Faulse beauté, qui tant me couste cher,
Rude en effet, hypocrite doulceur,
Amour dure, plus que fer, à mascher;
Nommer te puis de ma deffaçon soeur.
Charme felon, la mort d'ung povre cueur,
Orgueil mussé, qui gens met au mourir,
Yeulx sans pitié! ne veult droict de rigueur,
Sans empirer, ung povre secourir?

Mieulx m'eust valu avoir esté crier
Ailleurs secours, c'eust esté bonheur:
Rien ne m'eust sceu de ce fait arracher;
Trotter m'en fault en fuyte à deshonneur.
Haro, haro, le grand et le mineur!
Et qu'est cecy? mourray sans coup ferir,
Ou pitié peult, selon ceste teneur,
Sans empirer, ung povre secourir.

Ung temps viendra, qui fera desseicher,
Jaulnir, flestrir, vostre espanie fleur:
J'en risse lors, se tant peusse marcher,
Mais las! nenny: Ce seroit donc foleur,
Vieil je seray; vous laide et sans couleur.
Or, beuvez fort, tant que ru peult courir.
Ne donnez pas à tous ceste douleur,
Sans empirer ung povre secourir.

Prince amoureux, des amans le greigneur,
Vostre mal gré ne vouldroye encourir;
Mais tout franc cueur doit, par Nostre Seigneur,
Sans empirer, ung povre secourir.

———

THREE BALLADS BY FRANÇOIS VILLON

I   BALLAD OF VILLON TO HIS LADY

False beauty who costs me dear, rude indeed, hypocritical sweetness, hard love, harder to chew than iron; I could even call you the sister of my undoing. Felonious charm, the death of a poor heart, concealed pride that puts men to death, pitiless eyes! cannot justice, without worsening his fate, come to the aid of a poor creature?

I had been better off had I cried out for help elsewhere, help that would have brought happiness: nothing could stop me from acting as I did, and now I can only escape in dishonor. Shame, shame, great and small! And what is this? I will die without having stuck a blow, or will pity now without worsening his fate come to the aid of a poor creature?

A time will come that will wither, discolor, fade your blossoming flower: then I will laugh, if I still can—but no, no: that would be foolish. I shall be old, you will be ugly and colorless. So drink deep while the brook still runs. Do not make everyone this unhappy, come to the aid of a poor creature without worsening his fate.

Prince of love, lord of lovers, I do not want to risk your displeasure; but by Our Lord, every kind heart should, without worsening his fate, come to the aid of a poor creature.

———————

II   *BALLADE QUE VILLON FEIT A LA REQUESTE DE SA MERE POUR PRIER NOSTRE-DAME*

Dame du ciel, régente terrienne,
Emperière des infernaulx paluz,
Recevez-moy, vostre humble chrestienne,
Que comprinse soye entre vos esleuz,
Ce non obstant qu'oncques riens ne valuz.
Les biens de vous, ma dame et ma maistresse,
Sont trop plus grans que ne suys pecheresse,
Sans lesquelz bien ame ne peult merir
N'avoir les cieulx, je n'en suis menteresse.
En ceste foy je vueil vivre et mourir.

A vostre Filz dictes que je suys sienne;
De luy soyent mes pechez aboluz:
Pardonnez-moy comme à l'Egyptienne,
Ou comme il feit au clerc Théophilus,
Lequel par vous fut quitte et aboluz,
Combien qu'il eust au diable faict promesse.
Preservez-moy que je n'accomplisse ce!
Vierge portant sans rompure encourir
Le sacrement qu'on celebre à la messe.
En ceste foy je vueil vivre et mourir.

Femme je suis povrette et ancienne,
Qui riens ne sçay; oncques lettre ne leuz;
Au moustier voy dont suis paroissienne,
Paradis painct où sont harpes et luz,
Et ung enfer où damnez sont boulluz:
L'ung me faict paour, l'aultre joye et liesse.
La joye avoir fais-moy haulte Déesse,
A qui pecheurs doivent tous recourir,
Comblez de foy, sans faincte ne paresse.
En ceste foy je vueil vivre et mourir.

II   BALLAD MADE BY VILLON AT THE REQUEST OF HIS MOTHER TO PRAY TO OUR LADY

Lady of Heaven, Regent of Earth, Empress of the Infernal Deeps, receive me your humble Christian to be counted among your elect, despite my having nothing of value. My Lady and my Mistress, your goodness is so much greater than my sins, and without that goodness no soul would deserve heaven—I say truly, in this faith I would live and die.

Tell your Son that I am his; may he absolve my sins: Forgive me as he forgave the Egyptian woman, or as he did the clerk Theophilus, who was forgiven and absolved by you, even though he had made a pact with the Devil; preserve me from doing likewise! Virgin who bears without sin the Sacrament we celebrate in the mass.—In this faith I would live and die.

I am a poor old woman who knows nothing, who cannot read; in the monastery where I am a parishioner there is a painted paradise with harps and lutes, and a hell where the damned are boiled: the latter frightens me and the other makes me joyful and glad. Grant me that joy, High Goddess, to whom all sinners must turn, filled with faith, without pretense or weakness. In this faith I would live and die.

———————

III   *BALLADE DES FEMMES DE PARIS*

Quoy qu'on tient belles langagières
Florentines, Veniciennes,
Assez pour estre messaigières,
Et mesmement les anciennes;
Mais, soient Lombardes, Romaines,
Genevoises, à mes périls,
Piemontoises, Savoysiennes,
Il n'est bon bec que de Paris.

De beau parler tiennent chayères,
Ce dit-on Napolitaines,
Et que sont bonnes cacquetières
Allemandes et Bruciennes;
Soient Grecques, Egyptiennes,
De Hongrie ou d'aultre païs,
Espaignolles ou Castellannes,
Il n'est bon bec que de Paris.

III   *BALLAD OF THE WOMEN OF PARIS*

Although they are said to be ready with their tongues, the women of Florence or Venice, able to say what they have to say, even those who are old, still, including Lombardy, Rome or Genoa, even I dare say Piedmont or Savoy, the best talkers are still from Paris.

They say the women of Naples are good at swearing, and that the Germans and Prussians are good at gossip, but—including Greece, Egypt, Hungary or some other country, even Spaniards and Castilians, the best talkers are from Paris.

Brettes, Suysses, n'y sçavent guères,
Ne Gasconnes et Tholouzaines;
Du Petit Pont deux harangères
Les concluront, et les Lorraines,
Anglesches ou Callaisiennes,
(Ay-je beaucoup de lieux compris?)
Picardes, de Valenciennes...
Il n'est bon bec que de Paris.

Prince, aux dames parisiennes,
De bien parler donnez le prix;
Quoy qu'on die d'Italiennes,
Il n'est bon bec que de Paris.

———————

The Breton and Swiss women barely know how to speak, nor do the Gascons or the women of Toulouse. Two fishwives on the Petit Pont would finish them off, and the women from Lorraine, England or Calais (am I getting them all in?), from Picardy or Valenciennes—the best talkers are from Paris.

Prince, give the Parisian women the prize for loquacity; whatever they say about the Italian women, the best talkers are still from Paris!

NOTES FOR *TROIS BALLADES DE FRANÇOIS VILLON*

Date: May 1910
Source: François Villon, *Oeuvres complètes.* Alphonse Lemerre, Paris 1892, pp. 60–61, 57–58, 85–86
Manuscripts: in the Bibliothèque Nationale, Paris
Publisher: Durand & Cie, Paris, 1910
First performance: Paule de Lestang, 5 February 1911

Orchestral version (by Debussy)
Date: October 1910
Manuscripts: in the Bibliothèque Nationale, Paris
Publisher: Durand & Cie, Paris, 1911
First performance: Debussy conducted the Concerts Sechiari, 5 March 1911 (with the baritone Clarke).

Comment: In an article in *Musica,* March 1911, Debussy wrote:

Tenez dernièrement, j'ai mis en musique, je ne sais pour quoi, trois ballades de Villon.... Si, je sais pourquoi: parce que j'en avais envie depuis longtemps. Eh bien, c'est très difficile de suivre bien, de "plaquer" les rythmes tout en gardant une inspiration. Si on fait de la fabrication, si on se contente d'un travail de juxtaposition, évidemment ce n'est pas difficile, mais alors ce n'est pas la peine. Les vers classique ont une vie propre, un 'dynamisme intérieur,' pour parler comme les Allemands, qui n'est pas du tout notre affaire.

(Oh, lately, I've set to music, I don't know why, three ballades by Villon.... Yes, I do know: because I've wanted to for a long time. Well, it's difficult to follow, to "strike" the right meter and still retain some inspiration. If you're just putting things together, content to juxtapose, of course it's not difficult, but then it's not worth the trouble either. Classic poetry has a life of its own, an "inner dynamism," as the Germans would say, which has nothing to do with us.)

TROIS POÈMES DE STÉPHANE MALLARMÉ

I *SOUPIR*

Mon âme vers ton front où rêve, ô calme soeur,
Un automne jonché de taches de rousseur
Et vers le ciel errant de ton oeil angélique
Monte, comme dans un jardin mélancolique,
Fidèle, un blanc jet d'eau soupire vers l'Azur!
Vers l'Azur attendri d'Octobre pâle et pur
Qui mire aux grands bassins sa langueur infinie
Et laisse, sur l'eau morte où la fauve agonie
Des feuilles erre au vent et creuse un froid sillon,
Se traîner le soleil jaune d'un long rayon.

———————

II *PLACET FUTILE*

Princesse! à jalouser le destin d'une Hébé
Qui poind sur cette tasse au baiser de vos lèvres,
J'use mes feux mais n'ai rang discret que d'abbé
Et ne figurerai même nu sur le Sèvres.

Comme je ne suis pas ton bichon embarbé,
Ni la pastille, ni du rouge, ni jeux mièvres
Et que sur moi je sais ton regard clos tombé,
Blonde dont les coiffeurs divins sont des orfèvres!

Nommez-nous... toi de qui tant de ris framboisés
Se joignent en troupeau d'agneaux apprivoisés
Chez tous broutant les voeux et bêlant aux délires,

Nommez-nous... pour qu'Amour ailé d'un éventail
M'y peigne flûte aux doigts endormant ce bercail,
Princesse, nommez-nous berger de vos sourires.

———————

THREE POEMS BY STÉPHANE MALLARMÉ

I   SIGH

My soul mounts up toward your forehead, o calm sister, where freckle-
strewn autumn dreams, and toward the wandering heaven of your angelic eyes, as, in a melancholy garden, faithful, a white fountain sighs
toward the blue sky!

Toward the tender blue sky of pale and pure October that mirrors its
infinite languor in the vast basins and leaves on the dead water where
the leaves' fulvous agony roams with the wind, making a chill wake, a
long trailing ray of the yellow sun.

II   VAIN PETITIONING

Princess! Envious of the fate of some Hebe who may be placed upon
this cup where your lips can kiss her, I unleash my passion even
though I am merely a modest abbé and will never appear, even naked,
on a piece of Sèvres porcelain.

Since I am not your bearded lapdog, your sweetmeat, your rouge, your
dainty pastimes, and your unseeing glance falls upon me thus, blond
with hair dressed by goldsmiths!

Choose us... you whose myriad raspberry laughters become a flock of
tame lambs that browse on our desires, bleating in ecstasies,

Choose us... so that Cupid with his fanlike wings may paint me with
my flute between my fingers putting this sheepfold to sleep, Princess,
choose us as the shepherd of your smiles.

III ÉVENTAIL[1]

O rêveuse, pour que je plonge
Au pur délice sans chemin,
Sache, par un subtil mensonge,
Garder mon aile dans ta main.

Une fraîcheur de crépuscule
Te vient à chaque battement
Dont le coup prisonnier recule
L'horizon délicatement.

Vertige! voici que frissonne
L'espace comme un grand baiser
Qui, fou de naître pour personne,
Ne peut jaillir ni s'apaiser.

Sens-tu le paradis farouche
Ainsi qu'un rire enseveli
Se couler du coin de ta bouche
Au fond de l'unanime pli!

Le sceptre des rivages roses
Stagnants sur les soirs d'or, ce l'est,
Ce blanc vol fermé que tu poses
Contre le feu d'un bracelet.

III FAN

O dreamer, take care to keep my wing in your hand with subtle falsehood so that I may plunge into pure pathless delight.

Each flutter with which the emprisoned stroke beats delicately back the
horizon sends you a twilight freshness.

Vertigo! see how space trembles like a great kiss that, mad to exist for
no one, can neither blossom nor subside.

Do you sense the wild paradise like buried laughter flowing from the
corner of your mouth into the depths of the concerted folding!

It is this, the sceptre of pink shores stagnating in golden evenings, this
shut white flight you lay against a bracelet's fire.

NOTE FOR *III ÉVENTAIL*

  [1] The title of the poem is *Autre éventail* (de Mademoiselle Mallarmé).

NOTES FOR *TROIS POÈMES DE STÉPHANE MALLARMÉ*

  Date: summer 1913
  Source: Stéphane Mallarmé, *Poésies*. Editions de la Nouvelle Revue
Française, Paris 1913, pp. 24, 18–19, 93–94.
  Manuscripts: in the Bibliothèque Nationale, Paris
  Dedication: "À la mémoire de Stéphane Mallarmé et en très respectueux
hommage à Madame E. Bonniot (née G. Mallarmé)"
  (In memory of Stéphane Mallarmé and in respectful homage to Madame E.
Bonniot [née G. Mallarmé])
  Publisher: Durand & Cie, Paris, 1913
  First performance: Ninon Vallin accompanied by Debussy at a concert of
the Nouvelle Société Philharmonique de Paris, Salle Gaveau, 21 March 1914.
  Comment: In a letter to Jacques Durand, 25 July 1913, Debussy wrote:

  Ce matin, j'ai remis au bon Choisnel le manuscrit des trois nouvelles
mélodies, dont j'ose dire "qu'ils" ne tiennent pas cet article-là rue St-Jacques!
Nous avons regretté—elles et moi—que vous ne puissiez les entendre! C'est
généralement un instant charmant, Dieu sait qu'îles sont rares!

  (This morning, I sent good old Choisnel [the engraver] the manuscript of
the three new songs, something I daresay "they" don't have much of in the Rue
St-Jacques [address of the Schola Cantorum]! We are sorry—the songs and myself—that you cannot hear them! It's generally a charming moment, and God
knows they're rare enough.)

NOËL DES ENFANTS QUI N'ONT PLUS DE MAISONS

— Claude Debussy

Nous n'avons plus de maisons!
Les ennemis ont tout pris,
  tout pris, tout pris,
  jusqu'à notre petit lit!
Ils ont brûlé l'école et notre maître aussi.
Ils ont brûlé l'église et monsieur Jésus-Christ
Et le vieux pauvre qui n'a pas pu s'en aller!

Nous n'avons plus de maisons.
Les ennemis ont tout pris,
  tout pris, tout pris,
  jusqu'à notre petit lit!
Bien sûr! papa est à la guerre,
Pauvre maman est morte!
Avant d'avoir vu tout ça.
Qu'est-ce que l'on va faire?
Noël! petit Noël! n'allez pas chez eux,
  n'allez plus jamais chez eux,
Punissez-les!

Vengez les enfants de France!
Les petits Belges, les petits Serbes,
  et les petits Polonais aussi!
Si nous en oublions, pardonnez-nous.
Noël! Noël! surtout, pas de joujoux,
Tâchez de nous redonner le pain quotidien.

Nous n'avons plus de maisons!
Les ennemis ont tout pris,
  tout pris, tout pris,
  jusqu'à notre petit lit!
Ils ont brûlé l'école et notre maître aussi.
Ils ont brûlé l'église et monsieur Jésus-Christ
Et le vieux pauvre qui n'a pas pu s'en aller!

Noël! écoutez-nous, nous n'avons plus de petits
  sabots:
Mais donnez la victoire aux enfants de France!

———

NOËL FOR CHILDREN WITHOUT HOMES

We have no homes! The enemies have taken everything, everything, down to our little beds! They have burned our school and the teacher too, they have burned the church and Mr. Jesus Christ and the poor old man who was unable to get away.

We have no homes. The enemies have taken everything, everything, down to our little beds. Of course Papa is away at war, poor Mama is dead, without having seen all that. What are we to do? Noël, little Noël, don't go to them, never go to them again, punish them!

Avenge the children of France, the Belgian children, the Serbian children, and the Polish children too! If we have forgotten any, forgive us. Noël, Noël, and above all no toys—just try to give us back our daily bread.

We have no homes! The enemies have taken everything, everything, down to our little beds! They have burned our school and the teacher too, they have burned the church and Mr. Jesus Christ and the poor old man who was unable to get away.

Noël! Hear us—we don't even have any little clogs to wear. But grant victory to the children of France!

NOTES FOR *NOËL DES ENFANTS QUI N'ONT PLUS DE MAISONS*

Date: December 1915
Source: Claude Debussy
Manuscripts: for voice and piano, for children's chorus and piano in the Bibliothèque Nationale, Paris
Publisher: Durand & Cie, Paris 1916
First performance: Jane Monjovet at a concert of the Amitiés franco-étrangères in the Grand Amphitheater of the Sorbonne, 9 April 1916.
Comments: When Henri Büsser asked for permission to orchestrate this song, Debussy replied:

Non, non j'ai déjà refusé cela à André Caplet. Je veux que ce morceau soit chanté avec un accompagnement des plus discrets. Il ne faut pas perdre un mot de ce texte inspiré par la rapacité de nos ennemis. C'est ma seule manière de faire la guerre.

(No, no, I have already refused it to André Caplet. I want this piece to be sung with the most discreet accompaniment. Not a word of this text must be lost, inspired as it is by the rapacity of our enemies. It is the only way I have to fight the war.)

Part II
Letters

Chronological List of Letters

Articles

TO ROBERT GODET*

Cher Ami,

Je vous attendrai avec joie Lundi à l'heure dite quoique moi aussi je sois morne et pas du tout "morgue anglaise," mais j'espère qu'en mêlant nos "*pâleurs*" et en agitant vigoureusement, il en résultera une mixture encore très convenable.

Votre affectueux
A. Debussy

––––––––––

TO ROBERT GODET

10 July 1889

Dear Friend,

I will expect you with joy on Monday at the appointed time, although I too am depressed and lack all "English stiff upper lip," but I hope that if we mingle our *"pallors"* and shake vigorously, we will come up with a mixture that will be highly suitable nonetheless.

Affectionately,
A. Debussy

———————

NOTE FOR LETTER TO *ROBERT GODET, 10 JULY 1889*

In *Le Jet d'eau*, the third of the *Cinq Poèmes de Charles Baudelaire* dated March 1889, Debussy used a little known refrain and then changed the word "lueurs" to "pâleurs" in the fourth line. This is the only change he made in any Baudelaire poem, and it was the last change he made in any text.

* From *Lettres à deux amis*, soixante-dix-huit lettres inédites à Robert Godet et G. Jean-Aubry. (Paris: Librairie José Corti, 1942), p. 89.

TO ROBERT GODET*

25 décembre (1889)

Je suis tout heureux, cher ami, et laissez parlez un peu ma petite sensibilité (ça ne sera pas long); oui, je suis heureux d'une amitié qu'un naïf orgueil avait pressentie, et aussi la secrète pensée que des peines aussi sincèrement subies devaient être un peu partagées. Mais tout ça c'était encore des vieilles façons de voir la vie. Enfin, heureusement nous ne sommes pas "modernes" et je vous aime bien, aussi je tiens à le dire et à l'assurer hautement.
— Tout ceci sans lampions ni orphéons, plutôt comme de quelqu'un à qui ça fait plaisir, sans plus.

Figurez-vous que je viens de côtoyer une fièvre typhoïde heureusement changée en pneumonie avec quelque chose de rébarbatif que je vous passe. Cela me tiens encore au lit et m'oblige à de cérémonieuses convalescences; vous savez, celles où un oeuf à la coque prend une importance vraiment stupéfiante, je pense que tout cela est la Revanche du Sang.[1]

Il faut croire que la Hollande va m'être infiniment sympathique d'abord pour ce que vous me dites concernant votre vie, puis, pour ce qu'elle a bien voulu laisser ma musique se mêler à ses personnels paysages; du reste cette musique n'est pas faite pour d'autres buts: se mêler aux âmes et choses de bonne volonté. Déjà la conquête de la vôtre est une fine gloire, plus belle que l'assentiment du public d'élite que dirigent sévèrement le binocle et l'hiératique index de notre si wagnérien Monsieur Lamoureux.

Je ne sais même pas pourquoi j'insiste aussi follement, sur ce point, parfaitement élucidé d'ailleurs.

J'ai peur des imprimeurs. J'espère pourtant vous envoyer les mélodies[2] avant le 6 janvier; en tout cas, soyez aimable en m'indiquant une suprême adresse.

Ma maladie a cruellement interrompu la *Fantaisie,*[3] peu de gens en sont inconsolables. On ne jouera pas mes envois cette année, la séance étant prise par les oeuvres de Vidal, le Festival Vidal, quoi! Mais, l'année prochaine nous aurons le Festival Debussy: ça sera vraiment charmant. J'espère que vous serez là et m'aiderez à souffrir.

Avant d'être malade, j'ai été voir *Tobie:*[4] je ne crois pas que mes réflexions sur cette oeuvre soient d'une utilité bien absolue.

TO ROBERT GODET

25 December (1889)

I am overjoyed, my dear friend, and allow me to give vent to my petty feelings (it won't take long); yes, I'm happy because of a friendship a naïve pride had foreseen, and also because of the secret thought that sorrows that are suffered so sincerely must be shared. But all that was still an old-fashioned way of looking at life. In brief, we aren't "modern"—fortunately—and I am fond of you, so I want to inform you plainly.—Without sound and fury, but just as someone who takes pleasure in doing so, that's all.

Imagine, I've just escaped having typhoid fever, fortunately transformed into pneumonia plus something rather grim which I shall spare you. This keeps me in bed and forces me to suffer through a formal convalescence; you know, when a soft-boiled egg assumes startling importance, I think it's all the Blood's Revenge.[1]

I am forced to believe that I'll find Holland infinitely to my liking, first because of what you tell me about your life, and then because it has kindly allowed my music to mingle with its landscape; that music was made for no other purpose, as far as that goes: to mingle with souls and things full of good will. The conquest of yours is one triumph already, better than the acceptance of the elite audience our Wagnerian Monsieur Lamoureux leads so severely with his pince-nez and his hieratic index finger.

I'm not sure why I am so wildly insistent on this point, however clearly expressed.

I don't trust printers. However, I hope to send you the songs[2] before January 6; in any event, be kind enough to indicate to me a permanent address.

My illness has interrupted the *Fantaisie*[3] in a cruel way, but few people are inconsolable. They won't be performing my submissions this year, the concert being taken over by Vidal's works, the Vidal Festival! Next year, however, we'll have the Debussy Festival, it will be truly charming. I hope you will be there to help me get through it.

Before I fell ill, I saw *Tobie*:[4] I don't believe my comments on that work are of any absolute value.

NOTES FOR LETTER TO *ROBERT GODET, 25 DECEMBER (1889)*

[1] The title of a current play.
[2] The *Cinq Poèmes de Charles Baudelaire.*
[3] The *Fantaisie pour piano et orchestre,* which Debussy had begun in October.
[4] A play by Maurice Bouchor, the first performance of which took place on 15 November 1889.
* From *Lettres à deux amis,* pp. 90–92.

Petite réunion chez Mercier, pour y entendre deux chants d'*Endymion* traduit de Keats. C'est très beau, une fois la couleur admise; des paysages assez humides, et une *Diane* très *"vais m'en aller"* là où d'autres insisteraient.

J'ai vu votre ami Dardel, qui m'a l'air bellement simple, et avec un beau rire. — Le Mercier traducteur m'a semblé très supérieur au Mercier quotidien, ou du moins, il laisse cette enveloppe couverts de rébus faciles à deviner, mais agaçants par le nombre, d'autant plus que c'est un homme qui est très bon après tout. — Nous sommes naturellement allés chez Vachette, où Monsieur Jean Moréas a pris Schopenhauer sous sa protection, sans y être autrement invité, pourquoi ça? alors Mercier l'a attaqué, pendant ce, Dardel souriait, ce qui du reste était la seule attitude convenable à ce débat.

Accueillez sans rigueur ce bavardage de convalescent, mais moi aussi j'aime assez à me figurer que vous êtes là, sans cela j'ai des tendances à de grosses tristesses, il fait si laid et sans rien pour amuser l'oeil, puis de belles recherches qui n'aboutissent pas! (c'est peut-être mieux).

Enfin, je vous quitte avec le regret de vous dire au revoir pour si longtemps encore.

Votre
C. A. Debussy

A small gathering at Mercier's to hear two songs translated from Keats's *Endymion*. Very lovely, once one gets used to the color; fairly humid landscapes and a *Diana* very *"I'm off and away"* where others might linger over it.

I saw our friend Dardel who appears to me a simple creature with a fine laugh. The translating Mercier seemed to me far above the everyday Mercier, or at least he has that envelope covered with rebuses that are easy to figure out but annoying because there are so many, particularly since he's a very good man in the end. Of course we went to Vachette, where Monsieur Jean Moréas took Schopenhauer under his protection, why, without anyone's having asked? and then Mercier attacked him, during which Dardel smiled, which was the only suitable attitude to take where that debate was concerned, for that matter.

Don't look on this convalescent chatter too strictly, but I too like to imagine you are here, without that I'm prone to grow extremely sad, the weather is so awful and there's nothing amusing to look at, and then there are such fine experiments that come to nothing (perhaps it's best).

Well, I leave you with the regret at having to say *au revoir* for so long a time.

Yours,
C. A. Debussy

_____

NOTES FOR LETTER TO *ROBERT GODET, 25 DECEMBER (1889)*

The phrase "vais m'en aller" is the last line of *Rescousse,* a poem by Tristan Corbière that was included in Verlaine's article on this poet in his volume *Les Poètes maudits,* published in 1884. Debussy was undoubtedly familiar with this work, having shown interest in Verlaine as early as 1882 when he set four of his poems.

"Si de mon âme
La mer en flamme
N'a pas de lame;
— Cuit de geler...
Vais m'en aller!"

(If the burning sea is not ruffled by any soul, enough of freezing, *"I'm off!"*)

TO RENÉ PETER*

n.d. (1893?)

Je me reveille et ma première pensée est pour te demander si tu
veux dîner avec moi. Cela me parait un reveil *"tout soie."*
   Tu dis oui et je t'embrasse.

Claude

———————

TO MME ARTHUR FONTAINE*

samedi (fin 1893)

"Les chandeliers étaient passés."
V. Hugo

Chère Madame

Soyez remercié ainsi que Monsieur Fontaine du charmant envoi
des chandeliers. Ils sont en tous points conformes à mon désir.
Dieu seul sait comme ces aventures-là sont rares.
   Veuillez croire à ma respectueuse amitié et veuillez aussi en
assurer Monsieur Fontaine.

Claude Debussy

———————

TO RENÉ PETER

undated (1893?)

I wake up and my first thought is to ask you if you want to have dinner with me. That seems to me a *totally silky* awakening.
Say yes, and I'll hug you.

Claude

TO MADAME ARTHUR FONTAINE

Saturday (late 1893)

"The chandlers had passed by."
V. Hugo

Dear Madame,

I thank you and Monsieur Fontaine for the charming candlesticks. They are exactly what I wanted. God knows that that is a rare occurrence.
Please accept my respectful friendship and impart the same to Monsieur Fontaine.

Claude Debussy

NOTE FOR LETTER TO *RENÉ PETER, n.d. (1893?)*

The word "soie" is repeated in each verse of *De grève*, the second *Proses lyriques*, composed in 1892. It is found in the second line of the first stanza and in the last line of each stanza.
* From René Peter, *Claude Debussy* (Paris: Gallimard, 1944), p. 208.

NOTE FOR LETTER TO *MME ARTHUR FONTAINE*

The quotation at the top of this letter is taken from the last line of Victor Hugo's Ballade VI from *La Fiancée du Timbalier*. Debussy had moved to a new apartment in July 1893, and the candlesticks were given to him by M. and Mme Fontaine to celebrate this occasion. Debussy's knowledge of Hugo's poems was surely greatly influenced by Pierre Louÿs, of whom he was seeing a great deal at the time and who was a great admirer of Hugo's poems.
"Les timbaliers étaient passés."
(The kettledrummers had passed by.)
* From a private collection.

TO PIERRE LOUŸS*

"Dimanche sur les villes"
et aussi sur Séville
(mars 1895)

Cher ami

Si tu as été si longtemps privé de mes nouvelles c'est que la maladie vient de me visiter, et que je fus le pâle convalescent qu'on voit se traîner de fauteuil en fauteuil suivant la marche du soleil.

Enfin, c'était attendrissant!...

D'ailleurs mon silence semble s'accorder merveilleusement avec le tien! Mettons que nous eûmes chacun un "long point d'orgue" dans la symphonie que représente notre amitié!

J'espère que ce n'est pas une cause pareille qui me fait ne plus rien savoir de toi. Et si tu veux me faire plaisir écris-moi promptement et longement.

J'étais malade lorsque l'on joua la pièce de Lebey, ça me paraît ne point avoir trouble la marche des constellations.

Bien amicalement
ton
Claude Debussy

TO PIERRE LOUŸS

"Sunday in the towns"
and also in Seville
(March 1895)

Dear Friend,

If you've been deprived of my news for so long, it's owing to my having been ill, and I am that pale convalescent to be seen dragging himself from chair to chair to stay in the sun as it shifts.

In short, 'tis a tender scene!...

For that matter, my silence seems to accord wonderfully with your own! Let's say that we both have experienced a "lengthy pedal point" in the symphony of our friendship!

I hope that my not hearing from you has not been for the same reasons. And if you want to make me happy, write at once and at length.

I was ill when Lebey's piece was performed. It doesn't seem to me to have disturbed the progress of the constellations.

Your friend,
Claude Debussy

NOTE FOR LETTER TO *PIERRE LOUŸS*

"Dimanches sur les villes" is the first line of *De soir,* the last of the four *Proses lyriques,* which were published in 1895. This letter was addressed to Pierre Louÿs in Spain.

* From a private collection.

TO RENÉ PETER*

6 *mai 1898*

Mon cher René,

Tu dois me couvrir d'injures de ce que je n'ai pas répondu à ton charmant petit mot?

Voilà le drame...: j'ai eu la fièvre avec tout ce que cet état comporte de parfait abrutissement; a part ça, ce fut une fièvre comme tout le monde, et l'on y chercherait en vain une marque de génie particulier.

Assieds-toi et causons:

J'ai bien l'intention de couvrir de musique la Ballade de l'Enfant qui a reçu des fleurs sur la tête.[1] Jusqu'ici j'ai fouillé les recueils de chansons populaires; je songe, d'ailleurs, à cesser ces recherches et tâcher de trouver quelque chose qui ne doive rien à personne.

Tâche donc de venir me voir Vendredi, avant ou après le déjeuner.

A toi,
Dir,
Yours,
Tibi.
Claude

Mon gosier de métal parle toutes les langues.

————

TO RENÉ PETER

6 May 1898

My dear René,

Have you been saying terrible things about me because I haven't answered your charming note?

Here is how things have been...: I've had a fever, with all the total collapse that condition entails. Aside from that, it was a fever like any other, futile to endow it with any special talent.

Sit down and let's have a chat:

It is my decided intention to cover the Ballad of the Child who received flowers on her head with music.[1] Up until now, I've been leafing through collections of folk songs, but I guess I'll abandon such investigations and try to find something that owes nothing to anyone else.

So try to come to see me on Friday, before or after lunch.

A toi,
Dir,
Yours,
Tibi.
Claude

My metallic throat speaks all languages.

NOTES FOR LETTER TO *RENÉ PETER, 6 MAY 1898*

The last sentence (below the signature) is the second line of the fourth stanza of Baudelaire's poem *L'Horloge*. This line appears, slightly altered, in the first paragraph of an article in *Gil Blas*, 1 May 1903: "Mon gosier de métal ne parle pas toutes les langues, hélas." (My metallic throat does not speak all languages, unfortunately.)

It is interesting to note that Jules Laforgue used this same line in a letter to the poetess Sanda Mahali, dated 26 March 1882. We know that Debussy was familiar with Laforgue's correspondence from his letter to Paul Dukas of 19 May 1917.

[1] The reference is to the *Berceuse,* finished in 1899.

* From *Claude Debussy,* p. 213.

TO RENÉ PETER*

Es-tu bien sûr que la personne qui agite tes nuits (avant de s'en servir) ai vraiment habité cette planète? n'est-ce pas plutôt quelque fantôme odorant et léger, vaporisé par ta subtile imagination?...

Pour moi elle ne veut rien savoir et c'est exactement *la grande Isis dont nul n'a pu soulever le voile!* Aucune de mes tentatives policières n'ont réussi. Rien ne me réussit en ce moment, si ce n'est la dèche.

Veuille ne pas m'en vouloir de cet "échec à la dame" et crois-moi

Ton
Claude

————

TO RENÉ PETER

Saturday
19 August 1899

Are you quite certain that the person who gives you restless nights (before taking advantage of them) ever truly lived on this planet? Might it not rather be some sweet-smelling and airy phantom your subtle imagination has conjured up?

It wants nothing to do with me, and is exactly like *the great Isis whose veil none could rend*! None of my detective work has borne fruit. Indeed, nothing at the moment bears fruit for me, except for poverty.

Please don't blame me for "capturing your queen," and believe me

Yours,
Claude

NOTE FOR LETTER TO *RENÉ PETER, 19 AUGUST 1899*

The quotation is taken from *Le Concile féerique* by Jules Laforgue, a poet whose works were well known to Debussy and whom he mentions in his letters. Laforgue's influence can be seen in the *Proses lyriques*. For example, from this same poem comes the line: "Et la Vie et la Nuit font patte de velours" where in *De soir* Debussy gives: "Et la nuit à pas de velours" (see first line of the fifth stanza).

From *Le Concile féerique*:
"C'est moi qui suis *la grande Isis*!...
Nul ne m'a retroussé mon voile!"
(It is I who am *the great Isis*!...
Whose veil none could rend!)
* From *Claude Debussy*, pp. 209–210.

TO GEORGES HARTMANN*

Lundi 18 décembre 1899

Cher Monsieur Hartmann

Pardonnez-moi d'insister déplorablement sur le "post-scriptum" de ma dernière lettre, mais je suis réellement très gêné, et vous seriez très bon si vous vouliez m'aidez? J'ai des tas de médicaments à acheter pour Lilly et vous savez combien:
  "Les soirs illuminés par l'ardeur du charbon" sont coûteux!...
  Répondez-moi et dites-moi ce que vous en pensez, cela le plus vite qu'il vous sera possible.

En toute affection
Claude Debussy

————

TO GEORGES HARTMANN

Monday, 18 December 1899

Dear Monsieur Hartmann,

Forgive me for having to refer deplorably to the "post scriptum" of my last letter, but I am truly in a bad way and you would be doing me a great kindness if you could assist me? I have to buy many medicines for Lilly, and you know how expensive:
   "Evenings lit with the glow of the coals" can be!...
Reply letting me know your decision as soon as you can.

Affectionately,
Claude Debussy

———————

NOTE FOR LETTER TO *GEORGES HARTMANN*

   In asking financial aid from his publisher friend, Debussy uses the first line of the second stanza of *Le Balcon,* the first of the *Cinq Poèmes de Charles Baudelaire.*
   * From a private collection.

TO RAOUL BARDAC*

samedi 24 février 1906
et même dimanche 25

Mon cher Rara,

vous excuserez la date de cette lettre et... ma paresse!

Maintenant *"regonflons des souvenirs d'hiver"*—comme dirait le Faune de M. Mallarmé revu par Willy. — Et quel hiver! Il pleut, les arbres ont l'air de veufs inconsolables, les fleurs sont à l'intérieur et *la volaille est à l'extérieur*—pour changer—des gens, pleins d'esprit, essaient de remplacer le manque de tout cela par des descriptions symphoniques. C'est ainsi que nous avons réentendu *Shéhérazade*[1]... qui ne gagne pas en vieillissant, et c'est plus bazar qu'oriental. Il faut dire aussi que Chevillard ne ressemble pas du tout à la Princesse Boudour.... Il agite des bras de camelot, un dos d'agent cycliste, ce qui ne constitue précisément pas une vision de beauté.

Nous entendîmes aussi *Un jour d'été à la montagne* de Vincent d'Indy. C'est du d'Indy de derrière les Cévennes. Comme je ne suis pas exactement renseigné sur l'atmosphère de cet endroit, je ne peux guère vous en parler. Il m'a semblé qu'on y faisait un emploi immodéré du basson, on s'y étonne d'y entendre un piano. Je croyais que l'on ne rencontrait les pianos que sur les montagnes suisses?

Vous n'avez pas eu de chance avec la Société Nationale.[2] Il ne faudrait pas en prendre plus de dépit que cette aventure n'en comporte. D'abord, vous étiez mal soutenu, puis vous ne faites partie d'aucuns des groupes auxquels on accorde le droit de mettre les pieds dans la musique. Permettez-moi de ne pas trop déplorer que Colonne ne vous joue pas cette année.... Vous avez le temps de préparer votre jeu, profitez-en pour ne pas risquer des parties qui, sans être mauvaises, seraient peut-être nulles. Vous avez de la facilité, certainement des dons, mais vous ne vous défierez jamais assez du chemin que vous fond prendre vos idées. Cela vous fait parfois aboutir à quelque chose de décousu, et en même temps de pressé, qui donne l'impression déconcertante que vous avez voulu finir à tout prix. — Vous savez combien j'aime peu le développement parasite qui a trop servi à la gloire des Maîtres pour que nous ne cherchions pas à la remplacer par un choix d'idées plus rigoureux, une ligne plus normalement soucieuse de la valeur qu'elles prennent sur l'horizon ornemental ou orchestral, et surtout, qu'elles y respi-

TO RAOUL BARDAC

Saturday, 24 February 1906
and even Sunday the 25th

Dear Rara,

you will forgive the date of this letter and... my laziness!

Now, *"Let's expand on winter memories once again,"* as Mr. Mallarmé's *Faune* might have said had Willy edited him.

And what a winter! It's raining, the trees are like inconsolable widows, the flowers are inside and the "poultry is outside"—for a change—and some of the overweening are attempting to make up for this lack with symphonic descriptions. Such our rehearing *Shéhérazade*[1]... which hasn't improved with age, being more bazaar than oriental. In addition, one is forced to admit that Chevillard in no way resembles Princess Boudour.... He waves his arms like a political demonstrator, his back works like that of a cop on his bicycle, all of which gives an effect quite the opposite of beautiful.

We also heard a *Summer Day in the Mountains* of Vincent d'Indy. It's d'Indy beyond the Cevennes. Since I have no precise data on the climate in that area, I can't tell you much about it. It seemed to me that they employ the bassoon to an immoderate degree, and it's rather surprising to hear a piano in the region. I thought pianos were only found in the Swiss mountains?

You haven't had much luck with the Société Nationale.[2] You mustn't let that adventure upset you more than it should. First, you lacked the proper backing, and then, you don't belong to any of the cliques that have official permission to go into music.

Allow me not to be too sorry that Colonne isn't playing anything of yours this year.... You have time to plan your strategy, take advantage of it, so that you don't run the risk of playing a hand that, although it might not be bad, might very well be worthless.

You have talents and gifts, but you never sufficiently trust the path down which your ideas take you. Sometimes, that leads you into something that is somewhat disjointed and even hasty, giving the disconcerting impression that you were trying to end it at all costs. You know how little I enjoy the parasitical kind of overworked development in which the Masters have gloried all too often, and we should try to replace it with a more rigorous choice of ideas, a line more normally careful of the value such notions can assume on the ornamental or orchestral horizon, and see to it above all that the ideas can breathe, instead of succumbing as they do all too often to the richness or banality of

NOTES FOR LETTER TO *RAOUL BARDAC*

[1] By Rimsky-Korsakov.
[2] The reference is to the songs composed by Raoul Bardac that were badly sung at a concert of the Société Nationale de Musique.
* From the Bibliothèque Nationale, Paris.

rent, tant elles succombent si souvent sous la richesse ou la ba-
nalité du cadre. Enfin, ayez de la patience! C'est une vertu ma-
jeure—et même domestique—avec laquelle on arrange bien des
choses.

Je ne voudrais pourtant pas vous gâter une jolie journée
avec une pluie de considérations esthétiques et morales? Ça sert
si peu.... L'esthétique n'est en somme qu'une valeur qu'on
transpose selon les époques, et j'ai bien peur que la morale lui
ressemble?

La description de l'emploi de vos journées est délicieuse,
tant les heures où l'on ne fait rien me paraissent judicieusement
distribuées. Vous avez raison... il vaut mieux faire mariner son
cerveau dans un bain de bon soleil. Voyez les fleurs et les in-
stantanés—pendant que cette matière nerveuse est encore sus-
ceptible de reflexes.

Ramassez des impressions. Ne vous dépêchez pas de les no-
ter. Parce que la Musique a cela de supérieur à la Peinture,
qu'elle peut centraliser les variations de couleur et de lumière
d'un même aspect. C'est une verité bien mal observée, malgré sa
simplicité. Du reste... oubliez même toute la musique, de temps
en temps.... C'est une opinion de pion que celle qui décréta qu'il
fallait beaucoup écrire pour savoir écrire.... Et puis, il n'est pas
de bon goût d'importuner les gens que l'on prétend le mieux
aimer, par des demandes quotidiennes.

Votre Maman est merveilleusement grippée... vous savez
combien elle est contradictoire à tous médicaments, ce qui
n'arrange pas les choses.

La petite Claude[3] va, une fois de plus, changer de nourrice.
Cette dernière est, dit-elle, trompée par son mari! Elle ira donc
constater elle-même son malheur—c'est d'une psychologie dou-
teuse et d'une économie domestique déplorable.

Je ne parlerai pas de ce que je fais... car tout en écrivant très
peu de musique, elle me déplait beaucoup. J'attribue cela, faute
de mieux, à l'état du ciel.

Au revoir, mon cher Rara
Ma sincère amitié
Claude Debussy

their surroundings. Well, have patience! It's a major, even domestic, virtue that enables us to work things out for the best.

Still I don't want to spoil your lovely day with a shower of aesthetic or moral considerations. It's of so little use.... In sum, aesthetics is nothing but a value that changes key according to the period, and I fear that morality is a similar case?

Your description of how you spend your time is delightful, all those hours spent doing nothing seems to me a very fitting schedule. You are right... better marinate your brain in a bath of sunshine. Look at the flowers and snapshots—while your nervous tissue is still able to react to them.

Return with impressions you have collected. Don't be hasty in noting them down. Because Music is superior to Painting in that it can bring together in a single unit the color and light variations of a glance. This is a truth that is widely overlooked, despite its simplicity... you might even abandon music altogether, from time to time.... The opinion that maintains that a person must write a great deal in learning how to write is stupid.... And it's not good taste to harass the people one is supposed to be most fond of by making daily demands on them.

Your mother has a splendid case of the flu... you know how against any kind of medicine she is, which doesn't help matters.

Young Claude[3] is once again going to have a change of nurse. The latter has, she says, been deceived by her husband! So she is off to verify her misfortune for herself—dubious psychology and deplorable domestic science.

I won't speak of what I've been doing... for although I am writing very little music, that little displeases me a lot. For want of anything else, I attribute this to the condition of the heavens.

> *Farewell, my dear Rara*
> *my sincere friendship*
> *Claude Debussy*

NOTES FOR LETTER TO *RAOUL BARDAC*

The pun which opens this letter is a reference to line 66 of Mallarmé's eclogue *L'Après-midi d'un Faune*:
"*O nymphes, regonflons des souvenirs divers.*"
(O nymphs, let us swell various memories.)
Debussy had earlier been the butt of one of Willy's choice comments, this one in reference to his *Cinq Poèmes de Charles Baudelaire*. (The poems he drew from Baudelaire's *Les Fleurs du mal*, The Flowers of Evil.) "Debussy qui jette l'engrais de sa musique sur les Fleurs de Baudelaire." (Debussy who strews the compost of his music around the Flowers of Baudelaire.)
When using the phrase "la volaille à l'extérieur," although one often seen posted on shop fronts, Debussy may have been reminded of a passage in Chapter XI of *Mon Amie Nane*, a novel by his friend P.-J. Toulet, which he enjoyed very much. It was published in 1905.
[3] Debussy's daughter, later referred to as Chouchou.

TO LOUIS LALOY*

Vendredi 8 novembre 1907

Cher ami,

Pardonnez à des besognes stupides mon retard à vous demander de venir dîner avec nous lundi prochain.

Vous avez bien raison de regretter la tristesse, si prenante, des arbres revêtus de *"froidure et de pluye"* mais vous oubliez l'avenue du Bois-de-Boulogne[1] où tout cela vous attend avec l'amitié de votre

Claude Debussy

TO LOUIS LALOY

Friday, 8 November 1907

Dear Friend,

Forgive stupid duties for having made me late in inviting you to dine with us next Monday.

You are quite right to miss the attractive sadness of trees garbed in *"cold and rain,"* but you're forgetting the Avenue du Bois-de-Boulogne,[1] where all of that awaits you, along with the friendship of your

Claude Debussy

NOTES FOR LETTER TO *LOUIS LALOY*

The quotation is from the second line of the first stanza of *Le temps a laissié son manteau,* the first of the *Trois Chansons de Charles d'Orléans.*

[1] Debussy lived at 80 Avenue du Bois-de-Boulogne (now 24 Square du Bois-de-Boulogne).

* From *Revue de Musicologie,* numéro spéciale, 1962, p. 27.

TO ANDRÉ CAPLET*

Caplet vous êtes très gentil... mais! *"Caplet, vous n'êtes qu'un villain,"* comme disait Charles d'Orléans en parlant de *"l'Yver."*
      M'expliquerez-vous jamais cette disparition subite? À moins
que vous n'ayez été enlevé par des femmes turques ou que vous
mettiez le Bottin en musique, je ne vous vois aucune excuse!
      Voulez-vous venir à *Boris Godounov* jeudi prochain? puis
dîner samedi avec Ducasse, grand amateur de bridge?
Répondez-moi le plus tôt possible pour *Boris.*
      Votre amie Chouchou vous envoie son plus jolie sourire et
"veut voir" Monsieur Caplet. Dolly a voulu vous téléphoner,
mais le 546 n'a rien voulu entendre.
      Madame Debussy se réserve le plaisir de vous remercier elle-
même, et je vous serre affectueusement les deux mains.

Claude Debussy

———————

TO ANDRÉ CAPLET

Monday, 18 May 1908

Caplet, you're very nice... but! *"Caplet, you're nothing but a rascal,"* as Charles d'Orléans said of *"winter."*

Will you ever give me an explanation for that sudden disappearance? Unless you were kidnapped by Turkish women or you're setting the telephone directory to music, I cannot see what other excuse you can have!

Do you want to come to *Boris Goudonov* next Thursday, and then dine on Saturday with Ducasse, the great bridge player? Reply as soon as possible for *Boris*.

Your friend Chouchou sends her prettiest smile and "wants to see" Monsieur Caplet. Dolly tried to call you, but the number 546 was unwilling to reply.

Madame Debussy is claiming the pleasure of thanking you herself, and I shake both your hands affectionately.

Claude Debussy

NOTE FOR LETTER TO *ANDRÉ CAPLET*

This is one of the few instances where Debussy cites the source of his quotation. The poem referred to here is *Yver, vous n'estes qu'un villain,* the title and first line of the third of the *Trois Chansons de Charles d'Orléans*.

* From *Letters inédites à André Caplet,* 1908–1914, recueillies et présentées par Edward Lockspeiser (Monaco: Éditions du Rocher, 1957), p. 35.

TO ALEXANDRE CHARPENTIER*

27 septembre 1908

Mon vieux

Nous vous attendons mercredi prochain pour dîner, à moins que ce mercredi là ne vous plaise justement pas.

As-tu remarqué combien *le chant de la pluie* ressemble à un solo saxophone?

Naturellement si vous venez, ne te donne pas la peine de répondre.

Affectueux souvenirs à ta femme.

Ton vieux dévoué
Claude Debussy

––––––––––

TO ANDRÉ CAPLET*

Lundi (1910?)

Cher André Caplet,

Voici de la copie (*des feuilles et des branches*) que vous voudrez bien examiner d'un oeil secourable mais sévère. Voulez-vous mettre le paquet chez votre concierge, chez lequel je ferai passer demain vers midi.

Votre vieux porteur de lyre,
Claude Debussy

––––––––––

TO ALEXANDRE CHARPENTIER

27 September 1908

Old Friend,

We are expecting you for dinner next Wednesday, unless that particular Wednesday doesn't happen to suit you.
    Have you noticed how *the song of the rain* resembles a solo saxophone?
    Of course if you're coming, don't bother to reply.
    Affectionate wishes to your wife,

Your old devoted
Claude Debussy

TO ANDRÉ CAPLET

Monday (1910?)

Dear André Caplet,

Here is the copy (*leaves and branches*) which you will be so good as to examine with a benign but severe eye. Would you leave the package with your concierge, and I'll send someone by for it around noon tomorrow.

Your old lyre bearer,
Claude Debussy

NOTE FOR LETTER TO *ALEXANDRE CHARPENTIER*

In the song *Il pleure dans mon coeur*, the second of the *Ariettes oubliées*, Debussy changed the last line of the second stanza from "le chant de la pluie" to "le bruit de la pluie." But here he uses Verlaine's original wording.
    * From a private collection.

NOTES FOR LETTER TO *ANDRÉ CAPLET*

The words in parentheses are taken from the first line of *Green*, the fifth *Ariettes oubliées*. The "copie" may refer to the *Petite Pièce pour clarinette et piano* that Jacques Charlot had recently transcribed for piano two hands.
    The phrase "porteur de lyre," with which he signs himself, is found in the first line of the eighteenth stanza of Banville's *L'Âme de Célio*, a poem from *Les Exilés* from which Debussy had earlier set two poems.
    * From *Lettres inédites à André Caplet*, p. 83.

TO JACQUES DURAND*

Mon cher Jacques,

La santé de mon père m'a inquiété tous ces jours derniers; on le
menaçait d'une intervention chirurgicale, laquelle, à son âge,
n'était pas sans danger; enfin, hier, après une consultation avec
le Dr Hartmann, je suis un peu rassuré.

    Vous voyez bien que la chanson dit vrai:

Il n'est bon   gîte que   Bel - E- -bat![1]

Et je suis même sûr que votre charmant bureau de la place de la
Madeleine vous manquait.

    Dites-moi quand vous venez à Paris, j'ai hâte de vous serrez
la main.

    Toute l'amitié de votre

Claude Debussy

———————

TO JACQUES DURAND

My dear Jacques,

I've been concerned recently about my father's health; there was talk of an operation, which was not without danger at his age; in short, after a consultation yesterday with Dr. Hartmann, I am somewhat reassured.

As you see, the song is true:

The best lodging is in Bel-Ebat![1]

And I'm sure you missed your charming office on the place de la Madeleine.

Tell me when you will be coming to Paris, I'm eager to see you. In all friendship, your

Claude Debussy

NOTES FOR LETTER TO *JACQUES DURAND*, 22 JULY 1910

A rare example of a musical notation in a letter. The three bars are taken from the *Ballade des femmes de Paris*, the third of the *Trois Ballades de François Villon*. The words are a parody of the last line of each verse of that song.

[1] Bel-Ebat was the name of Jacques Durand's country house near Fontaine-bleau.

Debussy used the actual words of this last line in a letter to G. Jean-Aubry, 8 January 1911.

* From *Claude Debussy, Lettres à son éditeur* (Paris: Durand & Cie, Dorbon Aîné, 1927), p. 89.

TO JACQUES DURAND*

17 septembre 1910

Mon cher Jacques,

Aujourd'hui, j'ai reçu les "Ballades." C'est parfait, quoique jeusse aimé que le parchemin fût un peu plus *"jaulni"*... un temps viendra où tout cela sera *"desseiché,"* la musique aussi! En tout cas, l'édition est jolie.

Si vous sortez d'un lumbago pour rentrer dans les rhumatismes, il faut sincèrement vous plaindre et maudire, une fois de plus, les fantaisies de la saison.

Enfin, prenez patience et surtout tâchez de venir bientôt à Paris, puisque cela sera le signe que vous allez bien.

En tout amitié.

Claude Debussy

TO JACQUES DURAND

17 September 1910

My dear Jacques,

I received the "Ballades" today. Perfect, although I could have wished the parchment were a bit more *"yellowed"*... the day will come when it will all be *"withered,"* the music included! In any event, it's a pretty publication.

If you are to emerge from lumbago only to go on to rheumatism one must only pity you sincerely and curse once again the vagaries of the season.

So be patient, and above all try to come to Paris soon, since that will be the signal that you're feeling well.

In friendship,

Claude Debussy

NOTE FOR LETTER TO *JACQUES DURAND, 17 SEPTEMBER 1910*

Durand had just published the *Trois Ballades de François Villon*. Debussy took words from the first and second lines of the third stanza of the first of these ballads, *Ballade de Villon a s'amye,* to thank his publisher friend.

* From *Lettres à son éditeur*, p. 91.

*TO HIS WIFE EMMA**

Chère Petite Mienne,

Tout seul dans ce train si déplorablement "Orient-Express" qui semait une petite gare triste à gauche, une autre à droite, comme on jette rageusement des pierres. Comme c'est triste, et comme *la douceur du foyer* n'est pas seulement une expression littéraire!

Mon compagnon de voyage, vieux monsieur genre Freuder, moins le lyrisme, a eu l'excellente idée de chercher un autre compartiment, prétendant que, l'un et l'autre, nous aimerions mieux être seuls.... (Merci, vieux Monsieur, merci beaucoup!) Naturellement il n'a pu être question de dormir une minute, pas même à l'aide des *Mémoires d'Outre-Tombe* dans lesquels M. de Chateaubriand prend trop souvent une attitude "dessus de pendule" ou "Je sais tout." Alors je me suis transporté suggestivement dans notre maison. Je t'ai vue dans notre grand lit, Chouchou dans son petit lit, et j'ai eu beaucoup de mal à m'empêcher de pleurer.... Car, après tout, j'ai plus de sensibilité qu'on semble le croire dans certains milieux, surtout que je vous aime infiniment toutes les deux. Lors même que j'eusse pu en douter par simple dilettantisme, cette expérience m'en convaincrait, avec la force douloureuse d'un clou enfoncé dans la tempe.

TO HIS WIFE EMMA

29 November 1910

Dear Petite Mienne,

Alone in this train, deplorably "Orient Express," that strews behind it a sorry little station on its left, another on its right, as one pitches pebbles in ill-temper. How sad it all seems, how it makes *the sweetness of the hearth* more than a mere literary phrase.

My traveling companion, an elderly gentleman who looks like Freuder—less lyric—got the excellent idea of seeking out another compartment on the pretense that we'd both prefer being alone.... (Thank you, old Gentleman, thank you so much!) Of course, no question of a minute's sleep, even with the help of *Mémoires d'Outre-Tombe*, in which Monsieur de Chateaubriand too often assumes a pontifical, know-it-all attitude. Thus my thoughts transport me back to our home. I saw you in our big bed, Chouchou in her little bed, and I had great difficulty in restraining my tears.... After all, I do have more feelings than people in certain circles appear to think, above all I love you both infinitely. Even if I had been so frivolous as to doubt that, this experience would have disabused me with all the painful force of a nail driven into the forehead.

NOTES FOR LETTER TO *HIS WIFE EMMA, 29 NOVEMBER 1910*

The expression "la douceur du foyer" (the sweetness of the hearth) is found not only in the fourth line of the first stanza of *Le Balcon*, the first of the *Cinq Poèmes de Charles Baudelaire*, but also in the last line of Baudelaire's *Crépuscule du soir*. It also appears in stanza 24 of Banville's *L'Âme de Célio*, a poem Debussy referred to in a letter to André Caplet.

* From *Lettres de Claude Debussy à sa femme Emma*, presentées par Pasteur Vallery-Radot (Paris: Flammarion, 1957), pp. 77–79.

En arrivant à Vienne, je trouve le Dr. Béla von Angyan, jeune homme mûr et déjà directeur de la Maison Rozsavölgyl, très gentil, très Hongrois, c'est-à-dire un peu "schmouzeur," mais passionné de musique jusqu'à l'extrême gauche. Tout de suite il m'avertit que l'Hôtel Sacher est quelque chose dans le gout du Ritz ou du Carlton. Comme je ne suis ni Américain du Sud, ni de la famille Rothschild, je n'hésite pas à accepter la chambre qu'il a retenue à l'Hôtel Krantz, confortable et plus en rapport avec ma fortune. Nous dînons ensemble, il paie le dîner, puis s'en va vers une tante très riche qu'il faut ménager. Je remonte, défais mélancoliquement mes sacs, en constate la prodigieuse eurythmie; jolie occasion pour m'attendrir sur tes vertues domestiques, à laquelle je ne manque pas. Je pense à ce que serait cette chambre médiocre, si tu étais avec moi, avec ton génie de l'arrangement.... Hélas! elle restera médiocre et un peu tumultueuse.... Tout m'agace. J'ai les nerfs en "huits" et trouve que la position de compositeur de musique exige quelquefois les qualités de forte indifférence qui font la supériorité des commis-voyageurs.

Dire qu'hier encore *"je t'avais sur ma poitrine . . . ,"* comme dit à peu près Mlle Bilitis, et que je vais aller me coucher, n'ayant rien, désirant tout; c'est à demeurer stupide; c'est l'impossibilité de trouver la vie belle; c'est aussi l'état d'une âme désemparée, mais qui t'aime de la tendresse la plus forte.

Sur tes lèvres
Ton Claude

————

Upon arriving in Vienna, I met Dr. Béla von Angyan, a mature young man who is already director of the Maison Rózsavölgyl, very kind, very Hungarian—that is, a bit of a "shmoozer"—but so passionate about music that he's almost revolutionary. He advised me that the Hotel Sacher is rather like the Ritz or the Carlton. Since I'm neither a South American nor a Rothschild, I at once took the room he had reserved for me at the Hotel Krantz, comfortable and more in keeping with my fortune. We dine together, he pays, and then he goes off to a very rich aunt who requires his attentions. I come up to my room, unpack my valises in a melancholy way, noting the immense eurythmics that task entails; a fine opportunity to ponder your domestic virtues, which I don't fail to do. I think what this ordinary room could be if only you were here with me, with your genius for arranging things.... Alas, it will remain ordinary and somewhat disordered.... Everything upsets me. My nerves are at sixes and sevens, and I find that the job of composer sometimes demands those characteristics of strong indifference that make traveling salesmen such superior people.

To think that yesterday *"I had you upon my chest . . . ,"* as Mademoiselle Bilitis says, more or less, and that I'm going to go to bed with nothing, wanting everything; it's completely stupid; it's an inability to find life lovely; it's also the condition of a soul deprived, but a soul that loves you with the greatest tenderness.

On your lips,
Your Claude

NOTES FOR LETTER TO *HIS WIFE EMMA, 29 NOVEMBER 1910*

The last reference is to the first stanza of *La Chevelure*, the second of the *Chansons de Bilitis.*

TO HIS WIFE EMMA*

Moscou
4 décembre 1913

J'en ai tellement gros sur le coeur, que je ne sais pas par où commencer.... Tâchons de mettre de l'ordre dans mes regrets, qui peuvent être contenus en un seul: le regret de toi, chère petite Mienne à moi. Je me sens affreusement dépareillé et si je veux m'appuyer sur le "côté coeur," c'est la pire douleur, puisque c'est en toi qu'il trouve son appui; on dirait, romantisme à part, que l'on marche sur mon âme.

En apparence, rien n'est changé: je vis, je marche, je mange de ces nourritures immondes et prétentieuses que l'on ne treuve que dans la Compagnie Internationale des Wagons-Lits. Mais je ne suis plus qu'une mécanique que je regarde fonctionner, en m'étonnant de me voir faire des gestes identiques dans un milieu différent, même hostile, et qui n'ont plus ce charme du quotidien, où la discussion de savoir à quelle sauce on mangera le poulet peut devenir une joie, si tu n'es pas agacée par les affaires intérieures.

Ce détail n'est prosaïque qu'en surface, car il est rempli de moments délicieux. Tu ne sais pas comme tu es gentille avec tes grosses lunettes, au milieu de ces "damnés livres," comme ta nuque est jolie lorsque tu penches la tête sur ces "damnés livres" (bis). Vais-je aller t'embrasser?... Ah! bien oui! Ne suis-je pas prisonnier du Nord-Express, qui m'emmène vers Moscou avec une précaution de train omnibus?

C'est à peu près à ce moment que j'ai reçu ta première dépêche, qui m'a couru après, parce que le nom de Claude étant exclusivement réservé aux femmes en Russie, le conducteur du train a d'abord interrogé toutes les dames du train....

A partir de Varsovie, c'est la steppe infinie, on peut le dire, et, c'est aussi "Exposition générale de Blanc".... Il neige doucement, obstinément, ça peut même ne jamais finir. La locomotive pousse des meuglements comme la vache qui la regarde passer, seulement il n'y a pas de vaches, probablement pour ne pas les déconcerter. En somme, c'est le décor de la révolte de *Boris Godounov* en plus triste, plus miséreux. Il n'y a que les gendarmes qui ont bonne mine. Cela sert au restant de la population. *Bogé Tsaria Khrani*!

Comme tout est ligué contre moi! Va-t-il falloir vivre avec le coeur à jamais serré?

TO HIS WIFE EMMA

Moscow
4 December 1913

I'm so heartsick that I don't know where to begin.... Let's try to put my sorrows in order, they can all be summed up in one: missing you, my dear Petite Mienne. I feel frightfully bereft, and if I try to lay my heart where it yearns to be, it's even more painful, since that means you; all romanticism aside, it's as though someone were trodding on my soul.

On the surface, nothing has changed: I live, I walk, I eat the un-imaginable and pretentious meals that occur solely on trains of the Compagnie Internationale des Wagons-Lits. However, I'm nothing but a machine and I watch it working, astonished to see myself making the same gestures in different, even hostile surroundings devoid of familiar charm, where a discussion about what sauce to have with the chicken is a joy when you're not bothered by household affairs.

Such a detail only seems prosaic, for it contains moments of de-light. You don't know how nice you are with your big spectacles sur-rounded by those "accursed books," how pretty is your neck when you bend your head over those "accursed books." (bis). Shall I come to kiss you? Ah, of course! I'm a prisoner on the Nord-Express that takes me to Moscow with all the carefulness of a local train.

At almost this very moment I got your first dispatch, it's been catching up with me. Since Claude is a name exclusively set aside for women in Russia, the conductor asked every lady on the train first....

From Warsaw on, endless steppes, rightly named, and like an im-mense "white sale."... It's snowing softly, stubbornly, it may never end. The locomotive moos like the cow that watches it go by, only there are no cows, probably not to upset them. In sum, it's the scene of the revolutionaries in *Boris Goudonov*, sadder, more poverty stricken. The only creatures who look healthy are the policemen. That makes up for the rest of the population. *Bogé Tsaria Khrani!* [Long live the Tsar!]

And everything is leagued against me! Must one forever live sick at heart?

NOTE FOR LETTER TO *HIS WIFE EMMA, 4 DECEMBER 1913*

* From *Lettres de Claude Debussy à sa femme Emma*, pp. 100–105.

(Ce qui précède a été écrit tant bien que mal, et je le recopie scrupuleusement pour te mettre au courant.)

Arrivé avec une heure de retard et l'humeur la plus noire, je suis accueilli par une députation de la Société musicale de Moscou. Un long monsieur me fait un discours que je ne comprends pas... Enfin Koussevitzky m'arrache à ces manifestations, et nous arrivons à son hôtel. (Sa femme est une grosse dame qui parle français cordialement, et du nez.) Deux boulegogues me font fête, très laids, mais sympathiques.

Nous dînons. Il y a deux bouteilles d'eau d'Evian, comme chez nous. C'est bête, mais ça me donne envie de pleurer....

Je me déclare très fatigué, et Koussevitzky me fait visiter mon appartement... somptueux. Je pourrais facilement y loger "ma suite"! *Chagrin, déplaisir et déconfort*, comme disait ce pauvre Charles d'Orléans dans sa prison d'Angleterre.

Je me couche navré, dans un petit lit sans prétention. Au bout d'une heure, ne pouvant dormir, je me lève et marche comme un idiot à travers les pièces.... Je tombe dans un fauteuil, m'endors, et suis réveillé par le froid. Une vilaine aube, d'un blanc sale n'arrange pas mes affaires! Je me recouche, j'essais de trouver le sommeil en faisant des choses très bêtes, comme de compter jusqu'à mille, aller et retour. Mais on vient me demander ce que je prends pour mon petit déjeuner.... Ah, si je pouvais reprendre le train pour Paris.

Je m'habille, nous partons pour la répétition. Les musiciens m'accueillent debout et jouent une fanfare très exactement en mi bémol. Je les fais travailler avec une sorte de rage lucide et tracassière.... Ils sont gentils et bien disciplinés. C'est jeune, et plein de bonne volonté. Les contrebasses sont admirables; jamais, dans aucun orchestre, je n'en entendis de semblables. C'est à la fois, ferme et souple. (Il faut que tu saches que Koussevitzky a joué, paraît-il, merveilleusement de cet instrument.) Tout de même, il y aura beaucoup à faire. Ils n'ont jamais joué *La Mer*. Les "bois" sont excellents musiciens, mais ils sont lourds et canardants.

Vers la fin de l'après-midi, j'ai été avec Koussevitzky commander du caviar chez Elisseiw. Cette épicerie ressemble à un palais asiatique. On y trouve tout ce qui se peut manger, et l'on y débite cinq cents kilos de saumon fumé par jour. Un monsieur poli et vêtu comme un attaché d'ambassade m'a assuré que le caviar arriverait frais comme l'oeil!

(The above was written haphazardly and I am carefully recopying it to bring you up to date.)

Arrived an hour late and in a bad humor, I was welcomed by a deputation from the Moscow Société Musicale. A lengthy gentleman addressed a speech to me that I didn't understand.... Finally Koussevitsky tore me from such demonstrations and we got to his mansion. (His wife is a fat woman who cordially speaks French through her nose.) Two nice but very ugly bulldogs frolic around me.

We dine. There are two bottles of Evian water, just like at home. It's silly, but that makes me feel like crying....

I tell them I'm very tired, and Koussevitsky shows me through my rooms... sumptuous. I could easily accommodate my entire "suite" in them! *Sorrow, displeasure, and discomfort,* as poor Charles d'Orléans said in his English prison.

Heartbroken, I go to bed in a small, unpretentious bed. After an hour, unable to sleep, I get up and wander through the rooms like an idiot.... I fall into an armchair, fall asleep, and am awakened by the cold. An ugly, dirty white dawn does nothing to put things right! I return to bed, I try to fall asleep by doing silly things like counting to a thousand forward and backward. But I've just been asked what I want for breakfast.... Oh, if I could take the train back to Paris.

I dress and we leave for the rehearsal. The musicians receive me standing up and play a fanfare in the exact key of E-flat. I put them to work with a sort of lucid and exigent fury.... They are nice, well disciplined. All are young and full of good will. The double-basses are admirable; never in any orchestra have I heard the like. Firm and supple at the same time. (You should know that Koussevitsky was, it seems, a marvelous performer on this instrument.) All the same, there's a lot to be done. They have never played *La Mer.* The "winds" are excellent musicians, but heavy and tend to quack.

Toward the end of the afternoon, I went with Koussevitsky to order caviar at Elisseiw's. The shop is like an Asiatic palace. You can find anything edible there, and they sell 500 kilos of smoked salmon a day. A polite gentleman costumed like an embassy attaché assured me that the caviar would arrive as fresh as can be....

NOTE FOR LETTER TO *HIS WIFE EMMA, 4 DECEMBER 1913*

Debussy's special fondness for Charles d'Orléans is seen both in the way he refers to him in his letters and in his use of quotations not only from the poems he set, but also those from other poems by this poet. The quotation here, although not exactly as given in Ballade XIX, is certainly derived from it.

Douleur, Courroux, Desplaisir et Tristesse,
(Pain, wrath, displeasure and sadness,)

TO HIS WIFE EMMA*

Saint-Petersbourg
Le 9 décembre 1913
9 heures du soir

Chère petite Mienne,

Ton pauvre Claude est rompu...

A peine arrivé à Saint-Petersbourg, répétition; déjeuner en cinq sec et re-répétition. J'en sors, pâle comme ma chemise (non, elle est bleue), et je ne sais pas si c'est moi qui suis trop nerveux, mais il me semble que ça va plus mal qu'à Moscou. Koussevitzky m'assure que je me trompe.... Et puis zut, je ne peux pas en faire plus!

Excuse-moi si je ne peux te donner aucun renseignement sur Saint-Petersbourg. L'hôtel où nous sommes descendus est juste en face de la "Salle de la Noblesse" (oui, madame) où l'on repète et aura lieu le concert. Ce soir, je vais manger du pain et du fromage, puis me coucherai.... Ah! je les ai bien perdus *mes beaux sommeils d'enfant gâté!* .... Si j'arrive à m'endormir, c'est pour me réveiller un moment après. Naturellement, je me figure être dans notre bon grand lit.... Tu peux supposer tout ce que cette idée peut entraîner de mauvais quarts d'heure.

J'espère que tu as fini par trouver des raisons meilleures que les miennes pour ne pas continuer à me maudire, et que tu voudras bien continuer à m'honorer de ta confiance pour ce qui est du soin de t'aimer.

Ton Claude

———————

TO HIS WIFE EMMA

Saint Petersburg
9 December 1913
9 P.M.

Dear petite Mienne,

Your poor Claude is a broken man...
No sooner arrived in Saint Petersburg, rehearsal; lunch in five seconds and back to rehearsal.... I come out of it as pale as my shirt (no, it's blue) and I don't know whether it's just my nerves, but it seems to me worse than in Moscow. Koussevitsky assures me that I'm wrong.... Well, I can do no more!
Forgive me if I don't say anything informative about Saint Petersburg. The hotel we're staying at is right across from the Salle de la Noblesse (yes, madam) where we rehearse and where the concert will be given. This evening, I'm going to eat bread and cheese and go to bed. Ah, I've truly lost those *lovely spoiled child's dreams*!... If I do manage to get to sleep, I wake up a moment later. Of course, I imagine that I'm in our fine big bed.... You can envisage the unpleasant moments this notion gives rise to.
I hope you have finally found better reasons than I can to stop cursing me, and that you will go on trusting me so far as loving you is concerned.

Your Claude

NOTE FOR LETTER TO *HIS WIFE EMMA, 9 DECEMBER 1913*

This quotation is taken from the third to last line of *Apparition*. Debussy set this poem in 1884 but never published the song. (It was published posthumously.) In a small notebook containing sketches for *Soupir*, the first of the *Trois Poèmes de Stéphane Mallarmé*, which he composed in 1913, are sketches for a new version of *Apparition*—hence this reference, not to the 1884 song, but to the 1913 effort. (We have found no other quotation from a song Debussy did not publish himself.)
* From *Lettres de Claude Debussy à sa femme Emma*, pp. 116–117.

TO ROBERT GODET*

14 juillet 1914

Très cher,

L'accident, que vous savez, a eu des suites on ne peut plus fâcheuses: grippe; zona, qui tend les nerfs affreusement; enfin, pendant quatre mois et demi, je n'ai exactement pu rien faire! Naturellement ces choses-là aménent des tracas domestiques misérables et des heures où l'on n'aperçoit guère plus que le suicide pour en sortir.

C'est dans ces "conditions" que j'ai lu l'article de "Willy Schmidt." Si son auteur le prétend mal écrit, alors en verité vivent les gens qui écrivent mal, mais pensent délicatement. En tout cas, vous ne savez pas combien il a ranimé le pauvre être déclanché que j'étais à ce moment.

Depuis longtemps—il faut bien l'avouer!—je me perds, je me sens affreusement diminué! Ah! le "magicien" que vous aimiez en moi, où est-il? *Ça n'est plus qu'un faiseur de tours morose, qui bientôt se cassera les reins dans une ultime pirouette, sans beauté.*

Merci de m'avoir prévenu d'une autre menace, n'étant heureusement pas de ceux qui s'occupent de ma vie pour y semer des clous et des morceaux de verre cassé. Mais cessons ces doléances. Je vais passer quelques jours à Londres, pour des raisons d'économie domestique (si vous aviez quelque chose de pressé à me dire, vous pourrez m'écrire à Grosvenor Hotel, à partir du 16 jusqu'au 19 juillet)

vous êtes toujours mon vieux Godet,

j'en suis très fier

Claude Debussy

———

TO ROBERT GODET

14 July 1914

Dear Friend,

The accident, of which you know, has had the most annoying after-maths: flu, shingles—which are nerve-wracking; in short, for four months and a half I've been able to do precisely nothing! Of course, such things create awful domestic problems and hours when one sees no way out save suicide.

It is under such "conditions" that I read Willy Schmidt's article. Although its author maintains it's badly written, I say bravo for those who write badly but think with such delicacy. In any event, you don't know how it revived the poor sundered creature I was at the time.

For a long time now—might as well confess it!—I've been losing ground, I feel frightfully diminished! Ah, where is the "magician" in me you loved? *There's nothing left but a morose tumbler who will shortly break his back doing a final pirouette, devoid of beauty.*

Thanks for having warned me of a further threat, fortunately you are not among those who meddle with my life only to strew nails and broken glass in its path. However, enough of such complaints. I'm going to spend a few days in London for reasons of domestic economy (if you have anything urgent to tell me, you can write to me at the Grosvenor Hotel from 16 to 19 July).

You are, as ever, my old Godet,
I am very proud of that.

Claude Debussy

NOTE FOR LETTER TO *ROBERT GODET*

The last sentence of paragraph three is a reference to the last stanza of Banville's poem *Le Saut du Tremplin*. According to René Peter, Debussy alluded to this poem in a conversation with the clown Foottit, whom he knew and admired.

Here is the last stanza of Banville's poem:
"Enfin, de son vil échafaud,
Le clown sauta si haut, si haut
Qu'il creva le plafond de toiles
Au son du cor et du tambour,
Et, le coeur dévoré d'amour,
Alla rouler dans les étoiles."

(At last, from his tawdry platform, the clown jumped so high, so high that to the sound of horn and drum he burst through the canvas roof and, his heart consumed by love, flew off to somersault among the stars.)

* From *Lettres à deux amis*, pp. 141–142.

TO JACQUES DURAND*

Pourville
22 juillet 1915

Cher ami,

Ce jour,—comme disent les "business-men,"—j'ai mis le IIe Caprice[1] à la poste et j'ai reçu votre lettre. C'est un beau jour....
Vous verrez ce que peut "prendre" l'hymne de Luther pour
s'être imprudemment fourvoyé dans un "Caprice" à la française.
Vers la fin, un modeste carillon sonne une pré-Marseillaise; tout
en m'excusant de cet anachronisme, il est admissible à une
époque où les pavés des rues, les arbres des forêts, sont vibrants
de chant innombrable.

Je ne vois pas les choses si *vestues de noir* que vous.... À
mon humble avis, les Austro-Boches tirent les dernières flèches
d'un mauvais bois.

Des raisons plus fortes que la haine les forceront à une paix,
qui nous gênera, par crainte de tout perdre.

L'atmosphère de Paris, où se forme autant de pessimisme
que d'optimisme, où chacun veut sa tranchée pour le déjeuner
du matin, nous fait oublier, il me semble, notre habituel bon
sens. Rappelons-nous que la France en a vu bien d'autres, et
qu'elle est toujours "le plus beau royaume sous le ciel," malgré
ce besoin jaloux qu'a le restant de l'Europe—excepté les
alliés(?)—de la détruire.

Puisque vous admettez notre relèvement moral... à ce propos, notre prétendue décomposition ne venait-elle pas de cette
vague d'étrangers qui inonde Paris de ses horreurs variées, trou-
vant l'occasion de les accomplir plus librement qu'en leur propre
pays? L'âme française restera toujours claire et heroïque, y compris celle de l'apache Bonnot, qui sut mourir comme un beau
tigre, pour la plus vilaines des causes, c'est entendu, mais les
vertus dominatives ont plusieurs expressions.

TO JACQUES DURAND

Pourville
22 July 1915

Dear Friend,

I mailed the 2nd Caprice[1] and received your letter this day inst.—as "business-men" say. A good day.... You will note that Luther's chorale has been duly "reprimanded" for having strayed imprudently into a French-style "Caprice." Toward the end, there's a modest bell effect ringing a pre-Marseillaise; while begging pardon for that anachronism, it is permissible in an age when the very cobblestones in the streets, the trees in the forests, are vibrant with countless song.

I don't see things as *"dressed in black"* as you do.... In my humble opinion, the Austro-Boches are shooting off their last arrows, made of rotten wood.

More forceful reasons than hatred will bring them to make peace, which we will find upsetting out of fear of losing everything.

The atmosphere in Paris, which gives rise to as much pessimism as it does optimism, where everybody wants to get his share of tomorrow's breakfast, is making us abandon our habitual good sense, it seems to me. We must remember that France has been through all of this before, and that it is still "the loveliest kingdom under heaven," despite the jealous compulsion felt by the rest of Europe—with the exception of the allies(?)—to destroy it.

Since you admit our moral recovery... in this connection, doesn't our so-called decomposition arise from this wave of foreigners who are flooding Paris with their varied horrors, seizing on the opportunity to indulge such horrors more freely than they can in their own countries? The French soul will remain clear and heroic, even the soul of that crook Bonnot, who managed to expire like a tiger for the worst of causes—of course—but outstanding virtues have different ways of being expressed.

NOTES FOR LETTER TO *JACQUES DURAND, 22 JULY 1915*

[1] The *IIe Caprice* is Part II of *En blanc et noir*. This composition for two pianos four hands, composed and published in 1915, was originally entitled *Caprices en blanc et noir*. This *IIe Caprice* was dedicated to Jacques Charlot and had for its epigraph the Envoi from Villon's *Ballade contre les ennemis de la France*.

The short phrase in quotation marks is taken from the second line of the first stanza of *Pour ce que Plaisance est morte*, the third of the *Trois Chansons de Charles d'Orléans*.

* From *Lettres à son éditeur*, p. 138.

Encore une fois, si vous admettez notre "tournure," notre "cohésion," pourquoi ne croyez-vous pas à toutes ces volontés tendues vers la même fin, et qu'importent les boniments des fauteurs de gloire!

Ce sera dur, long, impitoyable aux douleurs; mais, pour nous, hommes de ville, contenons notre angoisse, travaillons pour cette beauté dont les peuples ont l'instinctif besoin, plus forts d'avoir souffert.

Excusez, mon cher Jacques, toutes ces phrases qui ne sont, tout de même, que "des mots, des mots . . . ," comme disait le prince Hamlet—frère de nos neurasthénies—si elles vous font sourire, elles dissiperont, pendant un moment, les nuages sinistres où se plaît votre présente inquiétude.

Nous vous envoyons, ainsi qu'à madame J. Durand, nos affectueuses pensées.

Votre vieux dévoué
Claude Debussy

P.S. — Je n'ai pu indiquer les mouvements métronomiques:[2] Monsieur Maelzel n'a plus de correspondants dans ce pays, depuis la guerre.

Je n'ai pas non plus de piano... jusqu'ici. Je n'en suis pas malade. Ce manque concentre l'émotion, en l'empêchant de se disperser dans des improvisations où l'on cède, trop souvent, au charme pervers de se raconter des histoires à soi-même.

Voilà que la Maison Pleyel m'annonce l'envoi d'un piano démontable...

Requiescat in pace!

Once again, if you admit our "standing," our "cohesion," then why can't you trust in these firm wills all bent on the same purpose, and what can the hanky-panky of the glory-mongers matter?

It will be difficult, lengthy, pitiless to sorrow; but we as civilized men must conceal our anxiety and work for that beauty the people instinctively need, people who are stronger for having suffered.

My dear Jacques, forgive all these lines which are, after all, only "words . . . words" (as Hamlet, our neurasthenic brother, said)—if they can make you smile, they may dissipate for a moment the dark clouds that are presently weighing on your mind.

We send to you and Madame Durand our affectionate thoughts.

Your old devoted
Claude Debussy

P.S. I was unable to indicate metronome markings:[2] since the war, Monsieur Maelzel no longer has any connections in this country.

Nor have I had a piano... up until now. It doesn't upset me. The lack has concentrated my feelings and prevented them from floating off into improvisations which all too often allow one to give in to the perverse charm of telling stories to oneself.

And now Pleyel informs me they have sent me a portable piano... Requiescat in pace!

NOTES FOR LETTER TO *JACQUES DURAND, 22 JULY 1915*

[2] For the above *Caprice.*

TO JACQUES DURAND*

Pourville
Samedi, 9 octobre 1915

Mon cher Jacques,

Vous savez mon opinion sur les mouvements métronomiques: ils sont justes pendant une mesure, comme *"les roses, l'espace d'un matin,"* seulement, il y a "ceux" qui n'entendent pas la musique et qui s'autorisent de ce manque pour y entendre encore moins!

Faites donc comme il vous plaira.

L'heure fatidique du départ s'avance!

J'écrirai pourtant jusqu'à la dernière minute, tel André Chénier, écrivant des vers, avant de mourir sur l'échafaud! Cette comparaison, quoique macabre, contient une part de verité.

Le cerveau est une machine bien délicate qui se fausse au moindre choc et l' "ambiance" n'est pas qu'un mot trop employé.

Aussitôt arrivé, je vous téléphonerai et vous me verrez, probablement, le lendemain.

Votre vieux dévoué
Claude Debussy

TO JACQUES DURAND

Pourville
Saturday, 9 October 1915

My dear Jacques,

You know my feelings about metronome markings: they're all right for a measure—like *"roses for a morning's span"*—but there are "those" who don't understand music and use this lack as an excuse to understand it even less!
Do as you like, therefore.
The fateful hour of departure draws nigh!
I, however, shall continue to write up until the last minute, like André Chenier composing verses before perishing on the scaffold! Albeit macabre, this simile contains a grain of truth.
The brain is a very delicate machine that can go awry at the least shock, and "ambiance" is not just a trite word.
As soon as I arrive, I'll telephone you and you will probably see me the next day.

Your old devoted
Claude Debussy

NOTE FOR LETTER TO *JACQUES DURAND, 9 OCTOBER 1915*

The quotation here is from the last two lines of the fourth stanza of François de Malherbe's poem *Consolation à M. du Périer*. Debussy also mentions the poet André Chénier in this letter. In both these instances, he is far afield from the poets of the songs.
"Mais elle était du monde, où les plus belles choses
  Ont le pire destin;
Et rose elle a vécu ce que vive *les roses*,
  L'espace d'un matin."
(But she was of the world in which the loveliest of things meet with the worst of fates; and rose she lived as live *the roses, for a morning's span*.)
* From *Lettres à son éditeur*, p. 158.

TO PAUL DUKAS*

Grand-Hôtel, Le Moulleau
Arcachon
10 septembre 1916

Cher ami,

Ma situation restant "inchangé" je n'ai pas cru devoir vous en abrutir avec des récits tendancieux. Nous partons pour Arcachon demain soir, non pas à cause de moi, mais surtout pour ma femme dont l'état ne s'améliore decidément pas. À mon retour, je vous dirai si ce voyage a eu d'heureux effets, jusque là, je n'ose me prononcer. Pourtant, je n'entendrai plus les bons clairons.... Est-ce suffisant pour éclater de rire?

À mon âge, le passé est déjà lourd a emporté avec soi; l'avenir n'est pas brillant... vous voyez bien qu'il n'y a pas de quoi "rire," ni même de sourire.

Excusez ma "*mérencolie*," comme disait mon oncle Charles d'Orléans, et croyez toujours à la vieille amitié de votre

Claude Debussy

TO PAUL DUKAS

Grand-Hôtel, Le Moulleau
Arcachon
10 September 1916

Dear Friend,

Since my condition is "unchanged," I thought it unnecessary to burden you with boring narratives. We are off to Arcachon tomorrow evening, not on my account but because of my wife, whose condition is not improving at all. Upon my return I'll let you know if this trip has had a propitious effect, until then I daren't predict. However, I'll no longer be hearing the fine bugle calls.... Is that enough to make one laugh?

At my age the past is already a heavy burden to carry about with one; the future isn't brilliant... you can see that there are no grounds for laughter, or even a smile.

Excuse my *"melancholia,"* as my uncle Charles d'Orléans put it, and believe always in the old friendship of your

Claude Debussy

NOTE FOR LETTER TO *PAUL DUKAS*

Time and time again, Charles d'Orléans refers to his "mérencolie" (melancholia) in the poems he wrote while a prisoner in England.
  * From the author's collection.

TO ROBERT GODET*

Grand-Hôtel, Le Moulleau
Arcachon
6 octobre 1916

Cher,

"Il n'arrive peut-être pas d'événements inutiles"... a dit Arkel dans une phrase dont la mélodie est dans toutes les mémoires. Malheureusement je n'ai plus le goût des "déplacements et villégiatures" et m'habitue maladroitement à ce riche climat, à la fureur des vents.

Vous expliquer pourquoi et comment nous sommes ici plutôt qu'à Singapour serait trop long:... la nécessité, Seigneur, le besoin d'échapper à une atmosphère trop lourde de mauvaises heures, et aussi pour cause d'hygiène. Ajoutez à cela que notre médecin n'était pas fâché d'envoyer promener nos coutumières doléances.

Enfin nous sommes partis un peu comme on se noie! je n'aime pas les départs, n'ayant aucun sens pratique des malles, paquets, etc.... À l'heure qu'il est (3 h. 35) je ne suis pas encore arrivé à decider si on doit tout emporter, ou simplement le strict nécessaire.

Nous sommes déjà venus à Arcachon il y a douze ans....

Présentement nous habitons au bout du bassin d'Arcachon, tout près de l'Atlantique,—rude et belle musique, jamais fausse pourtant. C'est d'ailleurs une faute commune que de croire, toutes les fois que l'on déchaine les éléments, qu'il faut absolument qu'ils soient en rapport de septième? Comme il se doit, l'hôtel est médiocre et je regrette intensément Pourville et "Mon Coin".... C'est probablement ma faute, mais je suis un vieil homme malade qui a augmenté sa collection de manies,—quelques-unes redoutables, comme celle d'avoir horreur de ces petites tables d'hôtel qui ont à peine 75 cent. Vous verrez que je ne rapporterai rien qui vaille de ce voyage, sinon le regret de l'avoir entrepris.

TO ROBERT GODET

Grand-Hôtel, Le Moulleau
Arcachon
6 October 1916

Dear Friend,

Perhaps, as Arkel said in a phrase whose music everyone remembers, "there are no useless events...." Unfortunately, I no longer have a taste for "displacements and vacations" and I am unsuited to adapt to this varied climate, to the wind's fury.

To explain to you why and how we happen to be here rather than in Singapore would take too long:... the necessity, good Lord, the need to escape from an atmosphere weighed down unduly with bad hours, and also for health reasons. Added to that, our doctor was not sorry to banish us and our usual complaints.

So we are leaving a little as one drowns oneself! I don't like departures, having no practical sense about trunks, packages, etc. At the present time (3:35) I still haven't decided if we should take everything, or only what is strictly necessary.

We were in Arcachon once before, twelve years ago...

We are now living at the end of the bay of Arcachon, near the Atlantic—a rude, lovely music, never out of tune. But then, it's a mistake, is it not, to think that every time the elements are let loose they will inevitably create sevenths? Of course the hotel is mediocre and I miss Pourville and "Mon Coin" intensely.... It's probably my fault, but I'm an old, sick man who has added to his collection of manias—some of which are quite formidable, such as a detestation for those tiny hotel tables that are barely 75 centimeters across. You can see that I'll come back from this trip with nothing worth while, other than the regret at having made it.

NOTES FOR LETTER TO *ROBERT GODET*

The letter opens with one of the many quotations from *Pelléas et Mélisande* that are found in Debussy's letters. This one is from Act I, Scene II.

* From *Lettres à deux amis*, pp. 158–160.

J'ai reçu ici votre dernière lettre qui est très belle. Souvent je la relis... il y circule une forte mélancolie, et j'y admire votre faculté de vous assimiler les paysages les plus déconcertants. Vous avez bien raison. Cependant croyez que ce n'est pas à la portée de tout le monde?

Pour continuer, *"ma songerie aimant à se martyriser,"* je ne me suis pas encore retrouvé. Cette horrible maladie a bouleversé mes plus belles facultés (*sic*), en particulier celle de trouver des façons inédites d'assembler les sons. Maintenant ce que j'écris me semble toujours de la veille, jamais du lendemain.... Alors je croupis dans ces *"usines du Néant"* dont se plaignait déjà notre Jules Laforgue. Ma santé n'est pas ce qu'il y a de mieux non plus! Excusez toute cette faiblesse, cher Godet! vous êtes mon seul ami (alias Roderick Usher[1]), naturellement j'en abuse.... D'avance, je retiens vos heures libres à votre prochain voyage à Paris (prenez vos tablettes et inscrivez-le!).

Je n'ai pas ici d'exemplaire de la *Sonate,* aussitôt rentré à Paris je vous l'enverrai, aussi l'orchestre de *Gigues.*

Il y a en face de l'hôtel une jeune fille que je ne connais pas, et à laquelle je vous jure que je n'ai jamais fait le moindre mal, qui joue du Franck pendant une bonne partie de l'après-midi. Seigneur! quand il y a la mer, et des couchers de soleil à pleurer! Si j'étais le soleil, j'irais me coucher ailleurs!

Au revoir, très cher Godet...

Votre maritime mais toujours vieux dévoué

Claude Debussy

I received your last letter here, it is very beautiful. I often reread it... it emanates a powerful melancholy and I admire in it your facility for assimilating the most disconcerting scenes. You are right to do so. Yet you must believe that not everyone is able to?

To continue, *my dreaming, fond of making me a martyr*, I have not yet regained my feet. This horrid disease has overturned my finest faculties, especially that of finding hitherto unknown ways of putting sounds together. Now what I write always seems to me yesterday's, never tomorrow's.... So I grind in the *"workshops of Nothingness"* our Jules Laforgue once complained about. Nor is my health the best part of it! Forgive all this weakness, my dear Godet! You (alias Roderick Usher[1]) are my only friend, so of course I take advantage of it.... I reserve in advance your free time during your next trip to Paris (take your notebooks and write it down!).

I haven't got a copy of the *Sonata* here, as soon as I return to Paris I'll send it to you, as well as the orchestral score of *Gigues*.

Across from the hotel a young girl with whom I am unacquainted, and to whom I've never, I swear, done the slightest harm, plays Franck for most of the afternoon. Good Lord! when there are seas and sunsets galore! If I were the sun, I'd go set somewhere else.

Au revoir, very dear Godet...

Your maritime, but always old devoted

Claude Debussy

NOTES FOR LETTER TO *ROBERT GODET*

The next quotation is from the sixth line of *Apparition*, the poem Debussy had set in 1884 and for which he left sketches for a new version in 1913. Debussy uses "se martyriser" here as in the 1884 manuscript, and not "me martyriser" as in the poem and the published version of the song (which appeared after his death).

The last quotation is from Laforgue's *Complainte des voix sous le figuier boudhique*, a phrase frequently found in Debussy's letters. Other examples are in a letter to Jacques Durand, 18 April 1906, and in an unpublished letter to Gabriel Mourey, 5 May 1910.

"— Vie ou *Néant*! choisir. Ah quelle discipline
Que n'est-il un Eden entre ces deux *usines*."

(— Life or *Nothingness*! take your pick. Ah, what a discipline. What a paradise exists between those two *workshops*.)

[1] Roderick Usher is the principal character in *La Chute de la Maison Usher*, a work Debussy started in 1908 and left unfinished.

TO PAUL DUKAS*

Cher ami, excusez moi... *"Je croupis dans les usines du Néant"*
(J. Laforgue—correspondances)
   Pendant ce temps, vous avez eu celui de revenir, ou même
de repartir?
   Alors, je vous écris rue Singer et vous y envoi le "Noël,"[1]
pour lequel vous voudrez bien avoir de l'indulgence! Il a été écrit
la veille du jour ou je fus opéré—Triste jour, suivi d'autres,
nombreux, ou de piqûres en piqûres, j'ai trainé une vie de convalescent nerveux qui attend, sans patience, des jours meilleurs.
C'est un peu—toute comparaison gardée—l'histoire de la guerre,
et j'ai bien lutté: je suis toujours envahi! Enfin, ne nous atten-
drissons pas, et continuons ce passionnant récit.
   La Sonate pour Violon et piano a été d'abord terminée, puis
jouée dans un concert donné au profit des soldats aveugles—
c'est ce qu'il y a de mieux dans mon histoire—par Gaston Poulet,[2] qui a l'air d'un tzigane, bien qu'il soit né tranquillement à
Paris.
   Quand puis-je vous voir, si vous êtes à Paris?

votre vieux fidéle
Claude Debussy

TO PAUL DUKAS

19 May 1917

Forgive me, dear friend... "*I am grinding away in the workshops of Noth-ingness*" (Jules Laforgue—correspondence)

During this time, have you returned, or perhaps gone off again?

So I'm writing to the Rue Singer to send you the *Noël*,[1] for which I beg your indulgence! It was written on the eve of my operation—Sad day, followed by many more, when I dragged out between injections a nervous convalescent's life impatiently awaiting better days. It's a bit like the story of the war—taking everything into consideration—and I fought valiantly; yet I was invaded nonetheless! Well, we shan't dwell on it, but get on with this enthralling narrative.

The Sonata for Violin and Piano was first finished and then per-formed at a concert given to benefit blinded soldiers—this is the best part of my saga—by Gaston Poulet,[2] who looks like a gypsy even though he was born tranquilly in Paris.

When can I see you, if you are in Paris?

Your old devoted
Claude Debussy

NOTES FOR LETTER TO *PAUL DUKAS*

Debussy gives Laforgue's correspondence as the source of this opening quo-tation. We have not been able to find it in the published volumes. Did Debussy have access to unpublished letters? A similar expression is found in the preced-ing letter.

[1] The *Noël des enfants qui n'ont plus de maisons*.

[2] The first performance of this Sonata was given by Debussy and Gaston Poulet on 5 May 1917.

* From the author's collection.

TO SERGE DE DIAGHILEV*

20 mai 1917

Mon cher Diaghilev

En sortant de la représentation des Ballets russes mercredi dernier, j'ai vraiment cherché à vous voir... j'ai téléphoner au Châtelet[1] mais je crois qu'il faudrait mieux essayer de téléphoner à Dieu....

Dandelot me donne votre adresse et la guigne me poursuit puisqu'on prétend que l'Hôtel Edouard VII ne répond pas.

Tout de même, il faut que vous sachiez ma joie d'avoir retrouver la beauté particulière des Ballets russes. *"C'est du rêve ancien"*... et c'est très mélancolique, parce que trop d'horreurs ont bouleversé la vie.

J'ai peur de ne pas être libre pour les deux représentations qu'annoncent les journaux. Si quelquefois il y avait un changement, m'autorisez-vous à user de votre complaisance?

Encore merci, cher ami, mes affectueux souvenirs. Vous souvient-il de l'Hermitage et des belles chansons que l'on nous chanta?

Votre bien dévoué
Claude Debussy

TO SERGE DE DIAGHILEV

20 *May 1917*

Dear Diaghilev,

I truly attempted to see you upon leaving the Ballets Russes performance Wednesday last... I telephoned the Châtelet,[1] but it would I think be simpler to try to get through to God....
    Dandelot gave me your address, and ill luck must be with me since they tell me the Hotel Édouard VII does not reply.
    However, I must tell you my joy at encountering again the special beauty of the Ballets Russes. *"Ancient dreams"*... and very sad, since life has been disrupted by all too many horrors.
    I fear I may not be free for the two performances announced in the newspapers. If it should happen that there is some change, do I have your permission to mention your name?
    Thank you once again, dear friend, and my affectionate remembrance. Do you recall the Hermitage and the beautiful songs they sang for us?

Your devoted
Claude Debussy

_____

NOTES FOR LETTER TO *SERGE DE DIAGHILEV*

    This phrase might have gone unnoticed had Debussy not used the quotation marks. It is taken from the last line of *De rêve,* the first of the *Proses lyriques.* One wonders if Diaghilev would have recognized the quotation.
    [1] The Théâtre du Châtelet.
    * From a private collection.

TO WALTER RUMMEL*

Cher ami,

Vous m'avez certainement excusé de n'avoir pas reçu l'hommage de mon admiration à l'issue de votre dernier récital?

On dit mal ces choses là en public... ou plutôt: on en dit trop, ou pas assez, cependant que l'intéressé vous contemple anxieusement ayant l'air de dire: Pourquoi me raconte-t-il des choses que je sais beaucoup mieux que lui? et c'est la tranquille vérité!

On ne félicite pas un beau coucher de soleil? On n'adresse pas ses félicitations à *la mer d'être plus belle que les cathédrales.*

Vous êtes une force de la nature... comme elle vous allez du plus grand au plus petit sans effort visible. C'est ainsi que vous comprenez l'âme du grand Sébastien Bach et celle du petit Claude Debussy, de telle façon que, pour un moment ils peuvent se trouver sur le même plan dans l'esprit du public....

De cela comme de toutes choses, soyez infiniment remercier, cher ami, et croyez toujours à l'affectueux dévouement de

votre vieux
Claude Debussy

TO WALTER RUMMEL

22 June 1917

Dear Friend,

You will surely have forgiven me for not having paid you the homage of my admiration at the end of your last recital?

Such things never come out well in public... or rather: one says too much or not enough, while the recipient anxiously looks at you as if to say: Why is he telling me these things that I know much better than he? and that's the simple truth!

One doesn't congratulate a beautiful sunset, does one? One doesn't congratulate *the sea for being more beautiful than cathedrals.*

You are a force of nature... like nature, you go from the greatest to the smallest without any apparent effort. This enables you to understand the soul of the great Sebastian Bach and that of the tiny Claude Debussy in such a way that, for a moment, they can stand on the same level in the public's mind.

For that, as for all else, let me extend my boundless thanks, dear friend, and ask you to trust in the affectionate devotion of

> *Your old*
> *Claude Debussy*

NOTE FOR LETTER TO *WALTER RUMMEL*

The quotation is from the first two lines of *La mer est plus belle,* the first of the *Trois Mélodies.*

* Formerly in the collection of Pasteur Vallery-Radot.

TO ROBERT GODET*

Chalet Habas, St-Jean-de-Luz
28 juillet 1917

Décidemment les "côtes" ne me réussissent pas. Et pourtant, la maison est charmante, basque comme construction, anglaise comme arrangement. Le propriétaire: Colonel A. L. Nicol est Anglais,—naturellement, depuis le commencement de la guerre, il est sur le front. Sa femme est à Londres, sur ce que vous voudrez?

Il semble que l'on va rencontrer S. Pickwick dans l'escalier. Le très beau portrait d'un vieux monsieur sévère et triste me poursuit et me hante. Quand je suis en retard le matin, il a l'air encore plus sévère et semble me reprocher ma nonchalance. Un peu partout: des fusils qui ont dû être terribles, des armes pour tribus dahoméennes. D'innombrables tableaux de famille,—dans le sens qu'ils ont été peints par un quelconque Nicol.

Au fond, petites montagnes sans prétensions. On ne voit pas la mer.... Il faut marcher pendant un quart d'heure pour y atteindre et se trouver en présence d'une baie,—comme toutes les baies,—où se baignent des gens qui pourraient être moins laids, et se repose un bateau charbonnier, utile, mais encombrant l'horizon. Plus loin, à Guéthary, qu'illustre la présence de P.-J. Toulet, célèbre humoriste, alcoolique obstiné, dont la figure représente un coucher de soleil peint par Van Dongen, la mer est très belle.

Tout cela pourrait encore s'arranger, s'il n'y avait "moi" qui abîme, démolit,—on dirait,—à plaisir? Donc jusqu'ici, rien de changé...

"Les morts
C'est discret
Ça dort
Bien au frais"
toujours votre vieux dévoué

Claude Debussy

Permettez-moi de ne pas m'excuser de vous avoir fait attendre presque un mois cette lettre inutile.

———————

TO ROBERT GODET

Chalet Habas, St-Jean-de-Luz
28 July 1917

The "shores" definitely don't agree with me. Yet the house is charming, built in the Basque style with English conveniences. The proprietor, Colonel A. L. Nicol, is an Englishman—naturally, since the outbreak of war he's at the front. His wife is in London, at whatever you like?

One has the feeling that one will meet S. Pickwick on the stairs. I am haunted and pursued by a very handsome portrait of a severe, sad old man. When I'm late in the morning, he looks even more severe and appears to reproach me for my carelessness. Everywhere: guns that must have been formidable, weapons for Dahomean tribes. Innumerable family portraits—in the sense that they were painted by some Nicol.

In the background are unpretentious little mountains. We can't see the sea.... You have to walk for fifteen minutes to get to it and find yourself at a bay—like all bays—where people who could be less unattractive swim and where there is a coal barge that is useful, but that blocks the view. Farther on, at Guéthary, made famous by the presence there of P.-J. Toulet, celebrated humorist and determined alcoholic, with a face like a Van Dongen sunset, the sea is lovely.

All of that might yet do the trick if it weren't for "me" falling apart, demolishing—so to speak—without cause. So up until now, nothing is changed....

The dead
Are discreet,
They repose
In much cold.

Ever your old devoted

Claude Debussy

I won't excuse myself for having made you wait nearly a month for this useless letter.

NOTES FOR LETTER TO *ROBERT GODET*

This is one of the last letters Robert Godet received from his friend, who died just eight months later. The quotation is found in Laforgue's short story *Hamlet*, the first in his book *Moralités légendaires*. This verse also appears in the fifth stanza of his poem *Complainte de l'oubli des morts*, but there with the word "Bien" changed to "Trop," in the last line.

Two earlier quotations from this same verse are found in articles Debussy wrote for *Gil Blas*, one on 26 January 1903 and the other on 13 April 1903.

* From *Lettres à deux amis*, pp. 176–177.

The three articles that follow serve as further examples of Debussy's use of quotations from poetry. They reveal him as a critic and writer just as the letters shed light on him as friend and husband.

LA REVUE BLANCHE

1 juin 1901

LA MUSIQUE EN PLEIN AIR

Voici venir le temps, où vibrant sur sa tige,
Chaque musique militaire s'évapore ainsi qu'un encensoir!

Et que Baudelaire veuille bien m'excusez.... En somme, pourquoi l'ornement des squares et promenades est-il resté le monopole des seules musiques militaires? Il me plairait d'imaginer des fêtes plus inédites et participant plus complètement au décor naturel. La musique militaire n'est-elle pas l'oubli des longues étapes et la joie des boulevards? En elle se totalise l'amour de la patrie qui bat dans tous les coeurs épars; par elle se rejoignent le petit pâtissier et le vieux monsieur qui pense à l'Alsace-Lorraine et n'en parle jamais! Loin de moi l'idée de lui enlever ces nobles privilèges; mais, encore une fois: dans les arbres, çà fait le bruit d'un phonographe en enfance.

Pour les arbres, il faudrait un orchestre nombreux avec le concours de la voix humaine. (Non!... pas l'orphéon! je vous remercie....) J'entrevois la possibilité d'une musique construite spécialement pour "le plein air," toute en grandes lignes, en hardiesses vocales et instrumentales, qui joueraient dans l'air libre et planeraient joyeusement sur la cime des arbres. Telle succession harmonique paraissant anormale dans le renfermé d'une salle de concert prendrait certainement sa juste valeur en

LA REVUE BLANCHE

1 June 1901

OUTDOOR MUSIC

Now is the time when, trembling on its stalk,
Each military band emits its perfume like a censer!

With apologies to Baudelaire.... In short, why does military band music have a monopoly on the adornment of public squares and promenades? I can easily imagine other festive occasions that would be more a part of such natural surroundings. Shouldn't military music be used to accompany long marches, to arouse the spectator? It embodies the patriotism that beats in every heart, it unites the humble pastry cook with the elderly gentleman dreaming tacitly of Alsace-Lorraine. It is not my intention to deprive them of such noble pastimes, but it must be noted that such music, filtered through the trees, sounds very like an old-fashioned phonograph.

To go with trees, there should be a large orchestra, with human voices. (No, not a "choral society," thank you very much!) I can envisage a possible music composed especially for the outdoors, large in scope, daring both instrumentally and vocally, to be played in the open air and to soar joyfully over the treetops. A harmonic progression that

NOTE FOR *LA MUSIQUE EN PLEIN AIR*

The two lines that serve as a heading for this article are a parody of the first two lines of *Harmonie du soir*, the second of the *Cinq Poèmes de Charles Baudelaire*.

plein air; peut-être trouverait-on là le moyen de faire disparaître
ces petites manies de forme et de tonalité trop précises qui en-
combrent si maladroitement la musique? Celle-ci pourrait s'y
renouveler et y prendre la belle leçon de liberté contenue dans
l'épanouissement des arbres; ce qu'elle perdrait en charme minu-
tieux ne le regagnerait-elle pas en grandeur? Il faut comprendre
qu'il ne s'agit pas de travailler dans le "gros," mais dans le
"grand"; il ne s'agit pas non plus d'ennuyer les échos, à répéter
d'excessives sonneries, mais d'en profiter pour prolonger le rêve
harmonique. Il y aurait là une collaboration mystérieuse de l'air,
du mouvement des feuilles et du parfum des fleurs avec la musique; celle-ci réunirait tous ces éléments dans une entente si
naturelle qu'elle semblerait participer de chacun d'eux.... Puis,
enfin, on pourrait vérifier décidément que la musique et la
poèsie sont les deux seuls arts qui se meuvent dans l'espace....
Je puis me tromper, mais il me semble qu'il y a, dans cette idée,
du rêve pour des générations futures. Pour nous autres pauvres
contemporains, j'ai bien peur que la musique continue à sentir
un peu le renfermé.

would seem strange when restricted to the concert hall would assume its true significance out-of-doors; perhaps this might be a way to do away with that inane obsession with finicky form and tonality with which music is so unfortunately oppressed? Music would certainly take a new lease on life and learn a fine lesson in freedom from the greening trees; what it might lose in charm of detail would it not gain in grandeur? It should be made clear that it is not a question of "larger" works, but of "greater"; not of making the echoes resound, of one fanfare after another, but of profiting from the opportunity to prolong the harmonic idyll. Such music would be a mysterious collaboration between the air, the movement of the leaves, the scent of the flowers, and music; music would join with all these elements in such a natural union that it would seem a part of each of them.... Finally, we would be able to prove once and for all that music and poetry are the only two arts that move in space.... I may be wrong, but it seems to me that this notion should be the dream of future generations. For us poor contemporaries, I'm afraid music will go on giving off a rather musty, indoor smell.

———————

GIL BLAS

30 mars 1903

À LA SOCIÉTÉ NATIONALE

Lundi dernier, la Société nationale donnait un concert à la Salle Pleyel, dont E. Risler, l'un des plus merveilleux pianistes de notre temps, et Mme J. Raunay, étaient les protagonistes. M. Risler joua une sonate de Beethoven, pour cor et piano, avec M. Pénable fils. C'est à la fois l'enfance du cor et l'enfance de la sonate.

Et puis, si vous saviez *"comme le son du cor est triste au fond de la Salle Pleyel"*!

Ensuite vint une suite pour piano, de M. G. Samazeuilh.... Oeuvre remplie de bonne volonté mais qui me paraît ne pas avoir assez de "bouteille"! Je veux dire qu'elle est un peu verte et que M. Samazeuilh s'est trop hâté de lui faire voir le monde. Elle contient beaucoup de l'influence de M. V. d'Indy; un tel maître est plus que recommandable et fait espérer beaucoup des prochaines oeuvres de M. G. Samazeuilh.

Mme Raunay a chanté avec un sentiment profond la série de mélodies que E. Chausson écrivit sur les "Serres chaudes" de Maeterlinck. Ces mélodies sont des petits drames d'une métaphysique passionnée que la musique de Chausson commente sans les alourdir; on voudrai même qu'il eût laissé plus de liberté à tout ce que l'on sent battre d'émotion intérieure dans sa très personnelle interprétation musicale.

Pour finir, les variations sur un thème de Rameau où Paul Dukas montra une fois de plus la hautaine maîtrise de son écriture. — Il y a bien des moments où Rameau lui-même ne serait pas fichu de retrouver son thème parmi tant de festons et d'astragales.

Mais je pense que Dukas a voulu simplement résoudre de fugitives énigmes? Il en résolut de plus considérables; aussi ne doit-on regarder dans ces "variations" que la curiosité du jeu de leurs lignes, et pour dire le fond de ma pensée; j'aime mieux Dukas sans Rameau.

Dans tant d'oeuvres, si différentes, M. E. Risler a montré une variété et une sûreté de moyens purement admirables.

GIL BLAS

30 March 1903

AT THE SOCIÉTÉ NATIONALE

Last Monday, the Société Nationale presented a concert at the Salle Pleyel by E. Risler, one of the most marvelous of today's pianists, along with Madame J. Raunay. Monsieur Risler performed a Beethoven sonata for horn and piano with Monsieur Pénable, junior. It was a work that hailed from the childhood of both the horn and the sonata.

If you could have heard *"how sadly sounded the horn from the depths of the Salle Pleyel"*!

Next came a suite for piano solo by Monsieur G. Samazeuilh... a work filled with good intentions, but, in my opinion, not sufficiently "aged." In other words, it was somewhat raw, and Monsieur Samazeuilh has been a trifle over-eager to serve it to the public. It contains much of the influence of Monsieur V. d'Indy, such a master is highly commendable and leads us to look forward to Monsieur G. Samazeuilh's future works.

Madame Raunay sang Ernest Chausson's song cycle to the *Serres Chaudes* of Maeterlinck with great feeling. These songs are mini-dramas, little metaphysical outpourings upon which Chausson's music comments without making them ponderous; one might even wish he had given freer rein to the inner feelings one can sense pulsating below the surface of his very personal musical interpretation.

Lastly, there were the variations on a theme of Rameau, in which Paul Dukas once again revealed his great mastery of his craft. There were moments when even Rameau himself would have had trouble recognizing his theme in such a thicket of festoons.

However, I feel that Dukas was simply trying to solve a few ephemeral puzzles. He managed to cope with the most difficult; we ought perhaps to regard these variations as evidence of his curiosity with regard to the interplay of their forms. In my opinion, I prefer Dukas without Rameau.

In all these very different works, Monsieur E. Risler displayed a totally admirable variety and surety of execution.

NOTE FOR *À LA SOCIÉTÉ NATIONALE*

This quotation is a parody of the last line of Alfred de Vigny's poem *Le Cor.* We have found no other reference to this poet in Debussy's letters or articles.

"Dieu! que le son du cor est triste au fond des bois."

(God! how sad is the sound of the horn in the depths of the woods.)

S.I.M.[1]

15 mai 1913

CONCERTS COLONNE

La douceur hypocrite d'avril termine la saison des concerts dominicaux. Nous ne reparlerons donc plus des Concerts Colonne, et laisserons se reposer la gloire restée,—avouons-le—les bras un peu ballants pendant cette dernière saison. Nul besoin de *"trompettes tout au haut d'or pâmé sur les vélins,"* ou plutôt l'or des trompettes se pâma sur les anciens nom pour ne pas se tromper.

Laissons aussi le déplorable "Cas Rust" qui mit aux prises ceux qui aiment la musique, sans morgue ni mauvaise humeur, avec ceux qui prennent soin des maîtres en préparant leur propre apologie—c'est excellent pour donner le ton aux "dernières paroles."

Le seul côté ironique dans cette histoire est qu'elle rajeunit Beethoven!... Il y prend figure de jeune révolutionnaire auquel on oppose le vieux professeur qui-ne-se-trompe-jamais. Pour un peu on lui reprocherait d'avoir écrit les derniers quatuors. N'insistons pas! la race des "Rust" est innombrable, en ce qu'elle représente ce besoin de médiocrité qui ne mourra jamais. Constatons tranquillement qu'il y a, de temps en temps, quelques Beethoven pour remettre toute musique au point.

D'autre part, plus nous allons, plus on dirait vraiment que le fait d'aimer la musique n'est possible qu'en de certains milieux, délicats et filtrés? Ce n'est pourtant pas l'aimer que de n'aimer qu'une façon d'en faire? Et pourquoi tant d'hypocrisie? Ne peut-on admettre simplement qu'on aime très peu la musique sur notre vaste terre? Est-ce d'avoir trop sollicité cet amour que la musique finira, non pas par en mourir, mais par se raréfier jusqu'à devenir une occupation aussi parfaitement chimérique que la recherche de la pierre philosophale?

A une époque comme la notre, où le génie des mécaniques atteint à une perfection insoupçonnée, on entend les oeuvres les plus célèbres aussi facilement que l'on prend un bock, ça ne coûte même que dix centimes, comme les balances automatiques. Comment ne pas craindre cette domestication du son, cette magie qui tiendra dans un disque que chacun éveillera à son gré. N'y a-t-il pas là une cause de déperdition des forces mystérieuses d'un art qu'on pouvait croire indestructible?

S.I.M.

15 May 1913

CONCERTS COLONNE

A hypocritically clement April has brought the Sunday concert season to a close. We shall therefore speak no more of the Concerts Colonne, and can allow them to rest on their laurels—not, let us admit, a very good crop this past season. No need for *"high trumpets swooning gold upon the vellum,"* or rather, the golden trumpets were blown for a lot of old names.

We pass over the deplorable "Rust Affair" that set those who love music without rancor or ill-temper against those who make it their business to look after the old masters by formulating appropriate apologies —a good way to get in the last word.

The only ironic note in this story is that it rejuvenated Beethoven. He comes out of it looking like a young revolutionary facing up to an elderly, hidebound professor. People were almost ready to reproach him for having composed his last quartets. But enough! The Rusts are an immense family and represent that eternal yearning for the second rate. We can happily cherish the thought that from time to time a Beethoven appears to set all music to rights.

On the other hand, must we admit that the love of music is possible only in certain delicate, purified circles? Does one truly like it if one likes only one way of performing it? Why so much hypocrisy? Can we not simply acknowledge the fact that in our great world music is liked very little? And because we have tried too hard to make it liked, might music not finally end up—not dying out—but becoming so rarefied that it begins to become as chimerical an occupation as the search for the philosopher's stone?

In an age like our own, when engineering genius has attained such unheard-of perfection, we can hear the most famous pieces of music as easily as we can order a beer—and it costs a mere ten centimes, like getting weighed! How can we help but fear this sonic domestication, this magic captured on a recording that anyone can evoke at will? May this not lead to a cheapening of the mysterious powers of an art hitherto regarded as indestructible?

NOTES FOR *CONCERTS COLONNE*

In the summer of 1913, Debussy composed the *Trois Poèmes de Stéphane Mallarmé,* returning once again to the poet he had used only twice before: *Apparition* in 1884 and *L'Après-midi d'un Faune* in 1894. The quotation here is from the last stanza of Mallarmé's *Hommage* (à Richard Wagner).

[1] Société internationale de musique.

Comment ne pas regretter les délicieux coureurs de route, diseurs de ballades, ménestrels au bon gosier qui gardaient ingénument la beauté des légendes, sans songer à en tirer d'autre profit que le pain quotidien. Maintenant on en tires des opéras où il y a assurément plus de musique, c'est-à-dire qu'elle fait plus de bruit; cet inconvénient est compensé par une grande richesse de mise en scène.

Nous avons aussi le "drame lyrique" qui emprunte également aux légendes.... Reste à savoir si nos âmes sont suffisament légendaires? En somme nous n'avons peut-être pas encore trouvé la forme lyrique répondant à notre présent état d'esprit.

L'erreur fondamentale vient de ce qu'il fallait considérer Wagner comme la géniale conclusion d'une époque et non comme un chemin ouvert sur l'Avenir! Rendre le développement symphonique responsable de l'action dramatique n'était qu'un pis-aller qui n'a jamais bien servi que Wagner et la pensée allemande. En l'adoptant, notre besoin de clarté ne pouvait que s'y affaiblir et même s'y noyer.

C'est pourquoi nous piétinons sans savoir exactement où nous allons. Plusieurs routes s'offrent pourtant à nous, où nous pourrions retrouver la trace, encore fraîche, de ce que nous avons égaré de la pensée française.

Nous ne parlerons de la musique dite "futuriste" que pour fixer une date.... Elle prétend rassembler les bruits divers des modernes capitales dans une totale symphonie, depuis les pistons des locomotives jusqu'à la clarine des raccommodeurs de porcelaine. C'est très pratique quant au recrutement de l'orchestre; seulement ça atteindra-t-il jamais à la sonorité, déjà satisfaisante, d'une usine métallurgique en plein travail? Attendons sans sourire, en pensant quel effet pourrait bien produire le finale du *Crépuscule des Dieux* sur un de ces ménestrels que nous évoquions tout à l'heure.

Ces réflexions manquent de gaieté, et il est étrange que les fantaisies du Progrés vous amènent à devenir conservateur. Qu'on se garde bien d'en conclure à une déchéance quelconque. Mais prenons garde à la mécanique qui a déjà dévoré tant de belles choses. Et si l'on veut absolument satisfaire ce monstre, abandonnons le vieux répertoire!

How we miss those entrancing wandering minstrels, those ballad-eers and full-throated traveling singers who innocently preserved the beauty of old legends without thought of any profit other than their daily bread. Nowadays, operas are based on them which certainly contain more music, that is, it makes more noise; an inconvenience made up for by a plethora of stage effects.

And we have the "lyric drama," also based on old legends... it remains to be seen whether our souls are legendary enough or not? In short, we have perhaps not yet found the lyric form best suited to the modern state of mind.

Our basic error has been to consider Wagner not as the genial end of an era but as a path toward the future! Making symphonic development responsible for dramatic action is a makeshift solution that was of service only to Wagner and German thought. In taking it over, we have only contaminated our need for clarity and eventually destroyed it.

That is why we are now plodding along without any precise notion where we are headed. Yet several routes are open to us along which we may find still fresh traces of where we have departed from French thought.

We are not speaking of "futurist" music, so called merely to fix a date.... It pretends to unite the various noises of the modern big city into a symphonic whole, from locomotive pistons to the porcelain repairer's bell. It's a practical method of recruiting orchestral personnel, but can it really ever compete with the already quite satisfactory sonority of a steel mill operating at full blast? We will bide our time, musing on the effect the final scene in *Götterdämmerung* would have had on one of those aforementioned minstrels.

These are far from happy thoughts, and it is strange how conservative the fantasies of progress tend to make us. Let us beware of becoming decadent, and of machinery, which has already devoured so many lovely things. And if we are truly bent on satisfying that monster, let's turn over some of the old repertoire!

———————

Part III
Compositions Based on Literary Texts

Chronological List of Compositions Based on Literary Texts

DANIEL
cantata for 3 soloists and orchestra

> *Date:* c. 1881
> *Source:* Emile Cicile
> *Manuscripts:* (1) sketch in a private collection in the United
States; (2) "Air de Balthazar," location unknown
> *Comments:* The text, a play in three scenes, is unpublished.
It was assigned for the Prix de Rome competition of 1868.

> *Opening lines:* "Versez que de l'ivresse
>   Aux accents d'allégresse
>   Circulent les doux feux.
>   Versez, et que l'aurore
>   Demain éclair encore
>   Nos ris et nos jeux."

(Intoxicate him, with lilting accents sound, let the sweet fires
descend and let tomorrow's dawn relume our laughter and our
games.)

HÉLÈNE
lyrical scene for soprano, chorus, and orchestra

> *Date:* c. 1881–1882
> *Source:* Leconte de Lisle, *Poèmes antiques,* édition nouvelle.
Alphonse Lemerre, Paris 1874, p. 89.
> *Manuscript:* fragment in a private collection in Paris
> *Comment:* At the end of the last page of the manuscript is
written: "Qui te l'a dis / Ce mot si doux je t'aime"
> (Who said to you / That word so tender I love you)

> *Opening lines:* "Franchis les mers Icariennes
>   Jeune Hélios au char doré
>   Et que les lyres Déliennes
>   Chante sur un mode sacré."

(Cross the Icarian seas, young Helos, with your gilded char-
iot, and let the lyres of Delos chant in sacred mode.)

SALUT PRINTEMPS
for women's chorus and orchestra

Date: May 1882

Source: Comte de Ségur

Manuscripts: (1) orchestral score in the Bibliothèque Nationale, Paris; (2) score for voice and piano on deposit in The Pierpont Morgan Library, New York

Publisher: for voice and piano, for chorus and orchestra, Choudens, Paris 1928

Comments: Both manuscripts are entitled *Le Printemps*.

The text was assigned for the preliminary examination for the Prix de Rome competition of 1882.

Opening lines: "Salut printemps, jeune saison
Dieu rend aux plaines leur couronne.
La sève ardente qui bouillonne
S'épanche et brise sa prison.
Bois et champs sont en floraison
Un monde invisible bourdonne
L'eau sur le caillou résonne
Court et dit sa clair chanson."

(Hail Spring, youthful season, let God grant the prairies their crown. May the ardent rising sap swell up and burst its prison. Woods and fields are in flower and an invisible world hums busily. The water runs resoundingly over the pebble and sings its clear song.)

INTERMEZZO
suite for cello and orchestra

Date: 21 June 1882

Source: Henri Heine, *Poèmes et Légendes, L'Intermezzo*, traduit par Gérard de Nerval, Nouvelle édition. Michel Lévy, Paris 1874, Canto XXXVIII, p. 104.

Manuscripts: (1) orchestral score, location unknown; (2) piano 4 hands, dated as above, location unknown; (3) score for piano and cello in a private collection in the United States

Publisher: for cello and piano, edited by Gregor Piatigorsky, Elkan-Vogel, Philadelphia 1944 (later withdrawn from publication)

Comment: This work was inspired by the following passage from Canto XXXVIII of *Intermezzo,* by Henri Heine, written on the title page:

"La mystérieuse île des esprits se dessinait vaguement aux lueurs du clair de lune; là, resonnaient des sons délicieux, là flottaient des danses nébuleuses; les sons devenait de plus en plus suave, la ronde tourbillonait plus entraînante."

(The mysterious isle of the spirits loomed dim in the moonlight; there, delectable sounds echoed, there, floated nebulous dances; the sounds grew ever more pleasing, the whirling dance grew more lively.)

CHOEUR DES BRISES
for woman's voice and orchestra

Date: c. 1882
Source: unknown
Manuscript: fragment at the Memorial Library of Music, Stanford University, Stanford, California

Opening lines: "Reveillez-vous, arbres des bois
Tressaillez tous à la fois
   forêts profondes
Et loin des rayons embrasés
À la fraîcheur de vos baisers
   livrez vos ondes."

(Awake, trees of the woods; bend together, dense forests, and far from the fiery rays abandon your movement to the cool of your kisses.)

HYMNIS
lyrical scene for soprano, tenor, and piano

Date: c. 1882
Source: Théodore de Banville, *Hymnis,* comédie lyrique en un acte. Tresse (éditeur), Paris 1880, pp. 4 and 37–39.
Manuscripts: (1) fragment in the Fondation Martin Bodmer, Cologny-Genève, Switzerland; (2) *Ode Bachique* in the Toscanini Memorial Archives, New York Public Library, Lincoln Center, New York; (3) further fragments, location unknown

Comments: The *Ode Bachique,* from the final scene, bears the dedication: "à Madame Vasnier."

Opening lines: "Il dort encore, une main sur la lyre!
        Il ne verra ni mon triste délire
        Ni ces longs pleurs qui tombent de mes
        yeux."

Ode Bachique "A toi Lyaeos
        Glorieux Bacchos [*sic*]!
        Dans l'ardeur qui me déchire
        Le coeur plein de toi
        Je t'offre, ô mon roi
        Ma fureur et mon délire."

(Still he sleeps, one hand upon the lyre! He shall see neither my sorrowful frenzy nor the slow tears streaming from my eyes.)

Ode Bachique
(To thee, Lyaeos, glorious Bacchos [*sic*]. In the ardor that transports me, my heart filled with thee, I offer to you, my king, my wrath and my frenzy.)

LE TRIOMPHE DE BACCHUS
orchestral suite

Date: c. 1882

Source: Théodore de Banville, *Les Cariatides,* Les Stalactites, *Le Triomphe de Bacchos* [*sic*] *à son retour des Indes.* G. Charpentier, Paris 1879, pp. 267–269.

Manuscripts: Allegro and *Andante cantabile,* for piano 4 hands (incomplete), in The Pierpont Morgan Library, New York

Publisher: with orchestration by M.-F. Gaillard, Choudens, Paris 1928

First performance: by M.-F. Gaillard, with l'Orchestre de la Société des Concerts du Conservatoire, in the Salle Pleyel, 2 April 1928

Comments: This work, inspired by Banville's poem, was intended to be in four parts, as noted on the title page of the manuscript: 1. Divertissement, 2. Andante, 3. Scherzo, 4. Marche et Bacchanale.

INVOCATION
for men's chorus and orchestra

>*Date:* 5–11 May 1883
>*Source:* Alphonse de Lamartine, *Oeuvres de Lamartine, Harmonies poétiques et religieuses.* Hachette et Cie—Furne, Jouvet et Cie, Paris 1879, p. 40.
>*Manuscripts:* (1) orchestral score in the Bibliothèque Nationale, Paris; (2) for men's chorus and piano 4 hands on deposit in The Pierpont Morgan Library, New York
>*Publisher:* for voice and piano, 1928; for men's chorus and orchestra, Choudens, Paris 1956
>*First performance:* by M.-F. Gaillard, with l'Orchestre de la Société des Concerts du Conservatoire and the Choeur mixte de Paris, in the Salle Pleyel, 2 April 1928
>*Comments:* The text was assigned for the preliminary examination for the Prix de Rome competition of 1883. Debussy was classed fourth.

>>*Opening lines:* "Élevez-vous voix de mon âme
>>Avec l'aurore, avec la nuit.
>>Élancez-vous comme la flamme
>>Répandez-vous comme le bruit!
>>Flottez sur l'aile des nuages,
>>Mêlez-vous aux vents, aux orages,
>>Au tonnerre, au fracas des flots."

(Voice of my soul, arise with the dawn, the night. Stream like flame, expand like sound! Soar on the wing of the clouds, mingle with the winds and the storms, the thunder and the crashing surf.)

LE GLADIATEUR
cantata for 3 soloists and orchestra

>*Date:* 19 May–13 June 1883
>*Source:* Émile Moreau, text published by the Institut de France, 1883
>*Manuscripts:* (1) complete score in the Bibliothèque Nationale, Paris; (2) nine pages in a private collection in Paris
>*First performance:* at a session of the Académie des Beaux-Arts in the Institut de France, 23 June 1883

Comments: The text was assigned for the competition for the Grand Prix de Rome of 1883. Debussy was awarded a Premier Second Grand Prix.

A reviewer, writing in *L'Art musical,* 28 June 1883, found it regrettable that the Institut was not able to award two first prizes as they found Debussy's compositions equal in all respects to that of the winner, Paul Vidal.

The work is unpublished.

Opening lines: "Mort aux Romains, tirez jusqu'au dernier.
Victoire où suis-je?
Rien qu'un rêve.
Voici le châtiment
D'une gloire trop brève."

(Death to the Romans, fire to the last man. O Victory, am I but a dream? Behold the punishment for too fleeting a glory.)

DIANE AU BOIS
comédie heroïque

Date: Paris, 1883–1884; Rome, 1885–1886

Source: Théodore de Banville, *Comédies.* G. Charpentier, Paris 1879, pp. 163–220.

Manuscript: Duo between Eros and Diane, for soprano, tenor, and piano, on deposit in The Pierpont Morgan Library, New York

First performance: B.B.C., Third Program, 9 November 1968

Comments: Begun at the Conservatoire, taken up again while at the Villa Medici as a possible first *envoi* from Rome, Debussy finally abandoned the work which he had planned to orchestrate.

On the back of the last page of this manuscript, Debussy copied out in pencil the three stanzas of Musset's poem *Chanson.* He used the first two stanzas for his song *Chanson espagnole.*

LE PRINTEMPS
for 4-part chorus and orchestra

Date: 10–16 May 1884
Source: Jules Barbier, *La Gerbe, Poèsies 1842–1883*, no. XXIV, *Le Printemps*, traduit d'Horace. Alphonse Lemerre, Paris 1884, p. 69.
Manuscripts: (1) orchestral score in the Bibliothèque Nationale, Paris; (2) incomplete piano and vocal score on deposit in The Pierpont Morgan Library, New York; (3) fragment in a private collection in Paris
Comments: The text was assigned for the preliminary examination for the Prix de Rome competition of 1884. Debussy was classed fourth.
The work is unpublished.
Opening lines: "L'aimable printemps ramène dans la plaine
 Zéphyr avec les oiseaux.
 Le navire sur le sable tend le cable
 Qui le traîne vers les eaux."

(Gentle spring draws Zephyr to the plain as it does the birds. The ship on the strand spells out its rope to the waters.)

L'ENFANT PRODIGUE
cantata for soprano, tenor, bass, and orchestra   .

Date: 24 May–18 June 1884 (first version); 1906–1908 (second version)
Source: Edouard Guinand, text published by the Institut de France, 1884
Manuscripts: (1) first version complete; (2) *Cortège* and *Air de danse*, 1906; (3) *Récit* and *Air d'Azaël*, 1908; in the Bibliothèque Nationale, Paris
Dedication: "À mon cher maître Ernest Guiraud"
Publisher: first version, for voice and piano, Durand, Schoenewerck & Cie, Paris 1884; second version, for orchestra and for voice and piano, Durand & Cie, Paris 1908
First performance: at the Institut de France, 27 June 1907, with Rose Caron (Lia), Van Dyck (Azaël), and Taskin (Siméon)
Comments: The text was assigned for the Prix de Rome competition of 1884. Debussy was awarded the Premier Grand Prix.

A critic writes in l'Art musical, *15 July 1884:*

"M. Debussy, qui a obtenu le premier prix, a bravement sauté à pieds joints sur l'émolliente poésie et a trouvé des accents émus, des pages d'une force très appréciable; en faisant, pour ainsi dire, abstraction de la poésie qui lui était offerte, il a osé chercher la couleur de la poésie."

(Monsieur Debussy, who was awarded first prize, has leapt audaciously with both feet into the soft and yielding poetry and has found there moving tones and pages of considerable strength; by, as it were, making abstract the poetry he has been provided, he has dared bring out its color.)

Debussy wrote to Jacques Durand on 17 July 1907:

"M. H. J. Wood veut décidément jouer *L'Enfant prodigue* et, à ce propos, il me semble qu'il vaudrait mieux que je le réorchestre... étant à peu près sûr que l'orchestre 'original' sent 'la loge,' 'le conservatoire,' et l'ennui."

(Mr. H. J. Wood truly wants to perform *L'Enfant prodigue* and in that regard, I feel it would be best were I to reorchestrate it... since I'm fairly sure that the "original" is redolent of the "studio," the "conservatory," and boredom.)

Then on 18 June 1908:

"J'ai vu Caplet qui veut bien m'aider un peu à revernir *L'Enfant prodigue*; cela ira donc assez vite et nous serons débarassé de cet illustre revenant."

(I've seen Caplet, who is willing to lend a hand in revarnishing *L'Enfant prodigue* so that it will be done fairly quickly and we'll be rid of this illustrious visitor from the past.)

ZULÉIMA
symphonic ode for chorus and orchestra

Date: 1885–1886
Source: Georges Boyer, *Zuléima,* after *Almanzor* by Henri Heine
Manuscript: not found
First performance: at the Académie des Beaux-Arts, December 1886
Comments: This was Debussy's first *envoi* from Rome.

In a letter to M. Vasnier, 19 October 1886, he wrote:
"*Zuléima* est morte et ce n'est certes pas moi qui la ferai res-
susciter, je ne veux plus en entendre parler, n'étant pas du tout
le genre de musique que je veux faire, j'en veux une qui soit
assez souple, assez heurté pour s'adapter aux mouvements lyriques de l'âme, aux caprices de la rêverie."

(*Zuléima* is dead and I'm certainly not going to be the one
who revives her, I don't want to hear about it ever again, for it's
not at all the kind of music I want to compose. I want music that
is supple, with sufficient contrast so that it can accommodate
itself to the soul's lyrical movements, to the caprices of reverie.)

LA DAMOISELLE ÉLUE
poème lyrique d'après D.-G. Rossetti, traduction française de
Gabriel Sarrazin

Date: 1887–1888; revised orchestration, 1902
Source: Gabriel Sarrazin, *Poètes modernes de l'Angleterre*, Dante
Gabriel Rossetti, *La Damoiselle bénie*. Paul Ollendorff, Paris 1885,
pp. 263–269
Manuscripts: (1) undated sketches, fourteen pages of music,
in the Bibliothèque Nationale, Paris; (2) piano and vocal score,
1888, in The Pierpont Morgan Library, New York; (3) undated
score (1902) for voice and orchestra, in the Bibliothèque Nationale; (4) piano and vocal score for the "Récitante," altered and
simplified, location unknown
Dedication: "à Paul Dukas"
Publisher: piano and vocal score (limited edition of 160
copies, with cover by Maurice Denis), Librairie de l'Art
indépendant, Paris 1893; orchestral score, A. Durand & Fils,
Paris 1903
First performance: the Société Nationale de Musique, under
the direction of Gabriel Marie, with Julia Robert (La Damoiselle)
and Thérèse Roger (the Récitante), in the Salle Erard, 8 April
1893
Comments: The 1888 manuscript bears the following inscription at the bottom of the last page:

"Ce manuscrit est offert à Bailly en souvenir de beaucoup de
5ʰ à 7ʰ qui me furent et me serons toujours de précieuse
esthétique, et aussi pour ma sincère amitié."

Claude Debussy
Mai / 93

(This manuscript is presented to Bailly for the many afternoon
meetings that were for me, and that will always be, so
esthetically precious, and also out of my sincere friendship.)

This work, Debussy's third *envoi* from Rome, was composed
in Paris after his return from the Villa Medici. He made many
changes in Sarrazin's translation of the poem. The first change is
in the title, where "élue" is used instead of "bénie"; other
changes occur in every stanza of the poem. Sarrazin omitted
stanzas 4, 6, 9, 11, 14, and 16 from Rossetti's text. Debussy
further omitted stanzas 3, 4, 11, and 13 from Sarrazin's text
(stanzas 3, 5, 17, and 19 in Rossetti's text). The three versions of
this poem are given in Appendix B.

In a letter to Chausson, 3 September 1893, Debussy wrote:

"Reçu une lettre de V. d'Indy, toute amicale, et des éloges à
faire rougir les lys qui dorment entre les doigts de la Damoiselle
élue."

(I've had a letter from V. d'Indy, very friendly, so full of
praise it would make the lilies resting in the Damoiselle élue's
fingers blush.)

AXEL
opera

Date: c. 1888
Source: Villiers de L'Isle Adam, *Axel*, in *La jeune France*, No-
vember, December 1885; February, March, April, June 1886
Manuscript: one scene in an unknown private collection
Comment: Vallas mentions this manuscript but gives no fur-
ther indication of its contents or location.

RODRIGUE ET CHIMÈNE
opera in 3 acts

Date: 1890–1892
Source: Catulle Mendés
Manuscripts: short score and working draft of Acts I and III, and piano-vocal score of Act II, dated 1892, on deposit in The Pierpont Morgan Library, New York
Dedication: "à Mademoiselle Gabrielle Dupont, avril 90"
Comments: Debussy undertook to write this work at the request of the author, a man of influence in literary and publishing circles, whom he was anxious to please. He took a dislike to the pomposity of the text and abandoned the work, saying that it had accidentally been burned.

To Gustave Charpentier, he wrote:
"C'est tellement contraire à tout ce que je désirais exprimer... le côté traditionnaliste de ce sujet appelle des musiques qui ne sont pas les miennes."
(It's so much the opposite of everything I wanted to express... the traditionalist aspect of this subject calls for a kind of music that isn't mine.)

To Robert Godet, 30 January 1892:
"Ma vie est tristement fiévreuse à cause de cet opéra, où tout est contre moi, et tombent douloureusement les pauvres petites plumes dont vous aimiez les couleurs."
(Owing to this opera, my life is dolefully frenetic, everything is against me, and pitiful little pens, whose colors you enjoyed, fall sadly down.)

PRÉLUDE À "L'APRÈS-MIDI D'UN FAUNE"
for orchestra

Date: 1892–1894
Source: Stéphane Mallarmé, *L'Après-midi d'un Faune*, Églogue par Stéphane Mallarmé, nouvelle édition. Léon Vanier, Paris 1887, pp. 11–16.
Manuscripts: (1) orchestral score, dated 1892 on title page and "sept. 1894" on last page, in the Bibliothèque Nationale, Paris; (2) particel, with dedication: "à ma chère petite Gaby—la vive affection de son dévoué Claude Debussy, Octobre 1899," on

deposit in The Pierpont Morgan Library, New York; (3) transcription for two pianos in the Bibliothèque Nationale

Dedication: "à Raymond Bonheur"

Publisher: orchestral score, score for two pianos, E. Fromont, Paris 1895

First performance: at a concert of the Société Nationale de Musique conducted by Gustave Doret in the Salle d'Harcourt, 22 December 1894; as a ballet with choreography by Vaslav Nijinsky, at the Théâtre du Châtelet, 29 May 1912

Comments: In a letter to the critic Willy (Henry Gauthier-Villars), 10 October 1896, Debussy writes:

"Le 'Prélude à l'Après-midi d'un Faune'? Cher Monsieur, c'est peut-être ce qui est resté au fond de la flûte du faune? Plus précisément, c'est l'impression générale du poème, car à le suivre de plus près, la musique s'éssouflerait ainsi qu'un cheval de fiacre concurrant pour le Grand Prix avec un pur sang. C'est aussi le dédain de cette 'science de castors' qui alourdit nos plus fiers cerveaux; puis c'est sans respect pour le ton! Et plutôt dans un mode qui essaye de contenir toutes les nuances, ce qui est très logiquement démonstrable.

"Maintenant cela suit tout de même le mouvement ascendant du poème, et c'est le décor merveilleusement décrit au texte avec, en plus, l'humanité qu'apportent trente-deux violonistes levés de trop bonne heure! La fin, c'est le dernier vers prolongé:

"Couple adieux, je vais voir ce que tu devins."

(The "Prélude à l'Après-midi d'un Faune"? My dear sir, perhaps it's what is left behind of the dream created by the last notes of the faun's flute? To be more precise, it's the over-all impression of the poem. (If one followed it more closely, the music would pant along like an old carriage horse competing with a thoroughbred in the Grand Prix.) And it's also contempt for the "beaver mentality" that has weighted down the best of our thinkers; and it's without respect for the key. And it's also done in a mode that attempts to embrace every nuance; which can be demonstrated very logically.

Now, it all follows the rising movement of the poem, nonetheless, and it's the wonderfully described setting of the text with, in addition, the human touch provided by thirty-two violinists who have gotten up too early! The end is the prolongation of the last line:

Couple farewell, I'm off to see what became of you.)

Note: Mallarmé's last line reads:
"Couple adieux; je vais voir l'ombre que tu devins."
(Couple farewell; I'm off to see the shadow you became.)

PELLÉAS ET MÉLISANDE
opera in 5 acts

Date: 1893–1902

Source: Maurice Maeterlinck, *Pelléas et Mélisande,* troisième édition. Paul Lacomblez, Bruxelles 1892.

Manuscripts: (1) fragments of Acts I, II, IV, and V, dated "juin–juillet 1895," in a private collection in Paris; (2) last scene of Act IV, dated "septembre–octobre 1893," on deposit in The Pierpont Morgan Library, New York; (3) Act IV Scene 4 complete, and fragments of Scenes 1 and 2 dated "September–October '93. May '95." in the Bibliothèque Nationale, Paris; (4) short score on deposit inThe Pierpont Morgan Library, dated "September 1893–1901"; (5) complete orchestral score in the Bibliothèque Nationale; (6) score for voice and piano dispersed, Act V and fragments of Act IV in the Bibliothèque Nationale.

Dedication: "à la mémoire de Georges Hartmann et en témoignage de profonde affection à André Messager"
(To the memory of Georges Hartmann and in token of profound affection to André Messager)

Publisher: piano and vocal score, 1902; Interludes only, 1905; full score, A. Durand & Fils, Paris 1907

First performance: at the Opéra-Comique, with André Messager conducting, Mary Garden as Mélisande and Jean Perrier as Pelléas, 30 April 1902

Comments: Debussy attended the first performance of the play at the Théâtre des Bouffes-Parisiens, 17 May 1893. Before the end of the year, he had gone to Ghent to ask Maeterlinck's permission to use his play as a libretto for an opera. He received permission not only to use the play but also to make numerous changes in the text. The libretto was published with the subtitle: "tiré du théâtre de Maurice Maeterlinck" (adapted from the dramatic work of Maurice Maeterlinck).

The answer to Debussy's quick decision to use this text may be found in an interview with his former professor Ernest Guiraud, which took place in October of 1889:

"Guiraud: Quel poète pourra vous fournir un poème?

"Debussy: Celui qui, disant les chose à demi, me permettra de greffer mon rêve sur le sien; qui concevra des personnages dont l'histoire et la demeure ne seront d'aucun temps, d'aucun lieu; qui ne m'imposera pas, despotiquement, 'la scène à faire' et me laissera libre, ici où là, d'avoir plus d'art que lui, et de parachever son ouvrage."

(Guiraud: What poet could provide you with a text?

Debussy: The poet who, by saying things only halfway, would enable me to graft my dream onto his own; who would create characters in a plot and setting that would be timeless, indefinite as to place; who would not burden me dictatorially with a fixed "scene to set," but would leave me free here and there to employ more art than he, to put the finishing touch on his work.)

Numerous quotations from this opera are to be found in Debussy's letters. An example is in the letter to Robert Godet, 6 October 1916.

LA SAULAIE
for baritone and orchestra

Date: 1896–1900

Source: La Saulaie, poème de Dante Gabriel Rossetti, traduction de Pierre Louÿs, in *l'Esprit français,* 10 September 1931 (from *The House of Life,* Sonnet XXIV, *Willowwood*)

Manuscript: one page (numbered 4) in the Memorial Library of Music, Stanford University, Stanford, California

Comments: The fragment begins with the fifth line (the fourth of Rossetti's poem).

Opening lines: "Mais il touchait son luth où j'entendais passer
Des paroles mystérieuses.
Nos yeux se rencontraient en silence
Dans le miroir de l'eau profonde.
Et peu à peu son luth devint la voix..."

(But touched his lute wherein was audible
The certain secret thing he had to tell:
Only our mirrored eyes met silently
In the low wave; and that sound came to be
The passionate voice...)

The text of Sonnets XXIV, XXV, and XVII (1870 edition; XLIX, L, LII of 1881 edition), translated by Pierre Louÿs, copied out by Debussy, is in the Bibliothèque Nationale. (These texts are given in *Correspondances de Claude Debussy et Pierre Louÿs*, pp. 190–191.)

In a letter to Robert Godet, 5 January 1900, Debussy wrote of La Saulaie:

"C'est très beau, très 'en vie,' on peut même y laisser un peu de la sienne avec quelques cheveux."

(It is very beautiful, very "full of life," one can even put one's own into it with a few setbacks.)

LES CHANSONS DE BILITIS, MUSIQUE DE SCÈNE
for 2 flutes, 2 harps, and celesta (poems by Pierre Louÿs)

Date: 1900–1901
Source: Pierre Louÿs, *Les Chansons de Bilitis*—traduites du grec par Pierre Louÿs, neuvième édition. Société du Mercure de France, Paris 1898, pp. 29, 49, 61, 69, 79, 99, 139, 225, 239, 257, 301, 313
Manuscript: (1) the original, given to Pierre Louÿs, has not been found; (2) incomplete score, celesta part missing, in the Bibliothèque Nationale, Paris
Publisher: with celesta part realized by Arthur Hoérée, Éditions Jobert, Paris 1971
First performance: at the Salle des Fêtes du *Journal*, 7 February 1901 (Nos. IV and XI were not included)
Comments: The poems are entitled as follows; the numbering is Debussy's:

I. Chant pastoral	VII. Le Tombeau sans nom
II. Les Comparaisons	VIII. Les Courtisanes égyptiennes
III. Les Contes	IX. L'Eau pur du bassin
IV. Chansons	X. La Danseuse aux crotales
V. La Partie d'osselets	XI. Le Souvenir de Mnasidika
VI. Bilitis	XII. La Pluie au matin

Debussy used music from six of these pieces for the *Six Epigraphes antiques*.

The following is taken from a review of the first performance that appeared in Le Journal, *8 February 1901:*

"Les *Chansons de Bilitis,* accompagnées de tableaux vivants dont la mise au point avait été minutieusement surveillée par Pierre Louÿs lui-même, et d'une musique captivante de M. de Bussy, ont obtenu un succés d'enthousiasme.... Une musique gracieuse, ingénieusement archaïque, accompagnait la voix de Mlle Milton et formait avec elle un rythme berceur, dont le charme s'ajoutait aux beautés antiques du poème."

(The *Chansons de Bilitis,* accompanied by *tableaux vivants* painstakingly arranged by Pierre Louÿs himself with captivating music by Monsieur de Bussy, was given an enthusiastic reception.... Graceful music, cleverly archaic, accompanied Mlle Milton's voice, and the whole created a soothing rhythm, the charm of which added to the antique beauties of the text.)

LE DIABLE DANS LE BEFFROI
conte musical in 2 acts and 3 tableaux

Date: 1902–1911

Source: Charles Baudelaire, *Oeuvres complètes de Charles Baudelaire,* vol. VI, *Nouvelles histoires extraordinaires,* par Edgar Poe, traduction de Charles Baudelaire. Michel Lévy, Paris 1869, pp. 249–253.

Manuscripts: (1) sketches without words, entitled "Notes pour L.D.d.l.B.—1ᵉʳ cahier. Aoüt 1903," in a private collection in Paris; (2) four pages corresponding to the first tableau, with violin solo, in a private collection in Paris

Text: six pages entitled "Notes pour *Le Diable dans le Beffroi,*" dated 25 August 1903, in a private collection in Paris

Comments: Debussy's text is a free adaptation of Poe's tale.

Although he signed a contract in 1903 with Durand in view of a production at the Opéra-Comique, signed a contract in 1908 with the Metropolitan Opera for a production of this work and *La Chute de la Maison Usher,* and the two works were listed in the program for the 1911–1912 season of the Opéra-Comique, neither work was ever completed.

In a letter to P.-J. Toulet, 28 August 1903, Debussy wrote:

"J'ai travaillé au *Diable dans le Beffroi,* excusez-m'en et n'y voyez aucun dépit, mais simplement le besoin de réaliser, musicalement, certains projets, qui, à les différer plus longtemps, me deviendrait un gêne."

(I've been working on *The Devil in the Belfry*, so forgive me and don't take it as neglect, but really as a need to succeed musically with some plans which, were they to be put off any longer, would begin to haunt me.)

To Robert Godet, 6 February 1911, he wrote:

"Les deux contes de Poe s'en trouvent remis à je ne peux dire quand!... je n'en suis pas fâché, à cause de beaucoup 'd'accents' qui ne me plaisent pas encore et d'une mise en place insuffisament rigoureuse, notamment pour *Le Diable dans le Beffroi,* dans lequel je voudrais arriver à une écriture chorale extrêmement simple, mais pourtant extrêmement mobile."

(The two Poe tales have been postponed until I don't know when!... I'm sorry, because of the many "accents" that continue to displease me and because of the insufficiently rigorous foundation, especially with regard to *The Devil in the Belfry,* in which I would like to manage an extremely simple and yet extremely mobile kind of choral writing.)

LE ROI LEAR, MUSIQUES POUR
for orchestra

1. Fanfare   2. Le Sommeil de Lear

Date: 1904–1906

Source: William Shakespeare, *Le Roi Lear,* traduit par Pierre Loti et Émile Vedel. Calmann-Lévy, Paris (1904).

Manuscript: not seen since its sale at auction in 1933

Publisher: with orchestration by Roger-Ducasse, Éditions Jobert, Paris 1926

First performance: for piano, by Léon Vallas at a meeting of "Musique vivante," 22 October 1926; for orchestra, at the Concerts Pasdeloup, conducted by A. Wolf, 30 October 1926

Comments: Debussy had suggested to the producer Antoine that he compose music for the forthcoming production of *Le Roi Lear.* The work was not finished on time and was finally abandoned. Seven parts were projected.

LA CHUTE DE LA MAISON USHER
opera in 3 scenes after Edgar Poe

Date: 1908–1917

Source: Charles Baudelaire, *Oeuvres complètes de Charles Baude-laire*, vol. VI, *Nouvelles histoires extraordinaires*, par Edgar Poe, traduction de Charles Baudelaire. Michel Lévy, Paris 1869, pp. 129–159.

Manuscripts: (1) early version of first scene in a private collection in Paris; (2) later version of first scene, for voice and piano, entitled "Etudes pour Fall H.U.," and single page entitled "Ce qui sera peut-être le prélude à *La Chute de la Maison Usher*," in the Bibliothèque Nationale, Paris; (3) two pages from first scene, location unknown

Texts: (1) first version in three scenes, dated August 1909–June 1910, in the Bibliothèque Nationale; (2) another version in three scenes in the Humanities Research Center, University of Texas at Austin, Texas; (3) single page, dated "VIII–09" in a private collection in France; (4) final version in two scenes in the Bibliothèque Nationale

Publisher: transcription for voice and piano and for voices and orchestra realized and arranged by Juan Allende-Blin, Éditions Jobert, Paris 1979

First performance: at the Hessischer Rundfunk de Frankfort-s/le-Main with the Radio-Sinfonie-Orchester, conducted by Eliahu Inbal, 1 December 1977

Comments: Debussy's text is a free adaptation of Poe's tale.

He signed a contract with the Metropolitan Opera in 1908 for a production of this work and *Le Diable dans le Beffroi* and the two works were listed in the program of the 1911–1912 season of the Opéra-Comique, but neither work was ever completed.

In 1917 he sent Durand the final version of the text.

In a letter to André Caplet of 1909, Debussy wrote:

"Monsieur E. A. Poe... cet homme, quoique posthume, excerce sur moi une tyrannie presque angoissante. J'en oublie des affections essentielles, et m'enferme comme une brute dans la Maison Usher, à moins que je tienne compagnie au diable dans le beffroi."

(Monsieur E. A. Poe... although deceased, that gentleman exercises an almost painful tyranny over me. I forget basic feelings and shut myself up in the House of Usher like an animal, unless the devil in the belfry happens to be with me.)

To Paul Dukas in 1916:
"Il est possible que *La Chute de la Maison Usher* soit aussi la chute de Claude Debussy. La destinée devrait bien me permettre de finir, je ne voudrais pas que l'on s'en tienne à Pelléas pour le dur jugement de l'avenir."
(It's very possible that *The Fall of the House of Usher* may also be the fall of Claude Debussy. Fate should really enable me to finish it, I wouldn't want *Pelléas* to be the only basis for the harsh judgment of the future.)

LE MARTYRE DE SAINT-SÉBASTIEN
mystery play in 5 acts

Date: February–May 1911
Source: Gabriel d'Annunzio, *Le Martyre de Saint-Sébastien.* Calmann-Lévy, Paris 1911.
Manuscript: score, with some pages missing, in the hand of Debussy, Caplet, and a copyist, in the Bibliothèque Nationale, Paris
Publisher: Durand & Cie, Paris 1911
First performance: at the Théâtre du Châtelet, 22 May 1911; costumes and scenery by Léon Bakst, choreography by Michel Fokine, orchestra conducted by André Caplet, D.-E. Inghelbrecht the chorus master, and Ida Rubinstein as Saint-Sébastien
Comments: In late 1910, Debussy was asked by d'Annunzio to collaborate on a play he was writing. He accepted immediately, without having seen the text. Interest in d'Annunzio's poetry as well as financial needs may have been responsible for this hasty decision. He later complained bitterly that he was given two months to compose something that should normally take two years. In order to complete the work on schedule, he asked André Caplet to help with the orchestration.
Debussy had just begun work on the ballet Khamma *when he wrote to Robert Godet, 6 February 1911:*
"C'est exactement à ce moment qu'est survenu Gabriel d'Annunzio avec *Le Martyre de Saint-Sébastien,* pour lequel j'ai accepté de faire de la musique de scène.... Je n'ai pas besoin de vous dire que le culte d'Adonis y rejoint celui de Jésus; que c'est très beau, par affirmation; et qu'en effet, si on me laissait le temps nécessaire, il y a d'assez beaux moments à trouver."

(At this very moment Gabriele d'Annunzio arrived with *Le Martyre de Saint-Sébastien,* for which I've agreed to do the music... I needn't tell you that in it the cults of Adonis and Jesus are intermingled; that it is very lovely and that, indeed, were I to be allowed sufficient time, there are some fairly lovely moments to be found in it.)

SIX ÉPIGRAPHES ANTIQUES
for piano 4 hands and 2 hands

Date: July 1914
Source: Pierre Louÿs, *Les Chansons de Bilitis*—traduites du grec par Pierre Louÿs, neuvième édition. Société du Mercure de France, Paris 1898, pp. 29, 139, 69, 257, 225, 313.
Manuscripts: both versions in the Bibliothèque Nationale, Paris
Publisher: Durand & Cie, Paris 1915
First performance: 17 March 1917(?)
Comments: These pieces are directly derived from the incidental music for *Les Chansons de Bilitis*. The titles and the order were changed. The former numbers are shown here in parentheses.

  I. Pour invoquer Pan, dieu du vent d'été (I)
  II. Pour un tombeau sans nom (VII)
  III. Pour que la nuit soit propice (IV)
  IV. Pour la danseuse aux crotales (X)
  V. Pour l'égyptienne (VIII)
  VI. Pour remercier la pluie au matin (XII)

Debussy had originally intended to make these pieces into an orchestral suite, but he wrote to Durand that "times are hard and life for me is even harder" and never went any further.

In neither the manuscript nor the published editions is any mention made of Pierre Louÿs or of *Les Chansons de Bilitis*.

ODE À LA FRANCE
for soprano solo, chorus, and orchestra

Date: 1916–1917
Source: Louis Laloy
Manuscript: incomplete orchestral sketch, partly without words, in the Bibliothèque Nationale, Paris
Publisher: for voice and piano, as realized by M.-F. Gaillard, Choudens, Paris 1928
First performance: by M.-F. Gaillard with the Société des Concerts du Conservatoire and the Choeur mixte de Paris, in the Nouvelle Salle Pleyel, 2 April 1928
Comments: Debussy asked Louis Laloy to write words for a patriotic work he wished to compose in which Jeanne d'Arc would figure as "la France douloureuse." This work, Debussy's last composition, was left unfinished and remained unknown until after his death.

> *Opening lines:* "Les troupeaux vont par les champs désertés
> Où les sillons ont gardés les charrues.
> Cette fumée est le feu des cités
> Dont l'ennemis a pris ramparts et rues.
> Il pretendait vaincre sans coup férir
> De mal rage il se venge en souffrance.
> Dieu! pourrez-vous voir sans la secourir
> La grande pitié du royaume de France?"

(The flocks wandered o'er the deserted fields, the plows in the furrows are stilled. The smoke is that of cities whose ramparts and streets have fallen to the foe.

He held that his victory was won without a blow's having been struck, and in his evil wrath he takes his revenge in suffering. Lord! can you look on the pitiful state of the Realm of France without giving it your aid?)

Vallas wrote of the first performance:
"Un jeune virtuose, adroit interprète des pièces de piano de Debussy, eut l'impertinence de développer l'esquisse et d'y superposer une orchestration postiche.... Manifestation qui ne parue ni digne ni opportune. Il ne semble point convenable d'apprécier une oeuvre qui n'était qu'une esquisse et dans le texte gravé de laquelle on ne sait quelles sont les parts respectives de l'auteur et des transcripteurs."

(A young virtuoso, a clever interpreter of Debussy's piano works, has had the impertinence to expand the sketch and to superimpose a false orchestration upon it.... A performance I found neither worthwhile nor appropriate. It seems to me far from fitting to be presented with a work that was no more than a sketch and with a printed score in which it is impossible to tell which parts are due to the composer and which to the transcribers.)

———————

Appendix A
The Original
Berceuse

*BERCEUSE**

— René Peter

Il était une fois une fée
qui avait un beau sceptre blanc,
il était une plaintive enfant
qui pleurait des fleurs fanées.

La fée en la voyant pleurer
détacha des fleurs de son sceptre
et les laissa doucement tomber;
l'enfant les noua dans ses tresses
et lui dit: " — En as-tu encore?"

Il en tomba mille et mille autres,
le long de ses yeux, le long de sa bouche,
des mauves, des jaunes et des rouges;
l'enfant en couvrit ses épaules
et lui dit: " — En as-tu encore?"

---

* This is the song as written by René Peter before Debussy gave it the
"accent Poitevin."

Il en tomba tout autour d'elle,
autant de parures nouvelles,
des colliers clairs, des ceintures d'or,
d'autres couraient le long de ses jambes,
cachant ses pieds sous les guirlandes.
" — En as-tu encore? En as-tu encore?"

La blanche fée enfin descendit,
elle ôta des cheveux de la petite fille
les fleurs répandues les premières
et qui étaient déjà flétries.
Mais l'enfant les lui prit des mains
et les jeta sur le chemin
avec de légers cris de colère.

Et la fée, la blanche fée dit:
" — Pourquoi jeter ces fleurs sur le chemin?
Tandis qu'elles passent d'autres naissent;
c'est ton bonheur, c'est ton bonheur que tu laisse."

Appendix B
La Damoiselle Élue

Three Versions:
Debussy,
Sarrazin and Rossetti

LA DAMOISELLE ÉLUE

— poème lyrique d'après
Dante Gabriel Rossetti

La Damoiselle *Élue s'appuyait*[1]
Sur la barrière *d'or* du Ciel,
Ses yeux étaient plus profonds que l'abime
Des eaux *calmes*, au soir.
Elle avait trois lys à la main,
Et sept étoiles dans les cheveux.

Sa robe flottante
N'était point *ornée* de fleurs brodées,
Mais d'une *rose blanche*, présent de Marie,
Pour le divin service justement portée;
Ses cheveux qui tombaient le long de ses épaules,
Étaient jaunes comme le blé mûr.

---

[1] The words in italics indicate the changes Debussy made in Sarrazin's text.

Autour d'elle des amants nouvellement réunis,
Répétaient pour toujours, entre eux,
Leurs nouveaux noms *d'extase;*
Et les âmes, qui montaient à Dieu,
Passaient près d'elle comme de fines flammes.

Alors, elle s'inclina *de nouveau* et se pencha
En dehors du charme *encerclant,*
Jusqu'à ce que son sein eût échauffé
La barrière sur laquelle elle s'appuyait,
Et que les lys gisent comme endormis
Le long de son bras étendu.

Le soleil *avait disparu,* la lune *annelée*
Était comme une petite plume
Flottant au loin dans *l'espace;* et voilà
Qu'elle parla à travers l'air calme.
Sa voix était *pareille* à celle des étoiles,
Lorsqu'elles chantent en choeur.

Je voudrais qu'il fût déjà près de moi,
Car il viendra,
N'ai-je pas prié dans le Ciel? Sur terre,
Seigneur, Seigneur, n'a-t-il pas prié,
Deux prières ne sont-elles pas une force parfaite?
Et pourquoi m'effraierais-je?

Lorsque autour de sa tête s'attachera l'auréole,
Et qu'il aura revêtu sa robe blanche,
Je le prendrai par la main et j'irai avec lui
Aux sources de lumière,
Nous y entrerons comme dans un courant,
Et nous y baignerons à la face de Dieu.

Nous nous reposerons tous deux *à* l'ombre
De ce vivant et mystique arbre,
Dans le feuillage secret duquel on sent
Parfois la présence de la colombe,
Pendant que chaque feuille, touchée par ses plumes,
Dit *Son Nom distinctement.*

Tous deux nous chercherons les bosquets
Où *trône Dame* Marie
Avec ses cinq servantes, dont les noms
Sont cinq douces symphonies:
Cécile, *Blanchelys*, Madeleine,
Marguerite et *Roselys*.

Il craindra peut-être, et restera muet,
Alors, je poserai ma joue
Contre la sienne, et parlerai de notre amour,
Sans *confusion ni* faiblesse,
Et la chère Mère approuvera
Mon orgueil, et me laissera parler.

Elle-même nous aménera, la main dans la main,
À celui autour duquel toutes les âmes
S'agenouillent, *les* innombrables têtes clair rangées,
Inclinées, avec leurs auréoles.
Et les anges venus à notre rencontre chanteront,
S'accompagnant de leurs guitares et de leurs citoles.

Alors, je demanderai au Christ, Notre Seigneur,
Cette grande faveur, pour lui et moi:
Seulement de vivre comme autrefois sur terre:
Dans l'Amour; et d'être *pour toujours*
Comme alors *pour un temps,*
Ensemble, *moi et lui.*

Elle regarda, prêta l'oreille et dit,
D'une voix moins triste que douce:
Tout ceci sera quand il viendra. Elle *se tu.*
La lumière tressaillit de son côté rempli
D'un fort vol *d'anges horizontal.*
Ses yeux prièrent, elle sourit.

Mais bientôt leur sentier devint vague
Dans les sphères distantes.
Alors, elle jeta ses bras le long
Des barrières *d'or.*[2]
Et posant son visage entre ses mains,
Pleura.[2]

---

[2] These words do not appear in the manuscript.

LA DAMOISELLE BÉNIE

— Dante Gabriel Rossetti
translated by
Gabriel Sarrazin

La Damoiselle bénie se penchait en dehors,
Appuyée sur la barrière dorée du Ciel;
Ses yeux étaient plus profonds que l'abime
Des eaux apaisées, au soir;
Elle avait trois lys à la main,
Et sept étoiles dans les cheveux.

Sa robe flottante
N'était point parée de fleurs brodées,
Mais d'une blanche rose, présent de Marie,
Pour le divin service justement portée;
Ses cheveux qui tombaient le long de ses épaules
Étaient jaunes comme le blé mûr.

Autour d'elle, des amants, nouvellement réunis,
Parmi des acclamations d'amour immortel,[1]
Répétaient pour toujours entre eux
Leurs nouveaux noms qui les ravissaient;
Et les âmes qui montaient à Dieu
Passaient près d'elle comme de fines flammes.

Elle s'inclina encore et se pencha
En dehors du charme qui l'encerclait:
Jusqu'à ce que son sein eût échauffé
La barrière sur laquelle elle s'appuyait,
Et que les lys gisent comme endormis
Le long de son bras étendu.

Le soleil était couché; la lune nouvelle
Était comme une petite plume
Flottant au loin dans l'abime; et voilà
Qu'elle parla à travers l'air calme.
Sa voix était semblable à celle des étoiles,
Lorsqu'elles chantent en choeur.

---

[1] Debussy omitted this line.

"Je voudrais qu'il fût déjà près de moi,
Car il viendra," dit-elle.
"N'ai-je pas prié dans le Ciel, — sur terre,
Seigneur, Seigneur, n'a-t-il pas prié?"
Deux prières ne sont-elles pas une force parfaite
Et pourquoi m'éffraierais-je?

Lorsque, autour de sa tête, s'attachera l'auréole,
Et qu'il sera vêtu de blanc,
Je le prendrai par la main et j'irai avec lui
Aux sources profondes de lumière;
Nous y entrerons comme dans un courant
Et nous y baignerons à la face de Dieu.

Nous nous reposerons tous deux sous l'ombre
De ce vivant et mystique arbre
Dans le feuillage secret duquel on sent
Parfois la présence de la Colombe,
Pendant que chaque feuille touchée par ses plumes
Dit distinctement Son Nom.

"Tous deux, dit-elle, nous chercherons les bosquets
Où est Madame Marie,
Avec ses cinq servantes, dont les noms
Sont cinq douces symphonies,
Cécile, Gertrude, Madeleine,
Marguerite et Rosalie.

Il craindra peut-être, et restera muet;
Alors je poserai ma joue
Contre la sienne, et parlerai de notre amour
Sans honte et sans faiblesse;
Et la chère Mère approuvera
Mon orgueil, et me laissera parler.

Elle-même nous amènera, la main dans la main,
A Celui autour duquel toutes les âmes
S'agenouillent, innombrables têtes clair-rangées,
Inclinées avec leurs auréoles;
Et les anges, venus à notre rencontre, chanteront,
S'accompagnant de leurs guitares et de leurs citoles.

Alors je demanderai au Christ notre Seigneur
Cette grande faveur pour lui et pour moi: —
De vivre seulement comme autrefois sur la terre
Dans l'Amour,—et d'être
Comme alors, pour toujours désormais,
Ensemble, Lui et moi."

Elle regarda, prêta l'oreille et dit,
D'un ton plus résigné que triste: —
"Tout ceci sera quand il viendra." Elle cessa.
La lumière tressaillit de son côté, remplie
D'un fort vol horizontal d'anges.
Ses yeux prièrent, et elle sourit.

(Je vis son sourir.) Mais bientôt leur sentier
Devint vague dans les sphères distantes:
Alors, elle jeta ses bras le long
Des barrières dorées,
Laissa tomber son visage entre ses mains,
Et pleura. (J'entendis ses pleurs.)

THE BLESSED DAMOZEL*

— Dante Gabriel Rossetti

The blessed damozel leaned out
    From the gold bar of Heaven;
Her eyes were deeper than the depth
    Of waters stilled at even;
She had three lilies in her hand,
    And the stars in her hair were seven.

Her robe, ungirt from clasp to hem,
    No wrought flowers did adorn,
But a white rose of Mary's gift,
    For service meetly worn;
Her hair that lay along her back
    Was yellow like ripe corn.

---

* From the 1881 edition of the poem.

Around her, lovers, newly met
   'Mid deathless love's acclaims,
Spoke evermore among themselves
   Their heart-remembered names;
And the souls mounting up to God
   Went by her like thin flames.

And still she bowed herself and stooped
   Out of the circling charm;
Until her bosom must have made
   The bar she leaned on warm,
And the lilies lay as if asleep
   Along her bended arm.

The sun was gone now; the curled moon
   Was like a little feather
Fluttering far down the gulf; and now
   She spoke through the still weather.
Her voice was like the voice the stars
   Had when they sang together.

"I wish that he were come to me,
   For he will come," she said.
"Have I not prayed in heaven?—on earth,
   Lord, Lord, has he not pray'd?
And not two prayers a perfect strength?
   And shall I feel afraid?

"When round his head the aureole clings,
   And he is clothed in white,
I'll take his hand and go with him
   To the deep wells of light;
As unto a stream we will step down,
   And bathe there in God's sight.

"We two will lie i' the shadow of
   That living mystic tree
Within whose secret growth the Dove
   Is sometimes felt to be,
While every leaf that His plumes touch
   Saith His Name audibly.

"We two," she said, "will seek the groves
    Where the lady Mary is,
With her five handmaidens, whose names
    Are five sweet symphonies,
Cecily, Gertrude, Magdalen,
    Margaret and Rosalys.

"He shall fear, haply, and be dumb:
    Then will I lay my cheek
To his, and tell about our love,
    Not once abashed or weak:
And the dear Mother will approve
    My pride, and let me speak.

"Herself shall bring us, hand in hand,
    To Him round whom all souls
Kneel, the clear-ranged unnumbered heads
    Bowed with their aureoles:
And angels meeting us shall sing
    To their citherns and citoles.

"There will I ask of Christ the Lord
    This much for him and me: —
Only to live as once on earth
    With Love,—only to be,
As then awhile, for ever now
    Together, I and he."

She gazed and listened and then said,
    Less sad of speech than mild, —
"All this is when he comes." She ceased.
    The light thrilled toward her, fill'd
With angels in strong level flight.
    Her eyes, prayed, and she smil'd.

(I saw her smile.) But soon their path
    Was vague in distant spheres:
And then she cast her arms along
    The golden barriers,
And laid her face between her hands,
    And wept. (I heard her tears.)

Appendix C
Poets
and Friends

d'Annunzio, Gabriele (1863–1938)   Italian poet, author of dramatic
works, and ardent patriot. Lived for many years in France, where he
was greatly appreciated. Author of the mystery play *Le Martyre de Saint-
Sébastien*, for which he asked Debussy to compose the music.

Bachelet, Alfred-Georges (1864–1944)   Composer of vocal and
instrumental works. Fellow pupil with Debussy at the Conservatoire.
Won the Prix de Rome in 1890. Appointed director of the Conservatoire
in 1918. The first version of *Chevaux de bois* was dedicated to him (1885).

Bailly, Edmond (1835–?)   Publisher, amateur composer, and owner of
the Librairie de l'Art Indépendant, a gathering place for young poets
and writers whom he was always ready to help. An admirer of
Debussy, he published the first editions of *La Damoiselle élue* (160 copies)
and the *Cinq Poèmes de Charles Baudelaire* (150 copies). The manuscript of
La Damoiselle élue was dedicated to him (1893).

Banville, Théodore de (1823–1891)   Poet and author of novels and
plays in verse. A master of rhyme and poetic fantasy and leader of the
younger school of poets. Debussy set eleven of his poems, but
published only one. He left unfinished compositions on the plays *Diane
au bois* and *Hymnis* and on the poem *Le Triomphe de Bacchos* [*sic*] *à son
retour des Indes*.

Bardac, Raoul (1881–1950)   Son of Emma and Sigismond Bardac. Amateur musician who had studied at the Conservatoire. A pupil and friend of Debussy who gave him advice on his compositions.

Bardac, Mme Sigismond   *See* Emma Debussy.

Baudelaire, Charles (1821–1867)   Poet, precursor of the Symbolists, translator of the tales of Edgar Allan Poe, and author of perceptive criticisms of art and literature. His single volume of verse, *Les Fleurs du mal*, marked him as one of the most influential poets of his century. Debussy set five of his poems and left unfinished compositions on two of the Poe tales: *La Chute de la Maison Usher* and *Le Diable dans le Beffroi*. Debussy wrote of him: "en même temps qu'un merveilleux artiste, un critique d'une compréhension unique."

Bonheur, Raymond (1861–1939)   Nephew of the painter Rosa Bonheur. Fellow pupil with Debussy at the Conservatoire, where they became friends in 1878 through their common interest in Banville. His musical output was small, and in later years he moved chiefly in literary and artistic circles. *Prélude à "l'Après-midi d'un Faune"* was dedicated to him (1894).

Bonniot, Mme E. (Geneviève Mallarmé) (1864–1918)   The daughter of Stéphane Mallarmé. *Trois Poèmes de Stéphane Mallarmé* was dedicated to the memory of the poet and to her (1913).

Bouchor, Maurice (1855–1929)   Minor poet best known for his dramas and mystical plays. Debussy left sketches for two songs set to poems from his *Poèmes de l'Amour et de la Mer*. (Chausson, a friend of Bouchor and Debussy, was working on songs to these poems at the same time.) Bouchor introduced Debussy to Robert Godet, who became his closest lifelong friend.

Bourget, Paul (1852–1935)   Author who early gave up poetry to write novels dealing with psychological and social problems. A close friend of Jules Laforgue. Debussy set nine poems from his last volume of verse, *Les Aveux*, published in 1882.

Caplet, André (1878–1925)   Composer and conductor. Won the Prix de Rome in 1901. Regular conductor of the Boston Symphony Orchestra from 1910 to 1914. He and Debussy met about 1907 and soon became close friends. He orchestrated two of the *Ariettes oubliées* (*C'est l'extase langoureuse* and *Green*) and *Children's Corner*, completed the orchestration of *La Boîte à joujoux*, directed the première of *Le Martyre de Saint-Sébastien*, and transcribed several orchestral works for piano. His compositions show the influence of Debussy. The best of his works are the religious compositions written toward the end of his life.

Charlot, Jacques (18?–1915)   Cousin and collaborator of Jacques Durand, in charge of the firm's production department. Killed in action in March 1915. Part II of *En blanc et noir* was dedicated to him (1915).

8891-1897). Debussy is known to have frequented it

Deguingand, Mme Émile (1852–?)   A pupil of Mme Moreau-Sainti, at whose singing classes Debussy was the accompanist. He dedicated *Fleurs des blès* to her (c. 1880).

Diaghilev, Serge de (1872–1929)   Russian impresario who with Fokine and Bakst created the Ballets Russes in Paris in 1909. He introduced ballets adapted to orchestral works, including Debussy's *L'Après-midi d'un Faune* and Rimsky-Korsakov's *Shéhérazade*, and collaborated with Stravinsky to produce *The Firebird, Petroushka*, etc. He produced *Jeux* in 1913.

Dolly (1892–   )   Nickname of Debussy's stepdaughter (Hélène Bardac), Mme Gaston de Tinan.

Doret, Gustave (1866–1943)   Swiss composer and conductor, who had been a pupil of Massenet. At his inaugural concert as conductor of the Société Nationale de Musique, he gave the first performance of the *Prélude à "l'Après-midi d'un Faune,"* 23 December 1913. The work was greeted with such enthusiasm that it was encored. At Doret's suggestion, Debussy orchestrated Satie's *Gymnopédies* 1 and 3. Doret conducted the first performance 20 February 1897. He is the author of *Temps et Contretemps*, a collection of souvenirs.

Dubois, Théodore (1837–1924)   Composer, organist, professor of harmony, and director of the Paris Conservatoire from 1896 to 1905.

Ducasse   *See* Roger-Ducasse.

Dukas, Paul (1865–1935)   Composer and professor of composition. He spent much of his life teaching at the Conservatoire, where he and Debussy had met as students. He was one of Debussy's closest lifelong friends among contemporary musicians. *La Damoiselle élue* was dedicated to him (1888). He is the author of *Écrits sur la Musique*.

Dupin, Etienne (1864–1899)   Wealthy banker and lover of music. He met Debussy in 1887, shortly after the latter's return from Rome, and invited him to go to Bayreuth with him in 1888 and 1889. With Chausson, he helped underwrite the *Cinq Poèmes de Charles Baudelaire*, which were dedicated to him (1889).

Durand, Jacques (1865–1928)   Debussy's sympathetic, and sometimes demanding, publisher (1889–1917), who was also a close friend. *Lettres à son éditeur* is a valuable and informative document. *La Mer* was dedicated to him (1905); *Jeux* was dedicated to Mme Durand (1913).

Fontaine, Arthur (?–?)   Brother of Lucien Fontaine. Debussy often was invited to his house in Paris, where he is known to have played extracts of *Pelléas* in 1899. In 1914, he advised Debussy to leave Paris in order to escape the German planes.

Fontaine, Mme Arthur (1865–1948)   (Later Mme Desjardins.) Amateur singer and sister-in-law of Chausson, at whose house she and her

husband met Debussy. She sang in the choral group founded by Lucien
Fontaine and worked with and was a great admirer of Debussy. *Clair de
lune* was dedicated to her (1891), as well as an undated manuscript of
De fleurs and *De soir* (c. 1893).

Fontaine, Lucien (186?–1956)   Patron of the arts and founder of an
amateur choral group which Debussy conducted from 1893 to 1904
(when Ravel replaced him). He was a witness (with Pierre Louÿs and
Satie) to Debussy's marriage to Lilly Texier (1899). A manuscript of
L'échelonnement des haies (1895) and of the 1898 version of *Dieu! qu'il la
fait bon regarder* and *Yver, vous n'estes qu'un villain* were dedicated to
him.

Fontaine, Mme Lucien (186?–1908)   Member of the choral group
founded by her husband, which met at their house. Debussy was also a
guest at their country house in Merçin. *Fantoches* (1891) and *Le Tombeau
des Naïades* (1898) were dedicated to her.

Freuder (?–?)   One-time German tutor of Raoul Bardac who would
occasionally visit Debussy.

Gaby (1866–1945)   Nickname of Gabrielle Dupont, also known as Gaby
Lhéry. Debussy's devoted mistress with the green eyes whom he met
about 1890 and who shared his life until 1898. The manuscript of
Rodrigue et Chimène was dedicated to her in 1890. The particel of the
Prélude à "l'Après-midi d'un Faune" was also dedicated to her (1899). In
1902, he sent her a copy of a special edition of *Pelléas et Mélisande*
inscribed: "À Gaby, princesse du mystérieux royaume d'Allemonde.
Son vieux dévoué Claude Debussy."

Garden, Mary (1874–1967)   Scottish soprano who made her debut at
the Opéra-Comique in 1900 (in *Louise*). Debussy chose her to create the
role of Mélisande in 1902. She made her American debut in New York
in 1907. The 1903 edition of the *Ariettes oubliées* was dedicated to her.
Debussy wrote of her performance in *La Traviata*, in 1903: "Toute
l'humaine souffrance d'un coeur sacrifié était contenu dans cette voix, et
cette compréhension d'un art va plus loin que la musique écrite."

Gautier, Théophile (1811–1872)   Poet and novelist. An early defender
of romanticism, he later turned to a more impersonal form of art and
was the first to expound the theory of "art for art's sake." Baudelaire
dedicated *Les Fleurs du mal* to him. Debussy set two of his poems,
neither of which was published.

Girod, André (?–?)   Author of the text of *Fleur des blés*.

Godet, Robert (1866–1950)   Swiss journalist and musicologist who had
studied harmony in Paris. He was a shy and erudite scholar with an
encyclopedic memory. Author of an important study of *Boris Goudonov*.
He met Debussy in 1888 and they soon became close lifelong friends.
L'échelonnement des haies and *Le son du cor s'afflige* were dedicated to him

(1891). *En sourdine* (second version) was dedicated to Mme Robert Godet (1891).

Gravollet, Paul (1863–?)   Pseudonym of Paul-Barthélémy Jeulin. Member of the Comédie Française, who later became a professor of diction. Author of a collection of poems entitled *Les Frissons*, for which he asked twenty-two composers to each set a given poem. Debussy was assigned no. 5: *Dans le jardin*. Among the other composers were Caplet, d'Indy, Ravel, and Widor. Gravollet later published a single volume of verse, *Les Floraisons*.

Guinand, Edouard (?–?)   Author of the lyric scene *L'Enfant prodigue*, for which students at the Conservatoire who were competing for the Prix de Rome in 1884 were required to write a choral setting. Debussy won the Premier Grand Prix with his cantata. He later set one poem from Guinand's single volume of verse, *Au courant de la vie*.

Guiraud, Ernest (1837–1892)   Composer of light operas and orchestral works. An intimate friend of Bizet. In 1880 Debussy joined Guiraud's composition class, of which Dukas was also a member, at the Conservatoire. Debussy and Guiraud remained friends long after the Conservatoire days. *L'Enfant prodigue*, the cantata with which Debussy won the Prix de Rome, was dedicated to Guiraud (1884).

Hartmann, Georges (1843–1900)   Generous and far-sighted publisher, who met Debussy in 1890. He published his works under the Fromont imprint, became his faithful friend, and provided him with a yearly income, as well as additional financial aid when requested. Founder (1873) of the Concerts de l'Odéon, which later became the Concerts Colonne. The *Nocturnes* were dedicated to him (1899). *Pelléas et Mélisande* was dedicated to his memory and to André Messager (1902).

Heine, Henri (Heinrich) (1797–1856)   German lyric poet and literary critic, who moved to Paris in 1831. Author of several volumes of verse and of prose. A friend of Laforgue, by whom he was much admired and who borrowed not so much his irony as what he termed "le gout allemand." Debussy's song *Tragédie* and the cantata *Zuléima* were both based on texts by Heine. *Intermezzo*, the fragment of a suite for cello and orchestra, was directly inspired by a passage from Heine.

Hocquet, Vital (1865–1931)   Pseudonym of Narcisse Lebeau. Plumbing contractor and lover of music whom Debussy met at the Cabaret du Chat Noir in 1890. Hocquet was involved in the weekly publication *Le Chat Noir*. He is said to have introduced Satie to Debussy. *De rêve* was dedicated to him (1892).

Hugo, Victor (1802–1885)   Prolific author of poems, novels, and plays. Leader of the Romantic movement. Debussy did not set any of his poems, saying that his writings were "flamboyantes de lyrisme et ne contiennent aucune sorte de musique." Hugo was greatly admired by

Pierre Louÿs, and it is possibly through his influence that Debussy became so well acquainted with his poems.

Hyspa, E. Vincent (1865–1938)   Poet and writer of satirical songs, a well-known figure at the Cabaret du Chat Noir, where he sang and recited his verse. Debussy set one of his poems, a ballad in true Chat Noir style. Hyspa's one volume of verse, *Le Ver solitaire,* was published in 1902.

Inghelbrecht, Désiré-Émile (1880–1965)   Conductor and composer. A friend and fervent admirer of Debussy. He served as the chorus master, under Caplet, at the first performance of *Le Martyre de Saint-Sébastien* in 1911 and conducted the first concert performance of this work in 1912. As musical director of the Théâtre des Champs-Elysées at its opening in 1913, he conducted the first performance of the *Marche écossaise.* In 1934, he founded the Orchestre National, which under his direction gave many concerts of Debussy's works, including a concert version of *Pelléas et Mélisande.*

Jean-Aubry, Georges (1882–1949)   Writer and critic who traveled extensively in Europe to introduce contemporary French music, chiefly that of Debussy. He introduced Debussy to the pianist Ricardo Viñes, who gave first performances of many of the piano compositions. Jean-Aubry was editor of *The Chesterian,* an English monthly journal, from 1919 to 1940.

Koussevitzky, Serge (1874–1951)   Russian-born conductor who in December 1913 invited Debussy to come to Russia to conduct his works in Moscow and Saint Petersburg. Conductor of the Boston Symphony from 1924 to 1949, and founder of the Berkshire Music Festival. Part I of *En blanc et noir* was dedicated to him (1915).

Laforgue, Jules (1860–1887)   Symbolist poet and originator of "vers libres," whose poems are marked by irony and humor. A close friend of Paul Bourget, who in 1881 proposed Laforgue for the post of reader to the Empress Augusta of Germany, which he held for four years. Debussy did not set any of his poems, but their influence can be seen in the *Proses lyriques.* Frequent references are also found in his letters to the poet he called "notre ami Jules."

Laloy, Louis (1874–1944)   Musicologist and critic. Author of a work on ancient Chinese music and founder of the *Mercure musical.* Friend of Debussy and his first French biographer (1909). Debussy's last composition (unfinished) is a setting for Laloy's *Ode à la France. Et la lune descend sur le temple qui fut (Images,* second series) was dedicated to him (1907).

Lamoureux, Charles (1834–1899)   Conductor and founder (1881) of the Concerts Lamoureux, which he conducted until his death. At these concerts he introduced many works by Wagner.

Lebey, André (1878–?)   Playwright.

Leconte de Lisle, Charles (1818–1894)   Poet who early translated the Greek tragedies, which greatly influenced his poetry. Later he became the leader of the Parnassian school of poets. Debussy set three of his poems and left an unfinished work based on the poem *Hélène*.

Lerolle, Henry (1848–1929)   Painter and friend of the Nabis and Impressionists. Brother-in-law of Chausson, through whom he met and became a friend of Debussy. *De soir* was dedicated to him (1893); the *Images oubliées* were dedicated to his daughter Yvonne (1894).

Le Roy, Grégoire (1862–1941)   Minor Belgian poet. Friend and classmate of Maeterlinck with whom he made one short trip to Paris in 1886. His collected poems, *La Chanson du Pauvre*, were published in 1907. Debussy set one of these poems.

Lhermite, Tristan (1601–1655)   Poet and author of plays and an autobiographical novel. Member of the retinue of the Duc d'Orléans. Debussy used verses from his best known poem, *Le Promenoir des deux amants*, for three songs.

Lilly (1873–1932)   Nickname of Rosalie Texier, Debussy's first wife.

Louÿs, Pierre (1870–1925)   Poet and novelist. He and Debussy met in 1893 and for ten years were very close friends. Best known for his novel *Aphrodite* and the prose poems *Les Chansons de Bilitis*. Debussy set three of these for his songs, composed incidental music to accompany the recitation of twelve others, and from these last chose six on which to base the *Six Épigraphes antiques*.

Maelzel, Johann Nepomuk (1772–1838)   German inventor of the metronome.

Maeterlinck, Maurice (1862–1949)   Belgian poet, dramatist, and essayist. His writings, full of symbolism, have a dreamlike quality, where fate dominates the characters. He is the author of the play *Pelléas et Mélisande*.

Malherbe, François de (1555–1628)   Court poet to both Henri IV and Louis XIII. Author of odes, sonnets, and paraphrases of the psalms. His poems are marked by clarity and precision.

Mallarmé, Stéphane (1842–1898)   One of the early Symbolist poets, whose obscure poems are full of allusions and suggestions. Translator of the poems of Edgar Allan Poe. He was brought to public attention when Verlaine included him in *Les Poètes maudits* (1884). Debussy attended his "Tuesdays," the meeting place of the young literary elite. He set four of his poems, and the *Prélude à "l'Après-midi d'un Faune"* was inspired by Mallarmé's Eglogue. The *Trois Poèmes de Stéphane Mallarmé* were dedicated to Mallarmé's memory and to his daughter (1913).

Meck, Alexandre de (1864–1911)   One of the eleven children of Mme de Meck, with whom Debussy spent three summers (1880–1882) while he was a pupil at the Conservatoire. He served as accompanist, teacher, and member of her trio. Alexandre, to whom he gave lessons in theory, was his particular friend. *Rondeau* was dedicated to him.

Messager, André (1853–1929)   Organist, conductor, and composer of operettas, the musical quality of which makes them models of their kind. He was a pupil of Saint-Saëns. Director of the Opéra-Comique, from 1898 to 1903, where he conducted the first performance of *Pelléas et Mélisande.* Later he was artistic director of Covent Garden and co-director of the Paris Opéra.

Moréas, Jean (1856–1910)   Pseudonym of Ioannes Papadiamantopoulos, Greek-born poet who settled in France in 1882. His best-known poems are the six-volume collection *Stances.*

Moreau-Sainti, Mme (?–?)   Daughter of an actress, Sainti, and a singer, Moreau, and widow of Baron Roux. She held singing classes for young ladies of the bourgeoisie. Recommended by Gounod and helped by Paul Vidal, Debussy obtained the post of accompanist at these classes in 1880. *Nuit d'étoiles,* his first published composition, was dedicated to her (1880).

Musset, Alfred de (1810–1857)   Romantic poet and author of plays in verse. (Many of his best works were written following a disastrous love affair with George Sand.) Debussy set four of his poems, though he never published any of them. Two are his earliest known songs.

Orléans, Charles d' (1394–1465)   Member of the royal family and author of ballads and rondeaux, of which he was the unrivaled master. He spent twenty-five years as a political prisoner in England. Debussy set five poems by this poet, whom he called: "doux prince aimé des muses et si gentil français." Frequent quotations from his poems are found in Debussy's letters.

Passerieu, François-Henri-Alexandre (1857–?)   Fellow student with Debussy at the Conservatoire. *Madrid, princesse des Espagnes* was dedicated to him and to Paul Vidal (c. 1879).

Peter, Alice (1872–1933)   Wife of Michel Peter (brother of René) and sister-in-law of Etienne Dupin. Debussy is said to have been briefly in love with her. *La Chevelure* was dedicated to her when it first appeared in *L'Image,* October 1897.

Peter, René (1872–1947)   Author of light comedies and tales. He met Debussy about 1890 and in 1898 introduced him to Lilly Texier, who was to become his first wife. Debussy and Peter planned to collaborate on several projects, none of which materialized. At Peter's request, Debussy composed a *Berceuse* (never published) for his play *La Tragédie de la Mort.*

Poulet, Gaston (1892–1974)   Violinist and conductor. He and Debussy gave the first performance of the *Sonata for Violin and Piano* at the Salle Gaveau, 5 May 1917.

Raunay, Jeanne (1869–1942)   A singer who made her career at the opera in Paris and in Monte-Carlo. She refused to give the first performance of the *Chansons de Bilitis,* saying that the morals of Bilitis were incompatible with her great talent.

Renaud, Armand (1836–1895)   A civil servant who devoted his spare time to writing. He published several volumes of verse as well as a series of essays on modern English poets. Debussy set one of his poems.

Risler, Edouard (1873–1929)   Virtuoso pianist and professor at the Conservatoire.

Roger-Ducasse (Jean-Jules Aimable Roger Ducasse) (1873–1954) Composer and professor of composition at the Conservatoire. He and Debussy were friends. Together they gave the first performance of *En blanc et noir,* 21 December 1916. He orchestrated the piano score of the *Rapsodie pour orchestre et saxophone,* which Debussy had left unfinished.

Rossetti, Dante Gabriel (1828–1882)   English poet and painter. One of the founders of the Pre-Raphaelite school of painting. His poetry was characterized by an idealistic romantic love of a mystical and dreamlike quality. Debussy's cantata *La Damoiselle élue* is a shortened form of *The Blessed Damozel.* Later Debussy planned to set one of the *Willowwood* sonnets from Rossetti's *House of Life.* Only a fragment remains of this work.

Rummel, Walter (1887–1953)   German pianist who settled in France and became an accomplished interpreter of French music. Debussy favored his interpretations of his music. Rummel gave the first performance of the twelve *Études* in 1916.

Rust, Wilhelm (1822–1892)   German pianist, composer, and organist. He published piano sonatas, which he attributed to his grandfather F. W. Rust. A scandal developed when it was discovered that he was the author of these works—the "Cas Rust." (See Debussy's account in *S.I.M.,* 15 March 1913.)

Samazeuilh, Gustave (1877–1967)   Composer and critic. Translator of songs by Schumann, Wagner, and Liszt. Transcribed more than one hundred orchestral works, chiefly those of French composers, for the piano, including *Nuages, Fêtes,* and *Sirènes.*

Sarrazin, Gabriel (1853–?)   Author of *Les Poètes modernes de l'Angleterre* (1885), *La Renaissance de la Poésie anglaise* (1889), *Les Grands Poètes romantiques de la Pologne* (1906). *La Damoiselle bénie* is found in the first of these volumes, where she is referred to as "la douce élue."

Schmidt, Wilhelm (1876–1952)   German author of plays, novels, and poetry. He wrote under the name of Wilhelm Schmidtbonn.

Stevens, Catherine (1865–1942)   Daughter of the Belgian painter Alfred Stevens, at whose house Debussy often dined in the early 1890s. There he accompanied Catherine, a gifted amateur singer, and played the piano four hands with her. He proposed to her, but she refused him. Two manuscripts of *En sourdine* are dedicated to her: one undated, the other dated 1892. (The published version is dedicated to Mme Robert Godet.)

Toulet, Paul-Jean (1867–1920)   Poet and novelist, a master of whimsy much appreciated by Debussy. He and Debussy met about 1906 and soon became good friends. In 1917, they planned a project on Toulet's adaptation of Shakespeare's *As You Like It*, which never materialized. His best-known novel, *Mon Amie Nane*, was published in 1905. His collected short poems, *Contrerimes*, did not appear until after his death. Debussy referred to him as "cette fine sauterelle aux tons passés."

Valade, Léon (1841–1894)   Minor poet and author of short plays in verse. With a friend (Albert Mérat), he translated Heine's *Intermezzo*. *Nocturnes*, a volume of verse in imitation of Heine, was published in 1880. Debussy set one poem from this volume.

Vasnier, Marie-Blanche (Mme Eugène-Henri) (1848–1923)   The wife of a civil servant eleven years her senior, she was an accomplished amateur singer with a soprano voice of unusual range. Debussy met her about 1880 at the singing classes of Mme Moreau-Sainti, in which she was a pupil. She and her husband befriended him and received him daily both in Paris and at Ville d'Avray. She became his first great love, and before leaving for the Villa Medici he had dedicated twenty-five songs to her. Soon after his return to Paris in 1887, their liaison came to an end.

Verlaine, Paul (1844–1896)   The most musical of all French poets and the one most favored by French composers. First associated with the Parnassians, he became the precursor of the Symbolists. In 1894, he was elected "Prince des Poètes." Debussy set eighteen of his poems—more than those of any other poet. The first five of these songs were composed in 1882, the last three in 1904. As late as 1913, Debussy was planning an opera-ballet based on the *Fêtes galantes*, a project which never materialized.

Vidal, Paul (1863–1931)   Composer of songs, light operas, and ballets. He won the Prix de Rome in 1883. A fellow student and friend of Debussy at the Conservatoire and at the Villa Medici. He became conductor at the Paris Opéra, musical director of the Opéra-Comique, and professor at the Conservatoire. *Aimons-nous et dormons* was dedicated to him (c. 1881), and *Madrid, princesse des Espagnes* to him and to Passerieu (c. 1879).

Vigny, Alfred de (1797–1863)   Poet, author of novels and plays, and translator of Shakespeare. An admirer of Victor Hugo, he became the leader of the Romantic school and remained one of its pillars. Debussy did not set any of his poems for his songs.

Villiers de L'Isle-Adam (1838–1889)   Author of short stories and plays. A friend of Banville and Baudelaire. His strange works, full of symbolism, were first published in *La Revue Fantaisiste*. Author of the play *Axel*, Debussy's lost composition of 1888.

Villon, François (1431–146?)   One of the first great French lyric poets. With him the Middle Ages can be said to end and modern poetry to begin. Debussy came to him late (1910) and then composed incomparable settings for three ballads from *Le Grand Testament*. In 1915, he chose a verse from Villon's *Ballade contre les ennemis de la France* for the epigraph of part II of *En blanc et noir*.

Willy (1859–1931)   Pseudonym of Henri Gautier-Villars. Clever and often caustic critic, who wrote under the name of "L'Ouvreuse." He was the first husband of the writer Colette.

Appendix D
A Selective Discography

The Songs*

Pierrette Alarie, soprano / Allen Rogers, piano
Westminster Gold WGM 8816 (1975)   (recorded 1959)

Pantomime	Fantoches
Clair de lune, first version	Romance
Pierrot	Zéphyr
Apparition	Rondeau
Mandoline	Noël des enfants qui n'ont
Beau soir	plus de maisons

John Alldis Choir
Argo ZRG 523 (1967)
Trois Chansons de Charles d'Orléans

Pierre Bernac, baritone / Francis Poulenc, piano
Odyssey 32 26 0009 (1974)   (recorded 1952)

Beau soir	Le Promenoir des deux amants
L'échelonnement des haies	

Julia Culp, contralto / Coenraad van Bos, piano
Rococo 5282 (1968)   (recorded 1917)
Nuit d'étoiles

---

* The recordings have been chosen so as to include, where possible, more than one interpretation of each song and a male as well as a female interpreter.

Suzanne Danco, soprano / Guido Agosti, piano
London LL 1329 (1955) (recorded 1951)
Chansons de Bilitis   Ariettes oubliées
Le Promenoir des deux amants

Ensemble vocal Philippe Caillard
Erato STU 70162 (1965)
Trois Chansons de Charles d'Orléans

Colette Herzog, soprano / Jacques Février, piano
DGG SLPM 138882 (1963)
Cinq Poèmes de Charles Baudelaire

Bernard Kruysen, baritone / Jean-Charles Richard, piano
Valois MB 729 (1968) (recorded 1961)
Mandoline   Noël des enfants qui n'ont
La mer est plus belle   plus de maisons
Le son du cor s'afflige   Le Promenoir des deux amants
L'échelonnement des haies   Fêtes galantes, second series
Dans le jardin   Trois Poèmes de Stéphane Mallarmé
Trois Chansons de France

Bernard Kruysen, baritone / Noël Lee, piano
Valois MB 939 (1972)   Telefunken SAT 22540 (1972)
Trois Chansons de France   Noël des enfants qui n'ont
Fêtes galantes, second series   plus de maisons
Trois Poèmes de Stéphane Mallarmé   Trois Ballades de François Villon
Le Promenoir des deux amants

Yolanda Marcoulescou, soprano / Katja Phillabaum, piano
Orion ORS 78312 (1979)
Green   Mandoline
Spleen   Trois Chansons de France
Chevaux de bois   Colloque sentimental
Le Jet d'eau   Fantoches

Janine Micheau, soprano / Aldo Ciccolini, piano
EMI-La Voix de Son Maître 2C 053-10016 M (1970) (recorded 1958)
Pantomime   Noël des enfants qui n'ont
Clair de lune, first version   plus de maisons
Pierrot   C'est l'extase langoureuse
Apparition   Il pleure dans mon coeur
Mandoline   L'ombre des arbres
Zéphyr   Green
L'échelonnement des haies   Spleen
Les Cloches   Le Jet d'eau
Romance   Rondeau
Paysage sentimental

Anna Moffo, mezzo-soprano / Jean Casadesus, piano
  RCA Red Seal LSC 3225 (1971)
    Cinq Poèmes de Charles Baudelaire   Romance
    Fêtes galantes, first series   Mandoline
    Voici que le printemps   Chansons de Bilitis

Roberta Peters, soprano / Leonard Hokanson, piano
  BASF MB 20799 (1973)   (recorded 1969)
    Rondel chinois   Pierrot
    Apparition   Fleur des blés
    Clair de lune, first version   Fêtes galantes, first series

Gérard Souzay, baritone / Dalton Baldwin, piano
  DGG SLPM 138758 (1967)   (recorded 1961)
    Beau soir   L'échelonnement des haies
    Mandoline   De soir
    Les Cloches   Le temps a laissié son manteau
    Green   Pour ce que Plaisance est morte
    Chevaux de bois   Fêtes galantes, first series
    Le Jet d'eau   Fêtes galantes, second series
    La mer est plus belle Le Promenoir des deux amants
    Le son du cor s'afflige

Maggie Teyte, soprano / Alfred Cortot (C) and Gerald Moore (M), piano
  Voix illustres FALP 50 021 (1964)   Angel COLH 134 (1962)   (recorded
  1936–1944)
    Fêtes galantes, first series (C)   Le Jet d'eau (M)
    Fêtes galantes, second series (C)   De rêve (M)
    Chansons de Bilitis (C)   De grève (C)
    Le Promenoir des deux amants (C)   De fleurs (M)
    Romance (M)   De soir (M)
    Beau soir (M)   Ballade des femmes de Paris (C)
    Green (M)

Jennie Tourel, mezzo-soprano / Erich Itor Kahn, piano
  Columbia ML 4158 (1949)
    Cinq Poèmes de Charles Baudelaire

Flore Wend, soprano / Noël Lee, piano
  Valois 707 (1966)   (recorded 1959)
    Fêtes galantes, first series   Chansons de Bilitis
    Ariettes oubliées   Trois Ballades de François Villon

With Orchestra

Camille Maurane, baritone
  Orchestre des Concerts Lamoureux
    Jean Fournet, conductor
  Epic LC 3355 (1957)
    Trois Ballades de François Villon

Bernard Plantey, baritone
Orchestre National de la Radiodiffusion Française
  D.-E. Inghelbrecht, conductor
  Ducretet-Thomson 320 C 154 (1962)
  Trois Ballades de François Villon

An Album of the Complete Songs

Les Mélodies de Claude Debussy
  Pathé Marconi EMI 2C 165—16371/74 (1980)   (recorded 1971, 1977,
  1978, 1979)
    Elly Ameling, soprano   Frederica von Stade, mezzo-soprano
    Michèle Command, soprano   Gérard Souzay, baritone
    Mady Mesplé, soprano   Dalton Baldwin, piano

  2C 165—16.371 A
    Nuit d'étoiles (Ameling)
    Fleur des blés (Ameling)
    Beau soir (Souzay)
    Mandoline (Souzay)
    La Belle au bois dormant (Command)*
    Voici que le printemps (Mesplé)
    Paysage sentimental (Mesplé)
    Zéphyr (Mesplé)
    Rondeau (Mesplé)

  2C 165—16.371 B
    Quatre Chansons de jeunesse (Mesplé)
      Pantomime   Pierrot
      Clair de lune (first version)   Apparition
    Rondel chinois (Mesplé)
    Aimons-nous et dormons (Mesplé)*
    Jane (Mesplé)*
    Calmes dans le demi-jour (En sourdine, first version) (Mesplé)
    Romance (Mesplé)
    Les Cloches (Command)

  2C 165—16.372 A
    Cinq Poèmes de Charles Baudelaire (Command)

  2C 165—16.372 B
    Les Angélus (Command)
    La mer est plus belle (Souzay)
    Le son du cor s'afflige (Souzay)
    L'échelonnement des haies (Souzay)
    Fêtes galantes, first series (Ameling)
    Dans le jardin (Ameling)

---

* First recording.

2C 165—16.373 A
Proses lyriques (Ameling)

2C 165—16.373 B
Ariettes oubliées (von Stade)
Trois Chansons de Bilitis (Command)

2C 165—16.374 A
Fêtes galantes, second series (Souzay)
Chansons de France (Souzay)
   Rondel: Le temps a laissié son manteau
   Rondel: Pour ce que Plaisance est morte
Le Promenoir des deux amants (Souzay)

2C 165—16.374 B
Trois Ballades de François Villon (Souzay)
Trois Poèmes de Stéphane Mallarmé (Ameling)
Noël des enfants qui n'ont plus de maisons (Ameling)

La Damoiselle élue

Montserrat Caballé, soprano
   Janet Coster, mezzo-soprano
   Ambrosian Ladies Chorus
   Symphonica of London
   Wyn Morris, conductor
Peters International, PLE 021 (1977)

Madeleine Gorge, soprano
   Jacqueline Joly, mezzo-soprano
   Choeur de femmes de la R.T.F.
   Orchestre Nationale de la Radiodiffusion Française
   D.-E. Inghelbrecht, conductor
Ducretet-Thomson 320 C 151 (1962)   (recorded 1955)

Barbara Hendricks, soprano
   Jocelyne Taillon, contralto
   Choeur de l'Orchestre de Paris
   Orchestre de Paris
   Daniel Barenboim, conductor
Deutsche Grammophon 2531 263 (1980)

Victoria de Los Angeles, soprano
   Carol Smith, contralto
   Radcliffe Choral Society
   Boston Symphony Orchestra
   Charles Münch, conductor
RCA Victrola AVM1–1412 (1976)   (recorded 1955)

Bidu Sayão, soprano
  Rosalind Nadell, contralto
  The Women's Chorus of the University of Pennsylvania
  The Philadelphia Orchestra
  Eugene Ormandy, conductor
  Columbia Special Products P 14187 (1977)   (recorded 1947)

Bibliography

General

Barraqué, Jean. *Debussy*. Paris: Editions du Seuil, 1962.

Bathori, Jane. *Sur l'Interprétation des mélodies de Claude Debussy*. Paris: Les Editions Ouvrières, 1953.

Bernac, Pierre. *The Interpretation of French Song*. New York: Norton, 1970.

Bonheur, Raymond. "Souvenirs et impressions d'un compagnon de jeunesse." *La Revue musicale*, numéro spéciale (1 May 1926): 3–9.

Debussy, Claude. *Monsieur Croche et autres écrits,* avec une Introduction et Notes par François Lesure. Paris: Gallimard, 1971.

Debussy et Edgar Poe. Documents inédits recueillis et présentés par Edward Lockspeiser. Monaco: Editions du Rocher, 1961.

Debussy on Music, the critical writings of the great French composer collected and introduced by François Lesure, translated and edited by Richard Langham Smith. New York: Knopf, 1977.

Debussy. Prelude to "The Afternoon of a Faun," edited by William W. Austin. New York: Norton, 1970.

Dietschy, Marcel. *La Passion de Claude Debussy*. Neuchâtel, Switzerland: La Baconnière, 1962.

Herbert, Michel. *La Chanson à Montmartre*. Paris: La Table Ronde, 1967.

Inghelbrecht, Germaine et D.-E. *Claude Debussy*. Paris: Costard, 1953.

Jarocinski, Stefan. *Debussy—Impressionism and Symbolism*. Translated from the French by Rollo Myers. London: Eulenburg, 1976.

Koechlin, Charles. "Quelques anciennes mélodies inédites de Claude Debussy." *La Revue musicale*, numéro spéciale (1 May 1926): 115–140.

Lesure, François. *Catalogue de l'oeuvre de Claude Debussy*. Geneva: Editions Minkoff, 1977.

Lockspeiser, Edward. *Debussy: His Life and Mind*, Vols. I and II. New York and London: Cambridge University Press, 1978.

Lockspeiser, Edward. *Debussy*, new edition with revisions and Preface by Richard Langham Smith. London: J. M. Dent, 1980.

Orledge, Robert. *Debussy and the Theatre*. London and New York: Cambridge University Press, 1982.

Peter, René. *Claude Debussy*. Paris: Gallimard, 1944.

Souffrin, Eileen. "Debussy lecteur de Banville." *Revue de Musicologie* XLVI (December 1960): 200–222.

Thompson, Oscar. *Debussy—Man and Artist*. New York: Dover Publications, 1965.

Tienot, Yvonne, and O. d'Estrade-Guerra: *Debussy: l'homme, son oeuvre, son métier*. Paris: Lemoine, 1962.

Trevitt, John. "Debussy inconnu: an inquiry." *The Musical Times* (September 1973): 881–886; (October 1973): 1001–1005.

Vallas, Léon. *Claude Debussy et son temps*. Paris: Albin Michel, 1958.

Vidal, Paul. "Souvenirs d'Achille Debussy." *La Revue musicale*, numéro spéciale (1 May 1926): 11–16.

Wenk, Arthur. *Claude Debussy and the Poets*. Berkeley and Los Angeles: University of California Press, 1976.

Correspondence

Lettres de Claude Debussy à son éditeur, publié par Jacques Durand. Paris: Durand, 1927.

Correspondance de Claude Debussy et P.-J. Toulet. Paris: Le Divan, 1929.

Lettres à deux amis, soixante-dix-huit lettres inédites à Robert Godet et G. Jean-Aubry. Paris: José Corti, 1945.

Correspondance de Claude Debussy et Pierre Louÿs, recueillie et annotée par Henri Borgeaud. Paris: José Corti, 1945.

Lettres inédites à André Caplet (1908–1914), recueillies et présentées par Edward Lockspeiser. Monaco: Editions du Rocher, 1957.

Lettres de Claude Debussy à sa femme Emma, présentées par Pasteur Vallery-Radot. Paris: Flammarion, 1957.

"Correspondance de Claude Debussy et de Louis Laloy (1902–1914)." *Revue de Musicologie*, numéro spéciale (1962): 3–40.

"Lettres inédites de Claude Debussy à divers." *La Revue musicale*, numéro spéciale 258 (1964): 109–119.

"Lettres inédites de Claude Debussy à Pierre Louÿs." *Revue de Musicologie*, tirage à part, Tome LVII (1971): No. 1.

Index of Titles

Index of First Lines